Meaning and Mind

Meaning and Mind

A STUDY IN
THE PSYCHOLOGY OF LANGUAGE

ROBERT F. TERWILLIGER
New School for Social Research

New York

OXFORD UNIVERSITY PRESS
London   Toronto   1968

Acknowledgments

The author wishes to express his gratitude for permission to reproduce figural material from the following works: Norman L. Munn, *Psychology: The Fundamentals of Human Adjustment* (Houghton Mifflin Company); Leonard Bloomfield, *Language* (Holt, Rinehart and Winston); and Simeon Potter, *Modern Linguistics* (Oxford University Press and André Deutsch Ltd.).

I would also like to take this opportunity to express my thanks to Elinor Yavneh for her secretarial assistance, to Phyllis Chesler for her invaluable criticisms of the manuscript, to Mr. Paul Whitfield of Oxford University Press for things too numerous to mention, and to my wife, Marlene, for helping to make this book possible.

New York   R.F.T.
February 1968

Contents

Contents

Introduction

This book presents a theory of language and meaning from a psychologist's point of view. From this point of view, language is treated as a mental activity or process which is essentially conscious, meaningful, and socially oriented. My concern, therefore, is with relatively global issues, with necessary theoretical assumptions rather than with the detailed, quantitative minutiae of language. For this reason, no effort has been made in this book to be either exhaustive or encyclopedic. Many areas covered here could have been presented more precisely and inclusively. However, my choice of which and how many factual and empirical details to present was governed by whether or not their inclusion would enhance the understanding of language as a dominant event in human life. I can only hope that nothing relevant to such an understanding has been ignored—particularly anything which would refute my own position.

In attempting to develop a theory of language, one must, of course, consider the theoretical attempts of other psychologists. My choice of which psychological theories of language to discuss has been guided by several factors. The scope or breadth of the theory is one. The nature of its underlying assumptions about man and about psychology is another. The degree to which it is accepted by the psychological community is a third. There are other reasons as well, but correctness or validity is not one of them. For it is the conclusion of this work that none of the existing theories can give an adequate psychological account or explanation of language.

I have tried, therefore, to propose some ideas that I feel will lead us toward a more fruitful theory of language. At this stage of their development, these ideas are broad and lamentably imprecise in many respects. I am nevertheless convinced that they are essentially correct. In order to evaluate their usefulness, some comments about my working assumptions are in order. First, I believe that the theorist's job is to specify necessities. That is, the psychological theorist must be prepared to answer the question: why and how is it necessary that people are as they are? It is not sufficient for the theorist to state simply that x occurs because of the presence of y—as, for example, B. F. Skinner, does. He must not only be able to specify the correlation between x and y, but in addition must be able to specify why this correlation *must* exist. The "must" may lie, of course, in the history of the individual, in his genes, in some factor of "human nature," or in, perhaps, a host of other factors. Wherein the necessity lies is a matter of debate and empirical investigation. Our job is to find it.

Second, I believe that an integral part of the nature of language is that it is conscious or that it involves conscious processes, i.e. that it is a mental process, as the title of this work suggests. Language, however, is not *totally* conscious. Thus, to understand language it is *necessary* to understand the nature of consciousness, those conditions which make something conscious and another thing not conscious. As the reader will see, I have no sympathy for the conception that consciousness is an epiphenomenon. But it most decidedly makes a difference, both theoretically and behaviorally, whether or not a process or event is conscious. Hence the necessity for understanding consciousness if one is to understand language.

Throughout the book, I have used terms that are not new to the discussion of language by psychologists. They are, however, occasionally given somewhat novel uses here. For example, other theorists have used the concept of *disposition* or *readiness to respond* (e.g. Charles Morris, *Signs, language and behavior*. New

York, Prentice-Hall, 1946). In prior usage these concepts were often tied to some particular model of learning or acquisition of behavior, such as Pavlovian conditioning. Such a model does not seem to me to be a fruitful starting place for a theoretical discussion of language. Hence my using dispositional concepts should not be taken as a preference for any particular form of learning or acquisition, but rather as a convenient (and hopefully accurate) expression of analytic and theoretical concepts. I have, of course, worked under certain broadly defined conceptions of the nature of language which shape my use of theoretical concepts. Thus I have used the concept of disposition as a device for explaining (a) the fact of consciousness, (b) the quality of a particular experience, and (c) the phenomenon of language and meaning. I would argue that a theory of language can be built only upon a theory of the mind, and it is the aim of this book to point the way toward such a theory.

The inclusion of the concepts of consciousness and mind in a discussion of the psychology of language is, of course, by no means universal among workers in this field. Without attempting to defend this inclusion—if, indeed, it needs any defense—I would point out that it has led me to certain "methodological" assumptions. Specifically, it has led me to assume that I am (and you are) a perfectly good source of data on problems of language and consciousness in general; that my observations of my own behavior and of the behavior of others in my immediate environment are as valid as—perhaps more valid than—data obtained by the use of more controlled methods of observation. I use my own data since I can observe things about myself more easily than I can observe the same thing in others in the laboratory. My self-observations are, however, subject to the usual criteria of scientific data, namely that others may presumably observe similar events—in themselves, or in others. Bear in mind that the extent to which you do not observe in yourself what I observe in myself does not invalidate the *fact* of my observing it; it does invalidate any generality I may presume about my self-observations, however. Logical niceties aside, what I am suggesting is this: certain critical facts about language—and of mental life in general—are directly open to one's own observations with an ease which is not permissible in the laboratory. These facts may not appear in the "experimental" literature either because of the methodological difficulty or because they are so obvious that no one thinks of studying them. There are facts which are so universal that they are often taken for granted. Yet it is just these "universal" things which cannot be taken for granted but rather must be explained. It is hoped that to some extent a return to the consideration of self-observation may facilitate such an explanation.

Finally, I would like to point out that any theory in psychology must eventually be evaluated in terms of its relevance to issues that are important to the life of human beings. Since language is the medium by which people communicate and influence one another personally, socially, and intellectually, any adequate psychological theory of language must have practical applications. Much psychological theorizing suffers from one of two faults: (1) either the connection between the theory and real-life affairs is so remote and abstract that the theory is for all intents and purposes useless for practical understanding, or (2) the switch from theory to practice involves a corruption of the theoretically derived concepts. The latter is particularly true when concepts are given precise laboratory definitions which cannot be applied directly to the practical world. I have herein attempted to show some practical applications of the skeleton theory which I am proposing. The success of this generalization from theory to practice must be left to the reader's judgment.

In summary, then, this book attempts to present the following: an outline of the nature, structure, and development of language (Chapter I-III); certain psychological theories of meaning and the author's critique and alternative theory (Chapters IV-VI); a discussion of the theories and problems raised by an attempt to account for the grammatical nature of language (Chapter VII); and various attempts to deal with the practical consequences of language, specifically with regard to certain language disorders (Chapter VIII), to the effects of language on other mental processes (Chapter IX), and to the social-manipulative uses of language (Chapter X).

Meaning and Mind

I
The Psychological Study of Language

The study of a particular problem or area within a much larger discipline may raise the issue of why one is interested in this particular problem. Why is the psychological study of language—which is sometimes called psycholinguistics—an important study? We may answer these questions by stating the aim of this book—and what conclusions we hope to draw from it. In discussing the problem of language from the viewpoint of the psychologist, we will draw upon other, divergent areas of psychology. In fact, what we want to show is that the psychological study of language raises questions which, when properly answered, may help to solve many issues in other areas of psychology as well—at least when human beings are the objects of psychological study. Moreover, we hope to show that the psychological study of language *touches* upon issues which are of considerable human and social import.

We will begin by attempting to define language. Obtaining a precise definition of anything is difficult. To obtain one for language is even more difficult since we all "know," from our own use of it, what language is. That is, we can easily become so bound up in our own language that we confuse giving a definition with merely giving a synonym for, or an example of, language. A proper definition must allow us to recognize any possible language in any possible species of animal. Simply giving a synonym for "language" (e.g. language is speech) will not permit this.

Let us begin by assuming that a language must have the following characteristics: (1) A *language is a system of behaviors and potential behaviors.* (2) *Language behaviors can influence the behaviors of other animals of the species. Language is communicative behavior.* (3) *Language behaviors are relevant or appropriate to states of affairs in the animal's environment, but they may be made without these states of affairs being immediately present.* (4)*Language behaviors may be inappropriate or wrong.* This may seem like a very cumbersome and overly technical definition. Could we not say instead that language is, for example, communication by symbols? This would be an unsatisfactory definition since the statement implies that language is a set of symbols and, hence, it only repeats the fact that a language is a language. It does not tell us how to recognize a language. We would have to define "symbol," "communication," and the like if we were going to use the latter definition. Although our definition requires further clarification, we will try to show that it leads to the conclusion that humans are the only animals we know of that can be said to have a language.

Those of us who are familiar with the nature of psychology as a discipline are aware that psychologists have not restricted their studies to human beings alone. Psychologists of one hundred years ago assumed that psychology was the study of the mind, while psychologists of the recent past often assume that psychology is the study or science of behavior. Both of these definitions are highly general. Certainly many, if not all, animal species seem to have what we might choose to call *minds* and all animals *behave*.

Whichever definition of psychology we take, it will necessitate the study of the behavior of many animal species. Psychology involves, in fact, the study of all animal behavior and/or mind. Many psychologists have assumed that there is sufficient commonality in animal behavior per se, that they may generalize accurately from the laws of behavior for one animal species to the behaviors of another species. We find, for example, a considerable amount of psychological research performed on the white rat. The selection of the rat as a research animal is dictated primarily for practical rather than theoretical reasons. The rat is an animal extremely easy to keep and care for. His size makes him easy to handle and relatively economical to construct apparatus for. But there is no reason to assume that his behavior is necessarily typical of the behavior of any other animal species.

Nevertheless, some psychologists still attempt to generalize from rat behavior to human behavior. Perhaps the most widely known statement of this position is to be found in the writings of the learning theorist E. C. Tolman. Despite the fact that Tolman is considered to be a relatively humanistic and cognitive—rather than mechanistic—psychologist, he said in his Presidential address to the American Psychological Association: "I believe that everything important in psychology (except perhaps such matters as the building up of a super-ego, that is everything save such matters as involve society and words) can be investigated in essence through the continued experimental and theoretical analysis of the determiners of rat behavior at a choice-point in a maze" (Tolman, 1938, p. 34).

Tolman's statement has an almost paradoxical aspect to it. It affirms the generality of laws derived from the study of rat behavior, while at the same time admitting that one cannot generalize from the behavior of lower species to human language behavior. We cannot, in fact, understand human language behavior from the study of any other animal species. We must study humans directly. Yet language is learned, and one of the things our study of lower animals presumably gives us is certain basic laws of learning. Can we then say that these laws of learning are applicable to the learning of language if language is not something typical of subhuman species? We will address ourselves to this among other problems later in the book.

Let us now consider four specific reasons for the psychological study of language.

LANGUAGE IS A UNIQUELY HUMAN BEHAVIOR*

Those subhuman species to which a language is sometimes attributed are bees, parrots, and porpoises. Von Frisch (1950) has shown how bees communicate information concerning the whereabouts of nectar-bearing flowers to other members of the hive. The specific communicative act is a ritual "dance" by the returning bee. This dance indicates the direction, distance, and nature of the nectar, and it is received by the other bees by imitation; that is, they actually follow the returning worker bee around in his dance. Let us look at this behavior in light of our tentative definition of language. It is clear that this bee dance influences the behavior of other bees, and that it is appropriate to certain environmental states of affairs. But can the dance be made in the absence of these states of affairs? Or can it refer to a potential state of affairs? The flower is, of course, not present in the hive at the time of the dance. On the other hand, no bee was ever seen dancing about yesterday's honey, not to mention tomorrow's. This alone makes us question whether the bee dance meets the criteria of a language. Moreover, bees never make mistakes in their dance. Their communications are never wrong, and they never communicate when there is no honey. By this criterion, they can be said not to have a language. Bees do communicate, however, which shows that language and communication are not identical. Communication is but one of the possible uses of language; and language is but one of the media through which communication may take place.

We must also consider parrots, porpoises, or members of any other animal species that mimic English. While it is conceivable that porpoises have a "language" of their own, this issue is independent of their talents as mimics of our language. Mimicry fails to meet two of the criteria for a language. First, mimicry is not usually an act of communication or social influence, either to a member of the same species or to a member of a different species.

* A discussion of this issue from a more linguistic perspective may be found in Hockett (1960).

Second, mimicry is rarely, if ever, appropriate to the environment. I may train a parrot to say /hello, Bob/ every time I enter a room. This makes his behavior in some sense appropriate to the environment. It is clear that he has not learned to greet people, however, since if I came up behind him, or called him on the telephone, I would not get /hello, Bob/ as a response.

The parrot's use of language does not constitute a *system* of behavior. A system, for our purposes, is a collection of *orders* of events. For example, events occur in a certain order. But only certain orders of events will belong to the system, while others do not. Different orders of the same events may belong to different systems, however. Our language is a system in this sense. Let us call words the events in the system called the English language. /The boy bites the dog/ and /the dog bites the boy/ then constitute different orders of the same events. Both belong to the same system, the English language. /The the bites boy dog/ is another ordering of the same events, but one which does not belong to that system. The parrot's use of words does not seem to belong to any language system. Any speaking human knows which orders of words belong to his language system and which do not. He can order words correctly or reorder them into new correct combinations. There does not seem to be any evidence to suggest that mimicked words can be reordered correctly by the mimicking animal. That is, any reorderings of words will not typically belong to the system of behaviors we call English. We may say the same thing in different terms if we say that the parrot's use of English is not productive (Hockett, 1960). He does not produce new, correct orderings of words. Words are not part of a behavior system for parrots or porpoises. As far as their speaking English, or any other known language is concerned, they do not have a language.

Within the limits of our knowledge, there is no species other than *Homo sapiens* which has a system of behaviors which meets our criteria for a language. The existence of a system of behavior which appears to be unique to a particular species poses a scientific challenge. It suggests that since there is a unique system of behavior, there may be unique psychological laws involved in it.

We are attempting as scientific psychologists, to create a system of laws for psychological events; hence, we cannot afford to ignore such a system. The study of the psychology of language is necessary then for the development of an adequate psychological theory.

LANGUAGE IS A "COMPLEX" BEHAVIOR

We have stressed the uniqueness of language, but we must also remember that it is a kind of behavior and will, therefore, have similarities with other behaviors. Psychologists have often been concerned with complex behaviors, particularly those which are sequentially ordered. A "complex" behavior, in this sense, is one which is assumed to be a result of the combination of other, previously acquired behaviors which, thus, become the "parts" of the complex. Language is a system consisting of orderings of words which are, in turn, orderings of sounds. Both the ordering of words and the ordering of sounds are sequential; they follow each other in time. Many other complex behaviors are sequentially ordered, just as language is. Psychology must try to understand the *mechanisms* whereby such sequential orderings take place.

The history of psychology is filled with examples of the study of sequentially ordered behavior. Yet we know distressingly little about these phenomena. For example, psychology has had a long history of studying rote memorization—the learning of words or nonsense words in a strict sequence or order—and of studying maze learning—which involves the learning of an ordered sequence of gross muscular responses. Yet we know little about even these. In fact, the study of maze learning was more or less abandoned some thirty years ago as being too complex. It was felt that we must learn about the simpler behaviors first before we can understand the complex ones which are presumably built from them.

We will not discuss in detail the assumption that complex things are constituted by the summing up of simple things. This appears to be an erroneous assumption since the "summing up" does not take account of the necessary order of the parts. Lashley (1951) has pointed out that there are a host of such sequentially ordered behaviors about which we are totally ignorant. It is often argued, for example, that the organization or ordering of events is controlled by our knowledge, perception, or sensation of our previous behavior. Each particular behavioral event is a result of the sensations produced by the immediately preceding behaviors. Yet, a violinist organizes the muscular control of his fingers in such a way that the correct sequence of notes which he produces is over before any muscular feedback from his fingers can take place. That is, he behaves correctly before it is possible for him to "know" whether he has played the correct notes or not. In language we have a similar problem; the movements of the speech organs produce precisely ordered correct sequences of sounds in such a short time that we cannot "know" that we are speaking properly until we have already finished speaking. As a system of behaviors, language is perhaps the paragon of sequentially ordered behaviors, and of complex behaviors in general. If for no other reason than to increase our knowledge about complex behaviors in general, the study of language would be important.

LANGUAGE IS A MEDIATOR

One of the questions of historical concern to American psychologists has been "What functions or purposes do particular behaviors serve?" If we ask this question of language, we immediately discover another reason for the psychological study of language. The functions served by language are many. Not only is language a device for communicating our ideas and intentions to others, but it is also a device for regulating our own behavior.

We may talk about this fact by saying that language is a *mediating behavior*. Traditionally it has been accepted that behavior is a response to stimuli. Stimuli may be defined as events affecting the sensory receptors of the organism. The determinants of a particular response are too numerous to list here. Indeed, not all are known. We can say, however, that some combination of the organism's genetic makeup and of his past experience with the stimuli in question, or with similar stimuli, determines what his behavior will be.

Yet this type of explanation is still not sufficient for accurate psychological explanation. The same physical stimulus event may "call out" totally different behaviors from an individual at different times, or from different individuals in the same situation. That there is no one-to-one correspondence between stimuli and behaviors is often attributed to the existence of internal mediators. For example, we might assume that when he encounters a particular stimulus, the individual makes some reaction to it which is internal (it may be entirely neural in nature) and that this internal reaction, in turn, determines the overt behavior which he makes. It is quite possible that in many cases there are such internal events which *mediate* between the overt external stimulus and overt muscular behavior. Psychologists often call these mediators "responses" because they are, in part, caused by stimuli and hence "function" as responses to stimuli.

Language is one possible mediating response. Suppose, for example, that you are faced with a strange object which has four legs supporting a flat surface, and that the surface is about as high off the floor as your mid-thigh. If you label this object to yourself as /chair/ or /bench/, you will behave differently with respect to it than if you label it as /table/. Consider the same object variously identified as /table/, /operating table/, or /dissecting table/. Here it should be even more obvious that the covert verbal response to the object will affect your overt response to it. Examples of this sort indicate that language may function as a mediator of behavior.

This, then, gives language a rather unique status in psychology. Language is not only a *behavior*, whose determiners must be studied per se, but it is also a *determiner and cause of behavior*. Few other objects of study can claim to be both a cause and an effect in the way that language can. Moreover, it is not just that language acts as a mediator which makes it important to study, but rather that language may be a mediator in extremely important behaviors. According to some theorists (Dollard and Miller,

1950) even the difference between events which are conscious and those which are unconscious may be a function of the presence or absence of verbal mediators—a debatable but provocative notion.

LANGUAGE IS A COGNITIVE ORGANIZER

In the preceding section we argued that language could function as a determiner of particular behaviors in particular stimulus situations. When we refer to language as a cognitive organizer, however, we are suggesting something of much greater scope. In essence we are suggesting the hypothesis, advanced by anthropologically oriented linguists (e.g. Whorf, 1956), which states that the nature of one's language *determines* his entire way of life, including his thinking and all other forms of mental activity.

From the viewpoint of linguistics any language can be described by enumerating two sorts of things: (1) a set of words or word roots which constitutes the vocabulary or *lexicon* of the language, and (2) a set of rules for combining the words or roots into whole *utterances* or sentences, which is the *grammar* of the language. To the linguistic relativists, of whom B. L. Whorf is perhaps the best known, one's entire manner of viewing, reacting to, and thinking about the world is determined by the nature of the lexicon and, more importantly, by the grammar of his native language.

Thus in English we distinguish between two wave lengths of light by calling one /blue/ and the other /green/. Speakers of Navaho do not make this distinction. While it is true that the Navaho retina (the layer of receptor nerves in the eye) responds to light in the same way as the retina of English speakers, it may also be true that in one real sense the Navaho do not see the difference between blue and green. To take a simple example, if you ask a Navaho for a can of paint of the color in question, you would probably be likely to get either blue or green, or more likely, something in between. This, of course, seems to be a rather unimportant matter. But such lexical differences extend from the area of simple concepts well into the concept systems which define the physical sciences, and into those concepts which make up major metaphysical and philosophic systems. These lexical differences may easily shape one's entire way of reacting to the world. Could a culture having a language which has no words for "time" develop physical sciences as we know them, for example? Or could a culture which has no concept of money develop a capitalist democracy such as ours? Perhaps of greater relevance are those issues which arise when two languages have the "same" word, but where each has slightly different meanings for it. Is it possible, for example, to understand certain behaviors of the governments of the USA and the USSR by considering that the languages of these countries assign somewhat different meanings to the term /democracy/? We shall return to this issue later in the book.

The question of grammatical differences is perhaps even more profound, and is therefore correspondingly more difficult to illustrate. Let us take a somewhat hypothetical example. As English speakers, our everyday, common sense "physics" tells us that there is a world of relatively permanent physical objects which have relatively fixed attributes such as size, shape, and color. To this world of objects, things happen; changes are made. The objects themselves, however, are seen as stable and fixed in character. But it is not necessary to conceive of the world this way. Some of the more advanced theories in physics do not, and for that matter neither did some of the ancient Greek philosophers. Heraclitus, for example, saw the world as "flux." The defining characteristic of physics for him was activity or change, not permanence in any form. Even in English a wave is alternatively an object (thing) or an event (part of a process).

A linguist relativist with some degree of fancy might argue that our everyday "physics" was a function of our grammar. That is, in English sentences we find a predominance of substantive words, nouns and adjectives referring to things and attributes (which are presumed to be more or less permanent), while there are fewer verbs (which denote change), and they are sandwiched into the middle of sentences. Actions and changes are not grammatically emphasized in our language. Moreover, not only is a particular vocabulary present, but it is *grammatically permissible* to talk about /a thing/ or /tables/ or /green/ or of /the essence of being/ or of /an action/ or even of /the essence of change/. Our language permits us to talk about things without expressing any action. It also permits us to describe actions themselves as though they were things. A linguistic relativist might argue, and with some force, that our thing-oriented view of the world is shaped and molded by the grammatical rules of our language, for our language is the means by which we conceptualize the world. There is, of course, always a problem about which is the cause and which the effect in any correlation between language and some other conceptual system. We return to this problem in later chapters.

We may conclude as follows: The hypothesis of linguistic relativity raises the rather distinct possibility that one psychological system, language, may influence other psychological systems such as perception and thinking. If this hypothesis is true, it has implications for practical, immediate life which are too important to ignore. Its validity is a fact which should be established beyond doubt. This suggests that the psychological study of language is not merely an interesting pastime for the academician, but a necessary study for the understanding of a great array of psychological and social problems. To the extent that we wish to understand man, the way in which he lives and the way in which he makes his world, the study of language appears to be logically necessary.

Let us now proceed to the actual psychological study of language. Here we hope to present not only some of the relevant facts about language, but also the speculations and theories offered by psychologists to account for it. None of these theories appear to be entirely satisfactory. As a result, we will offer some ideas of our own. Their validity may be judged in terms of their relevance to the human and social issues for which a psychological theory should account. The latter will be illustrated by the areas of language pathology and the use of language to influence others.

Bibliography

Dollard, J., and Miller, N. *Personality and psychotherapy*. New York, McGraw-Hill, 1950.

Hockett, C. F. The origin of speech. *Sci. Amer.*, 1960, 203, #3, Sept., 88-96.

Lashley, K. The problem of serial order in behavior. In L. A. Jeffries (Ed.) *Cerebral mechanisms in behavior*. New York, John Wiley & Sons, 1951.

Tolman, E. C. The determiners of behavior at a choice point. *Psychol. Rev.*, 1938, 45, 1-41.

Von Frisch, K. *Bees: their vision, chemical senses, and language*. Ithaca, Cornell University Press, 1950.

Whorf, B. L. *Language, thought and reality*. New York, John Wiley & Sons, 1956.

II
Linguistics

What Is a Language?

In the preceding chapter we gave a brief definition of language, but we did not attempt to justify or elaborate this definition. Now we will do so. Let us first restate the definition: (1) A language is a *system* of behaviors and potential behaviors; (2) these language behaviors may influence the behavior of other people; (3) language behaviors are relevant or appropriate to states of affairs in the user's environment but are in part independent of those states of affairs; (4) language behaviors may be inappropriate or wrong. Let us analyze this definition point by point.

A. BEHAVIOR AND POTENTIAL BEHAVIOR

For a psychologist the study of language concerns itself with something which users of the language *do*; that is, what a language is, is expressed in one or another type of behavior by the user of the language. This is not to imply that a language is necessarily spoken, for it clearly may be only written, or it may be gestural, as in American Indian sign languages or the languages of deaf mutes. However, to say that a language is nothing more than some kind of overt behavior is incorrect.

First of all, we cannot simply say that a language consists of all members of some class of behaviors, if by this we mean behaviors which people have actually done. A language is not sim-

ply all words or all sentences of that language which have in fact
been uttered. We must differentiate between the language itself
(*la langue*) and those utterances which have actually been made
in the language (*la parole*) (de Saussure, 1922). To identify a
given behavior as part of a language we must already know what
the language is. New sentences or utterances are constantly being
added to *la parole* without in any way effecting *la langue*. It is
possible to say something novel in any language, if only because
all languages permit some variety of repetition. Thus I can say
"Bob is a good boy," or "Bob is a good, good boy," or "Bob is a
good, good, good boy," and so on, repeating the word "good" as
often as I like. I can, in other words, create an *infinite* number
of gramatically correct sentences just by this device alone.

We have to conclude that *any* language is *infinite* in size, and
no language can be defined by any finite body of utterances, such
as by all utterances which have been made in that language. A
language consists not only of behaviors which have been made,
but also of behaviors which can be made. Not any behavior will
do, of course, but only certain specific behaviors, those which do
not break certain rules. That is, the *possible* utterances in the
language must be grammatically acceptable in order to appear as
actual utterances in that language. And to be grammatically acceptable, these utterances must not break certain rules. That
these rules exist verifies the fact that a language is a system of
behavior.

Before we discuss the concept of a system another point must
be made. A language is related to something which has been or
can be *done*—behavior or potential behavior. To the extent that
we wish to subject language to psychological study, we cannot
permit definitions only in terms of abstract or metaphysical entities. Any scientific study must *start* with phenomena which are
observable or tangible to the scientist. Thus language cannot be
identified as a set of meanings or essences to which words or
sentences refer, nor can it be identified with the states of affairs
to which words or sentences refer. This does not mean that words
or sentences have no meaning. It does deny, however, that there
are "meanings" in some Platonic world which we must consider

in order to understand language. We cannot prove this assertion, but a great deal of our discussion of meaning, which will follow, will be an attempt to justify it.

B. A SYSTEM

When we say that language is a *behavior system*, we mean that the events which make up language are not independent of one another, and that they occur in certain specific orders or follow certain rules. Moreover, the ways of ordering the events (words, for example) which are permissible within the system, are fewer than the logically possible ways. The system has rules, and to say that something has rules implies that certain orderings are permitted, and that certain other orderings are *not* permitted.

It is, perhaps, less obvious, and more interesting, that those events which make up a language (words, in the case of English) are not independent of one another. How one uses a particular word is not independent of the use of other words. It is not a function of its meaning alone, but is a function of at least some additional words, and perhaps of *all* the other words in the system. Consider a traditional example, the word /red/. In order to use /red/ properly, in order to know what the word /red/ means in any sense of that term, you must know both when to use it and when *not* to use it. Each word in the lexicon of a language, and each utterance made within the language implies a *discrimination*. Each utterance implies that something is so and so, and something else is not that way or need not be that way. To use /red/ properly you must also know when not to use it both grammatically and in reference to the world around you. You must have some category which is "not-red." In addition, since something cannot be red and not-red simultaneously, we see that other color names, as is the word /color/ itself, are dependent for their meaning on that of /red/ and vice versa, of course.

We need not stretch the imagination too far to see that /red/ is dependent for its correct grammatical use on other color words and on the existence and use of other adjectives. We could not use /red/ properly if we did not have rules for adjectival use. The

18   MEANING AND MIND

fact that there are rules for adjectival use implies that there are
ways in which one cannot use adjectives, and suggests further
that there are other classes of words whose rules of usage are not
adjectival rules. In other words, the appropriate use of /red/ is in
some sense dependent on or determined by the use of every other
word in the language. It is this lack of independence which makes
us call language a system. Language is not the only system of
behavior, but the fact that it is a system is a necessary, identifying characteristic of a language.

C. INFLUENCING OTHERS

We have defined language behaviors as ones which may influence the behavior of other users of the language. Needless to say,
we must emphasize the word "may." Language is not compelling,
the way a push or a punch is. But language is a tool for social
interaction and influence. Language is, by necessity, social, and
this characteristic of it is crucial. Any language is learned from
other people and is used, at least to some extent, to communicate
to others. The evident success of this communication testifies to
the fact that languages do not, and cannot, escape their social
heritage. A language which does not communicate is a sick, non-
functioning language.* Indeed, it is not a language at all.

Not only are all languages or dialects derived from social intercourse, but, in fact, no language can *ever* be anything but social.
There is no logical possibility of a truly private language. The
arguments of Wittgenstein (1953) and his followers would seem
to be telling here. As an example, consider the use of the word
/pain/. Pain is a sensation which is internal to the individual and
which may result from causes which are not directly observable
to anyone else, as in the case of a headache. We can take /pain/
then as an example of a word which presumably refers to some-

* Adults can, of course, invent languages which no one else can understand.
But in all cases these languages are derivatives of existing languages. They
are, in effect, codes of languages. These idiosyncratic languages are also used
for communication; in this case, however, the target of the message is either
the communicator himself, or some product of his fantasy life.

thing private to the experiencer, and which can thus be said to have a private meaning. It is the name of a sensation which you, the experiencer, and you alone, are aware of. But then we must ask how you could learn such a name.

Let us suppose that you have such a private experience at Time 1, and at that time you give the experience a name, say /fap/. Now at Time 2 the experience is repeated. How can you correctly apply the name to the experience at this second time? Well, you might say, you recognize it. But how do you recognize it? Are you not just saying that you see that it is a fap, therefore, you call it /fap/? But, if so, then you are just using the word to explain how you use it—clearly an illogical procedure. Recognition and actually using the word are so intertwined that one cannot be used to explain the other. In point of fact, if you digest this illustration, you will see that you cannot privately tag any experience to identify it for future use, for any such tag would suffer the fate of our word /fap/—you would never know whether or not it was used correctly, and, hence, you could not ever learn to use it correctly. But if you cannot learn a word or name by correlating it with a *private* experience, how do you learn names, and, in particular, how do you learn the names of so-called private experiences?

It seems to be an unavoidable conclusion that *no word can be learned completely privately*. Neither the first word nor any other in the vocabulary can be learned totally privately. If the first words must be taught by others, this means that all language, even what is thought of as most private—names for sensations and the like—must have a social, public, and communicable heritage.* No private experience, such as pain, can be labeled by a private word alone. To identify such a sensation for future use, the identifying markers—those things which tell us that pain is pain (for this argument it is unnecessary to define these identifying markers)—must be *independent* of a person's immediate experience. Others must be able to recognize that person's pain

---

* That something is *your* experience and that no one else can have that particular experience does not deny the possibility that someone else can know that you are experiencing it.

as similar to something they have experienced. If the person attempts to supply the identification himself, privately, he can never be sure that he is correct. But if the identification is independent of his own immediate experience, this problem is avoided. Words are labels of things only because their meanings and uses are independent of any particular individual. The word /pain/ has meaning because it is used by others, because it has a correct and an incorrect use, and because its meaning is taught by others to the experiencer. /Pain/ has meaning precisely because it is *not* a private label for a private experience. No word can refer to something which is totally private: *all* of language is social, even those parts which presumably refer to private events.

Now of course a person can invent words, and even invent labels for his own subjective experience. But to the extent that these are functional labels, true names or words which can be *used* in a language, they will always describe events which could be described by other words. That is, the invented words may be defined by other, social words (there is no such thing as an independent word or meaning since we are dealing with a system of behaviors). These defining words were learned in social situations and have meanings independent of the individual's private experience. Their meaning is provided by others. Thus for any word in any language, while it may in fact refer to something subjective, private, and not directly observable by another, its meanings and the rules for its use are public. To the extent that we are dealing with a language, we can say that while I may not be able to see what a word refers to I can *know* what it refers to. There are no private meanings for words. All language is social, for if it were not, it would not and could not be a language.

D. LANGUAGE BEHAVIORS ARE RELEVANT TO, BUT INDEPENDENT OF, STATES OF AFFAIRS

This part of our identification says essentially that a language conveys some kind of meaning and that it can refer to things. It says that a particular piece of linguistic behavior is not independent of what is happening in the world around the speaker. But it also says that language behavior is not simply *conditioned* to environmental events so that, given the event, the particular language behavior always appears as a response to that stimulus. Given the physical object, table, we do not always say /table/ or even think it. On the other hand, the word /table/ may be used correctly in the presence of a table and may be used incorrectly (sometimes) in the presence of other objects, such as refrigerators. The word /table/ *refers* to something in the physical environment and *in that sense only* can it be said to be a response to that physical object. This is, of course, not the psychologist's typical usage of the term "response."

But it is probably more accurate to say that language behaviors are *appropriate* to certain environmental events or, that they *refer* to such events, for there are many language behaviors which cannot *in any sense* be said to be *responses* to the events referred to. Consider /a perfect vacuum/, /the essence of being/, and /the world is not round/. Here we have utterances which clearly refer to states of affairs, but the states of affairs either (1) never have existed, (2) are not open to our direct experience, or (3) could not possibly exist. These linguistic behaviors, therefore, cannot be treated or understood as responses to their referents. A simple example of the fact that I can sit at my desk and talk of sailboats where none are present actually illustrates the problem equally well. My language here refers to some particular state of affairs in the world, but one which is not physically present at this time. Indeed, we can speak of a state of affairs that is totally imaginary.

It is characteristic of language that, while it refers to states of affairs, it can be used when the states of affairs are not present, when the states of affairs do not exist, or when the actual state of affairs is other than that spoken of. Statements may be true or false, with regard to the facts of the world about us, while they are all equally correct, linguistically. This poses a considerable theoretical problem. Psychologists have traditionally analyzed behavior by a stimulus-response model. This model has been suggested by the apparent fact that a world exists independent of man and that his behavior seems to be a function of that world.

Among other things, this analysis is reinforced by the neurologist's distinctions between afferent (sensory) and efferent (motor or response) nerves. As psychologists, if we wish to conceive of linguistic behavior as a response to some stimulus (as has been done), we are going to have to expend considerable effort in defining "stimulus." It will be no *simple* thing, and clearly the problem cannot be solved by trying to treat the physical referents of words as stimuli, since all words simply do not have such referents. Neither can we solve the problem by calling the *verbal* definers of words, stimuli, since then we would not understand how words can correctly refer to physical things. That language both can be a correct describer of experience and propose states of affairs which are directly contradictory to experience, suggests profound problems either for a theory of language or a theory of experience or both.

E. LANGUAGE BEHAVIOR MAY BE INAPPROPRIATE OR WRONG

It is a characteristic of language, as we have pointed out, that it is not completely caused by any particular environmental events. The use of the word /table/ is not dependent on the physical presence of table. The complexity of the stimuli to which any given utterance is the "response" is so vast that the utterance may in fact be made in a wide variety of situations. Some of these situations may be said to be erroneous. That is, the language behavior will be grammatically wrong or will be an incorrect description of events. The range of error in the possible uses of language extends from misstatements of fact or false statements, through grammatical errors, up to the completely inappropriate choice of words. The freedom of expression built into a language necessitates the freedom of being wrong in our usage of it. But even in the case of incorrect description of the facts, the utterance still remains part of the language; it will convey some sort of message to the listener; it will have a sense, though the sense is not that intended.

Our major point is this: without this possibility of error, we would not be dealing with a language. Consider some of the vocalizations made by birds. Crows will give a characteristic cry when humans approach and a different cry when the human danger is leaving—an "all clear" signal. This is clearly an act of vocal communication on the part of the crow. But equally clearly these cries do not constitute a language. Each of the particular vocal signals given by the crow seems to be a response to a definite and relatively small and distinct set of stimuli. These stimuli are external to the crow and are produced by particular states of affairs in the world around him. Without these stimuli the cry would not be made; with the stimuli present the cry will always be made. It is, among other things, the apparent determinism and certainty of these vocalizations by the crow which show that they are not part of a language. In a language we would see the crow "talking" about humans when they were not there, or mistaking cows for humans or some similar sort of act. For when we speak of language we are speaking of something that is *not completely certain*, that *cannot* be predicted completely from any set of events, whether those events are external to the organism or are part, perhaps, of his own behavior. That is, we cannot predict a person's use of words either by considering only his environment, or by considering only his previous linguistic behavior, or both.

While this is not the place to indulge in an extensive discussion of meaning, we must point out that language, as we have defined it, functions because of the uncertainty or unpredictability which it has; *it works because it permits one to be wrong*. We have already tried to establish the fact that communication can take place without the necessity of language. Both traffic lights and crows communicate to someone or other, but neither has a language. Likewise, vocal acts on the part of people may communicate and yet not be linguistic in nature. Consider a person who, following every statement of fact by someone else, says /you don't say/. This act is vocal, it technically is made up of words, and it communicates—the communication is mainly about a distressing state of fuzziness on the part of the speaker. But its very predictability, the fact that it always occurs in certain highly definable situations, makes it meaningless. It tells us nothing that we do not already know about either the speaker or about the world around him. Whatever is communicated is not related to the particular meanings of the words in the utterance. It is only because of the possibility of error, because of the existence of uncertainty, that language functions and conveys the vast amounts of meaning and information which it does. No system of behavior which is completely and precisely predictable can be linguistic.

As an aside, it is of some interest to speculate on whether or not machines can learn a language in view of this last issue. All existing computers are programmed to respond to a simple set of variables and to respond unequivocally to them. While it is possible to make such a machine highly sensitive to the statistical properties of a language, at some point the machine must be made narrowly deterministic; it must respond in one and only one way to a particular set of variables. And yet language cannot be completely predictable from a simple set of variables, e.g. only from the statistical properties of language (such as the relative frequencies of using words or combinations of words) and still be fully functioning as a language. Since the machine cannot go beyond some small set of predictor variables, we would have to conclude that it could not master a language. While a machine may be taught to substitute one group of signs for another, as in the case of translating machines, these substitutions must have a rigidity that will often produce linguistic nonsense. That is, of course, the current state of translating machines, but it would seem as though this might be a necessary state of such machines. No machine could translate properly because no machine can learn a language in the proper sense of that term. And no machine can learn a language because no machine can be programmed to accommodate the requisite number of variables nor the requisite lack of one-to-one correspondences between causes and effects. If one could build a machine that could, in fact, live in the world, it probably could learn a language. But then one would have built a very special kind of machine, the kind we call *Homo sapiens*.

Linguistics

Now that we have arrived at a means of identifying a language, we must describe the study of linguistics proper. While the psychology of language is concerned with the questions raised by the fact that *people* can use language, linguistics concerns itself with the nature and history of languages in general, independent of any particular users of the languages. Linguistics concerns itself not only with the study of the origins and history of languages in general, but also with the structure of languages, and of the necessary constituents and rules of languages.

HISTORICAL LINGUISTICS

It is well known that various languages have enough similarities so that they are said to belong to the same group or family; e.g. the Romance languages and the Germanic languages. Historical and comparative linguistics are concerned with the similarities among languages and with the possible historical antecedents of these similarities. Linguists have been able to derive, by careful study of modern languages, the hypothetical historical ancestors of these modern languages. By a careful study of the similarities among most modern European languages, and by taking into account the known recorded changes in those languages (for instance, all the documents recording the change of classical Latin into modern French), it has been assumed that these languages all have a common ancestor language.

This ancestor tongue, which is known as *Indo-European*, is a hypothetical language from which most modern European languages and also many of the languages of Asia, including Hindi, Sanskrit, and Persian, are generally presumed descended. The actual characteristics of this hypothetical ancestor language remain unknown, of course. There are no historical records which go back far enough to establish the facts of the matter.

We have room for much fascinating but basically futile speculation here. For instance, if there was such a common primitive tongue, where did it originate? One hypothesis is that the original speakers of Indo-European were located somewhere in the Caucasus mountains, and that they then migrated both west and east to the lands which they now occupy. This is all conjecture, but it suggests some further questions. What happened to the languages of the lands to which they migrated? There may in fact have been languages which were suppressed by incoming populations of Indo-European speakers. Archeological evidence indicates that Europe has been populated since the appearance of the earliest forms of man. We also see that there are certain languages in Europe which are not related to the Indo-European group. The Finno-Ugric group, which contains Finnish and Hungarian, is one, but this appears to be a later addition to Europe, arriving just before the Mongol hordes. Basque, on the other hand, appears to be a completely isolated tongue, both geographically and linguistically. Could it, in fact, be the descendant of some pre-Indo-European language? Unfortunately we cannot say, and doubtless never will be able to say, although it remains a distinct possibility.

The same cloudiness befalls another ever-popular question of historical linguistics: namely, how did languages arise? What was the first spoken language like? Hypotheses here have abounded since the time of the classical Greek philosophers. One theory has it that language developed from an attempt to imitate natural or animal sounds; another has it that language derives from emotional, expressive sounds made by humans, the grunts, screams, and laughs of extreme emotional states. Neither these theories nor any of the others offered carry any real conviction. Faults can be found with each, and even extreme eclecticism, the combining of all theories into one, produces no really satisfactory answer. We just do not know how languages originated, nor are we ever likely to know.

There is another myth which must be dispelled. There are *no* existing primitive languages, if by this one means either languages which are close to being some aboriginal single common language or languages similar to those spoken by some prehistoric man. There are languages which are spoken by primitive societies, i.e. those which do not have our advanced technology, but *linguistically* there are no primitive tongues. While many languages do not have as extensive vocabularies as does English, the lack of words is usually confined to the area of technology. There may have been no word in Bantu, for instance, equivalent to the English /refrigerator/, but that is because there were no such objects available to be named. A language cannot be considered to be less adequate because it fails to describe an environment which does not exist for its speakers, although it could become inadequate if the environment were radically altered, say by technological change.

Nor can a language be said to be more adequate than others on the basis of translation. That is, there is in some sense commonality among languages, for anything which can be said in one language can be translated into any other language. There does exist the question of the *ease* with which things may be said in different languages. In fact, it may be impossible to convey the full sense of any *single* utterance in one language by means of any *single* utterance in some other language. But here it is important to realize that this is a *mutual* problem. We cannot criticize Chinese because a Chinese translation of an English statement does not convey the full sense of the English, but instead conveys some slightly different sense. For we see that the English does not convey the full sense of the Chinese either. Both languages have, in this sense, failed. Thus it is, in fact, impossible to rank languages. None are better than any others. None may be said to be primitive while others are called advanced.

The comparative study of languages which we have been discussing is almost completely concerned with spoken rather than written languages. The family relations among languages are established by appealing to speech sounds, not to graphological conventions. In contrast to spoken language, written language is often a development of which we have historical record. It is, in general, of no great linguistic importance, although, as we shall see, it is of far greater psychological importance. Writing is

arbitrary in the way that speaking is not. The selection of an al-
phabetic notation rather than a syllabic notation or a hieroglyphic
notation or a character notation seems to bear little relation to
the grammar, vocabulary, and sound characteristics of the language per se. It is often a matter of historical coincidence or even
individual whim. Thus Chief Sequoia of the Cherokee invented
a syllabary for that language using letters borrowed from the
English alphabet as some of the signs. Or the Catholic monks,
who happened to be Greek speaking, borrowed from that alphabet to create the Cyrillic alphabet for Russian. Yet the original
Russians probably came from Sweden. And, equally by chance,
the Swedish language is written in the Latin alphabet. Graphological traditions are of little interest to our study of language. It
is the structural differences between spoken languages which present the most fascinating issues for the linguist and the psycholinguist.

THE CONSTITUENTS OF LANGUAGE

(1) *Sounds:* Languages are built of spoken sounds. The nature of
these sounds is clearly of concern to both the linguist, for they
are the building blocks of languages, and to the psychologist,
since they are behaviors, the occurrence of which must be explained and understood. Each language is in fact constructed
from a relatively small set of the large number of possible sounds
which the human vocal apparatus can produce.* It is customary
to refer to the basic speech sounds of a language as *phonemes*.
Each language, then, consists of a set of phonemes. The number
of phonemes in any language varies considerably from language
to language as do the particular phonemes which particular languages use. Thus French does not use the phoneme we represent
by /ch/ (sometimes called a diphthong since two letters are used
to represent one sound) as in /church/. English, on the other
hand, lacks the glottal stop which Arabic includes.

Identifying the phonemes within a language is a delicate prob-

* According to Cherry (1957) there are as many as 4096 possible distinct
phonemes.

lem. Essentially the process involves discrimination which can be seen if we define a phoneme as *a difference in sound which makes a difference*. Thus the /a/ in /pan/ is a different phoneme from the /i/ in /pin/ because if one changes from one to the other, one has changed the sense of the word. Changing a phoneme produces a different word or changes a word into something which is not a word. Changing a sound does not necessarily produce a different phoneme. In fact, a particular phoneme consists of a large array of physically different sounds. But all these sounds are alike in that they may be substituted in a particular word without changing the sense of that word. Dialectic differences illustrate some of the most extreme examples of this. Thus the /oi/ sound in /oil/ as spoken by a Midwestern American and the /er/ sound in the same word, when spoken by some natives of New York, constitute in one real sense two cases of the same phoneme. They are *allophones*; different sounds which are members of the same phoneme class.

Linguists generally insist that the study of phonemes, *phonemics*, is carried out without recourse to the question of meaning. That is, although a word must have meaning, that meaning is not necessary to the study of the speech sounds which make it up. This may seem to be a paradoxical statement at first since it is by observing changes in meaning that we know when we have changed from one phoneme to another. But there are two reasons why the linguist's contention is important. First of all, it is not necessary to know the particular meaning of a word in order to know that one has changed the meaning of the word. If we use the word /pan/ and the word /pin/ in the sentence, /Give me a ——./ we can tell that /a/ and /i/ are different phonemes because different objects are given to us. We do not need to know in advance what object /pan/ refers to. To be even more realistic, a mispronunciation will be corrected by a speaker of the language, thus indicating to the linguist that he has exceeded the permissible bounds of the phoneme in question—without requiring that the linguist know the meaning of the word.

That phonemics is carried out without recourse to meaning is a statement which ignores the question of whether there is meaning in phonemes per se. Are there phonemes which are, for example, regularly or commonly used in words which have a particular sense? Or is there a particular sense which is regularly granted by the use of a particular phoneme? These questions reflect the position known as *phonetic symbolism*, which hypothesizes that certain sounds do tend to *suggest* certain meanings and that all languages tend to use sounds similarly. We will devote some time to the discussion of phonetic symbolism in a later chapter. For the moment we should bear in mind that phonetic symbolism is a theory, not an established fact. And, even the most extreme adherents do not claim that particular sounds *always* mean the same thing. The point is that phonemics may be pursued irrespective of the truth of the phonetic symbolism hypothesis.

With or without recourse to meaning, determining the phonemic constituents of a language always remains somewhat arbitrary and hypothetical. It is perfectly possible to record *all* of the sound distinctions heard in a language, either by mechanical means or by the use of one of the elaborate phonetic alphabets available. But distinct sounds do not define phonemes. Some sounds are not phonemes at all in most languages, e.g. clicks of the tongue, although they may be in some, such as Hottentot. Moreover, some sound distinctions are phonemic, while other distinctions constitute allophones. Much of the difficulty here lies in the use of the phrase "a language," which implies that there is only one discrete set of sounds used by all speakers of the language. Yet, this is clearly not the case. All languages have dialects, speech variations shared by subgroups of people within the language community as a whole. These dialects are usually mutually understandable, although in some cases even this becomes strained. But to the objective observer they are all members of the same language, even though they consist of different sets of phonemes. Thus, while it may be perfectly plausible to isolate the phonemes for a particular speaker of a particular dialect, there may be difficulty in establishing a set of phonemes which are common to any large set of speakers. That is, we will not be able to absolutely specify *the* phonemes for *a* language.

Each language is a set of dialects which differ in their phonemic constitution.

For example, in Figure 1 we have presented the set of phonemes which the anthropologist and linguist Leonard Bloomfield (1933) presented as the phonetic constituents of Chicago English.

As you can see, Bloomfield specifies thirty-two primary phonemes in his description. Without in any way questioning its accuracy for Chicago residents, it is not applicable to the speaker who, for example, does not distinguish between the first two phonemes listed by Bloomfield: /alms/ and /odd/ have the same initial sound for me.

While establishing exactly what sounds "make a difference" may be a difficult procedure, one can establish the *physically possible* phonetic distinctions. That is, we can describe the sounds which you can possibly make by virtue of the fact that you are a human being with a particular vocal apparatus. These sounds are produced by physiological organs and differences in sounds are produced by altering these physiological organs and their behavior. The physically possible sound differences do not necessarily constitute phonemic differences. Feel for yourself the great difference in tongue position between making an /r/ and an /l/ and realize that a speaker of Japanese does not recognize this as a phonemic difference.

A diagram of the organs of speech (Munn, 1966) is presented in Figure 2. Speech sound production begins with exhaling. Nearly all known speech sounds are made by either releasing air from the lungs or by interrupting such released air. Only in the case of a few African languages, such as Hottentot, are sounds made by inhaling, and even in these languages the frequency of such sounds is rare. The clicking of the tongue (often written as "tsk tsk") is an example of such an inhaled sound. The shaping of the exhaled air to form the distinctive sounds of speech is performed by several organs. Going from the lungs outward, the first important organ of speech is the larynx or vocal cords. These cords are muscles which lie across the air passage leading from the lung, and which can be tightened, so that they vibrate with the passage

[a]	*alms*	[amz]	[i]	*pin*	[pin]	[r]	*rod*	[rɑd]
[ɑ]	*odd*	[ɑd]	[j]	*yes*	[jes]	[s]	*sod*	[sɑd]
[b]	*big*	[big]	[ǰ]	*gem*	[jem]	[š]	*shove*	[šov]
[č]	*chin*	[čin]	[k]	*cat*	[kɛt]	[t]	*tin*	[tin]
[d]	*dig*	[dig]	[l]	*lamb*	[lɛm]	[θ]	*thin*	[θin]
[ð]	*then*	[ðen]	[m]	*miss*	[mis]	[u]	*put*	[put]
[e]	*egg*	[eg]	[n]	*knot*	[nɑt]	[v]	*van*	[vɛn]
[ɛ]	*add*	[ɛd]	[ŋ]	*sing*	[siŋ]	[w]	*wag*	[wɛg]
[f]	*fan*	[fɛn]	[o]	*up*	[op]	[z]	*zip*	[zip]
[g]	*give*	[giv]	[ɔ]	*ought*	[ɔt]	[ž]	*rouge*	[ruwž]
[h]	*hand*	[hɛnd]	[p]	*pin*	[pin]			

[aj]	*buy*	[baj]	[ij]	*bee*	[bij]	,	[ɔj]	*boy*	[bɔj]
[aw]	*bough*	[baw]	[juw]	*few*	[fjuw]		[uw]	*do*	[duw]
[ej]	*bay*	[bej]	[ow]	*go*	[gow]				

["], placed before primary symbols, loudest stress: *That's mine!* [ðɛt s "majn!].

['], placed before primary symbols, ordinary stress: *forgiving* [for'giviŋ] ; *I've seen it* [aj v 'sijn it].

[ˌ], placed before primary symbols, less loud stress: *dining-room* ['dajniŋ ˌruwm] ; *Keep it up* [ˌkijp it 'op].

[ˌ], placed under one of the primary symbols [l, m, n, r], a slight stress which makes this primary phoneme louder than what precedes and what follows: *coral* ['karl̩], *alum* ['ɛlm̩], *apron* ['ejprn̩], *pattern* ['pɛtrn̩].

[.], placed after primary symbols, the falling pitch at the end of a statement: *I've seen it* [aj v 'sijn it.].

[¿], placed after primary symbols, the rising-falling pitch at the end of a question to be answered by speech-forms other than *yes* or *no*: *Who's seen it?* ['huw z 'sijn it¿].

[?], placed after primary symbols, the rising pitch at the end of a yes-or-no question: *Have you seen it?* [hɛv juw 'sijn it?].

[!], placed after primary symbols, the distortion of the pitch-scheme in exclamations: *It's on fire!* [it s ɑn 'fajr !], *Seven o'clock?!* ['sevn̩ o "klɑk?!].

[,], placed between primary symbols, the pause, often preceded by rising pitch, that promises continuation of the sentence: *John, the older boy, is away at school* ['jɑn, ðij 'owldr 'bɔj, iz e'wej et 'skuwl.].

Figure 1

of air producing the *vocalized* phonemes (e.g. /v/), or relaxed to produce the unvocalized phonemes (e.g. /f/). Moreover, the degree of tension can be varied such that the cords vibrate at a greater or lesser rate. The high vibration produces high speech tones, while the lesser vibration produces lower tones.

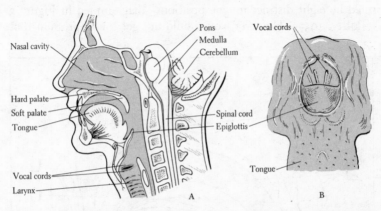

Figure 2. Speech Mechanisms. Note the position of the larynx and vocal cords. Drawing B gives a view of the area in blue from above.

At the rear of the roof of the mouth we find the soft palate, or velum, and the appendage dangling from it which is called the uvula. Both of these play a potential role in speech. The soft palate may be raised or lowered. In the former position, the passage leading from the mouth to the nasal cavities is closed, so that any sound is produced through the mouth—the so-called oral sounds. In the lowered position of the soft palate, the sound may resonate through the nasal passages, producing the nasal sounds /ng/. The uvula can be made to vibrate to produce a rolling or trilling effect. We have no uvular phonemes in English, but certain French and British dialects contain uvular /r/ sounds.

The tongue is popularly regarded as the major organ of speech, a belief which is somewhat justifiable because of the relatively large number of functions which the tongue can perform. It can, first of all, change the resonance patterns of the mouth cavity by changing its relative position (raised or lowered) and its degree of curvature. Strictly speaking, the tongue can assume a nearly infinite number of such positions, although not all such positions would result in sounds which were distinct phonemes in any particular language. In English, for example, we find that the eight distinct cardinal vowel sounds are typically accompanied by eight distinct tongue positions—diagrammed in Figure 3 (Potter, 1957). However, you should not get the impression that

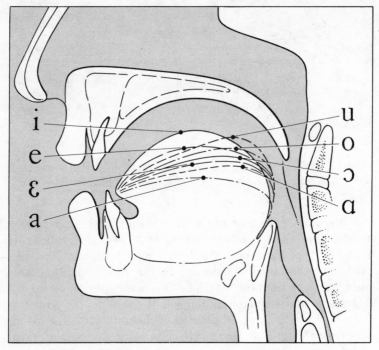

Figure 3. Tongue-positions of the cardinal vowels.

these sounds are produced only by tongue action and position. In general, the vowels are also differentiated by vocal cord activity and by lip position. In addition, the tongue plays a role by coming into contact with other parts of the mouth. It may, for example, touch the aveolar ridge, just in back of the upper teeth, to produce *aveolar* phonemes, such as the /d/ in *dog*. Contact with the teeth produces another set of phonemes, the *dentals*. The /t/ sound in French is an example of this, while the /t/ of English is more aveolar in nature.

The lips and teeth are the final organs of speech, playing a role, in general, in conjunction with other organs. Thus the *labio-dental* sounds are made by bringing the lower lip and the upper teeth into contact /f/. And as we have already seen, the tongue and teeth acting together can produce a particular set of phonemes. The lips can perform several functions. They can, first of all, stop or contain the passage of air by closing. They can release air either slowly or suddenly, in the latter case creating such *plosive* phonemes as /p/. Plosives may also be created by the vocal cords as in the glottal stop found in German but not typically found in standard English. The lips, furthermore, can assume several degrees of opening: relatively wide /a/ or relatively narrow /e/, rounded /o/, spread /e/, or neutral /i/ as in /it/.

If we take all of the various possible ways in which single speech organs can function and combine them in all possible ways, we can determine the total number of physically possible speech sounds—according to one calculation, 4096 (Cherry, 1957). Some combinations are not physically possible; we cannot produce nasal sounds with rounded lips, for example. The number of physically possible sounds is much larger than the number of phonemes actually found in any language. The phoneme set which makes up any language is always a *selection* from the possible number of phonemes. Those sounds which are not selected as part of the language suffer one of two fates: either they become allophones, and are treated as functionally identical to other sounds, or they drop out of one's behavioral repertoire completely and are never produced. There are sounds which could be phonemes, and which in fact are phonemes in other languages, which are not recognized as linguistic sounds by speakers of English, e.g. the rolled /ch/ sound found in Hebrew words like /chiam/. Some of these sounds which are dropped out of the speech patterns of particular linguistic groups are so little used that it becomes almost impossible for the adult speaker to make them. The uvular /r/ is an excellent example of this, as any teacher of French can no doubt testify.

It is clear that a human being has the physical apparatus to produce all known phonemes. There are no known racial differences in the vocal apparatus. Simplicity of phoneme content in a language does not indicate physical inferiority of the speakers or linguistic inferiority of the language. A human infant can be raised as a member of any language community and will speak that language as would a native born member of that community. It has been hypothesized that human infants produce all known sounds in their infancy and that in the process of learning their native languages they drop some and retain only those which actually are a part of the language of the parents. While this hypothesis is probably not true as stated, it is true that all or nearly all infants utter phonemes which are not part of the parental language and that those sounds which are not part of the parental language are not retained. In adulthood we may well find that some of the sounds which could be produced in infancy can no longer be produced easily. This leads to the belief that it takes some peculiar attribute verging on the abnormal to speak certain languages, particularly those languages which are phonetically quite different from the speaker's. Nevertheless, this is a complete misapprehension of the true state of affairs.

What we find in fact is that speech sounds are produced by the interplay of a small number of distinct organs. Each of these organs can assume a small number of distinct positions. The fact that the tongue, for example, can assume an infinite number of positions does not change the fact that the number of positions which will produce distinctly different sounds is a small, finite one. The combination of a finite number of organs in a finite number of positions (some of which are not physically possible combinations) produces a finite set of all possible phonemes. And a human being is at one time capable of making all of these sounds. The problem for the psychologist is to account for the selection among sounds; he must explain how it is that certain sounds come to be made frequently, while it becomes "impossible" to make others.

Moreover, the speaker acquires a truly astounding skill in the production of those distinct speech sounds which make up the phonemes of one's language. The ordinary spoken sentence, for example, which may take five seconds to utter, may contain fifty phoneme shifts—that is, not different phonemes, but changes from one phoneme to another during the course of uttering the sentence. This leaves about a tenth of a second for each phoneme shift to take place. The fact that the sentence is comprehensible at all testifies that most of these shifts are performed accurately, bearing in mind that there is considerable room for error permitted in any language. How such incredibly rapid muscular skills are performed and how they are organized and controlled by the central nervous system or other psychological processes is an unsolved issue at this time. But it is an issue the psycholinguist must eventually solve. No mentalistic explanation will suffice. A person does not think of phonemes when he speaks. If he thinks of anything, it is words or, more likely, complete ideas or sentences. In fact, he does not have time to think of the phonemes, even if he knows what they are. Speaking takes place too rapidly for this sort of thought. How such control is acquired and how it functions, then, are problems of considerable psychological import.

(2) *Morphemes:* The purpose of a language, as we ordinarily think of it, is to convey meaning. In a manner which we must explore, this meaning is conveyed by sounds, specifically by the set of sounds which are the phonemes of the language. We have, therefore, at least two distinct levels of analysis of language; one level which concerns itself only with sounds (phonemics) and another level which concerns itself with meaning. By the term "morpheme" we mean the smallest unit of a language which can be said to have meaning. We will not worry for the moment about what we mean by meaning. This will be discussed fully later.

Typically, a morpheme will consist of a temporally ordered

set of several phonemes. That is, a morpheme is a particular sequence of sounds which conveys meaning. There is neither a minimum nor a maximum length to a morpheme, however. In a few cases morphemes are formed from only one phoneme—for example, one of the pronunciations of the word /a/ in English, or the word /y/ in French. Probably the most frequently used length of morpheme, in English, would be three or four phonemes.

Morphemes may be divided into two types: those which can stand or be uttered by themselves, the *free morphemes*, and those which must be uttered in conjunction with other morphemes, the *bound morphemes*. Among the free morphemes we could class many of the words of the English language. Among the bound morphemes, for example, we would class the final /-s/ in all plural nouns. The /-s/ is a morpheme, since it conveys the meaning "more than one." It is bound, since it can never occur except when attached to some other morpheme. It also becomes convenient to speak of *allomorphs*, analogous to the allophones discussed earlier. Allomorphs are phonetically distinct ways of conveying the same meaning. Allomorphs are almost always bound, and one standard example is that of the final /-ed/ in the words /walked/ and /crawled/. The /-ed/ is a bound morpheme conveying the meaning of past time. The /-ed's/ in these two words are pronounced differently, as /t/ and as /d/, respectively. As phonetically distinct sequences conveying exactly the same meaning, they meet the definition of allomorphs. Some theories go so far as to identify the /a/ in /ran/, for example, as an allomorph of /-ed/ also, since it too conveys the same information. Whether or not such a step is necessary depends in part upon one's conceptions of grammar.

Languages differ strikingly from one another in terms of their morphemic structure. Western European languages, including English, consist mostly of free morphemes with only a minimum number of bound morphemes. The *inflected* languages, of which Latin is a well-known example, differ from the (relatively) uninflected ones like English or Chinese, in terms of the usage of bound morphemes. However, most of these inflected languages are still *isolating* languages. That is, they are made up of a large number of morphemes which can be used in isolation, independently of other morphemes. In inflected languages, however, we typically find bound morphemes fulfilling the functions assigned to free morphemes in the isolating languages. Thus in inflected languages bound morphemes replace the free morphemes which in English we use for verb auxiliaries, prepositions, and the like.

At the opposite extreme, we have the *agglutinative* languages, which have virtually no free morphemes. In these languages the minimum permissible utterance is a sentence of some kind. The sentence is "one word long"; that is, it is made up of a string of bound morphemes, none of which can permissibly be uttered alone. In English we can use a one-morpheme utterance—we can simply say /table/, for example. In an agglutinative language, such as Shawnee, we must use at least two morphemes. We would have to say something about the table. Such languages, which are built solely of bound morphemes, may be inflected or not, depending on whether they change morphemes for each particular meaning. Thus while all languages must, by definition, have morphemes, the particular form the morphemes assume varies from language to language.

(3) *The Rules of Language*: Language since it is a system, consists not only of a collection of parts, phonemes and morphemes, but a set of rules for ordering those parts as well. We typically call these rules the *grammar* of the language. While we will discuss grammar more fully later, some introductory comments should be made here.

The first thing which we discover upon looking at the strings of morphemes which make up the sentences of a language, is that they give rise to a new class of events. These events, sometimes called *secondary phonemes*, are the intonation patterns of the languages. Languages differ in terms of the role played by intonation. In some languages intonation of any sort conveys next to no linguistic meaning; it may tell you about the emotional state of the speaker, but that is another issue. In others, critical intonation patterns may be confined to sentences, or may be extended to individual morphemes. In the latter category, some dialects of Chinese differentiate among words in terms of the tonal quality or pitch of the phonemes; the same phonemic sequence spoken in a high pitch is a different morpheme than the sequence spoken in a low pitch. In the case of sentences, we find that English is a fine example of a language which uses intonational differences to convey meaning. Thus the sequence /have the men paid/ said with rising intonation becomes a question, while when said with a slightly falling one becomes an order. Here the intonational pattern is not only phonemic but morphemic; it conveys meaning. The sound patterning itself becomes, then, one of the factors which we must consider in understanding the organization of morphemes into sentences.

A somewhat closer look at the strings of morphemes or words which make up the sentences of our language will show that there appear to be two broad classes of words, the form-class words and the function words. Take, for example, the following sentence:

/The boy suddenly gave the present to his younger sister./

The word /boy/ in this sentence is, in one way, not necessary. We could substitute for it a large number of other words all of which would make perfect sense in the sentence. Instead of /boy/, we could just as easily have said /nobleman/, /pauper/, /beggar/, /thief/, /doctor/, /lawyer/, or /Indian chief/. /Boy/, then, is a member of a class of words, all of which could just as easily have occurred in that sentence, disregarding, of course, the question of whether the sentence is relevant to anything. But relevant or not, these words would have been *correct* with respect to any grammatical criterion. The *form class* is defined as all the words which could be used in a particular position in a given sentence or similar positions in other sentences. If you apply this definition to enough different sentences you will find, for example, that /boy/ and /present/ and /sister/ are members of the same form class, while the other words are not. C. C. Fries (1952) assumes that four form classes will encompass nearly all words in English (and most bound morphemes in agglutinating languages, presumably) with a few exceptions which we will discuss below. These form classes are:

(a) *Form Class* 1: All words which could occupy the positions of /boy/, /present/, or /sister/ in our example. In general, this class contains mostly what we are traditionally used to calling *nouns*. However, if we consider a sentence of the type of /cheese is good./, where /cheese/ is a form-class-1 word, we see that words such as /running/, /his/, and similar "almost-nouns" fall into this form class as well. They can be substituted for /cheese/ in this sentence. Ordinarily they would not be classified as nouns but as a gerund and a nominative pronoun respectively.

(b) *Form Class* 2: All words which would occupy the position of /gave/ in our example, or similar positions in other sentence forms. This category contains mostly verbs. While it would contain the /is/ in /cheese is good./, however, it would not contain the /is/ in /The boy is giving the present/. The latter /is/ is a verb auxiliary, one of the function words we will describe below. In our example, we can see that words such as /sent/, /threw/, /pushed/, /passed/, /handed/ are members of this class, since they can all be substituted for /gave/ and still produce sensible sentences.

(c) *Form Class* 3: Here we include all the words which could occupy the position of /younger/ in our example, or similar positions in other sentence forms. This form class is, of course, made up mostly of what we would traditionally call adjectives. Thus we could substitute /older/, /ugly/, /beautiful/, /noisy/, or the like for /younger/ and still have a perfectly correct and sensible sentence. But we could also substitute words which are less clearly pure adjectives, such as /running/, /waiting/, /sorority/, and the like. They also would be form-class-3 words. And as is evident from the example, /running/, a word can belong to several form classes.

(d) *Form Class* 4: This class appears to include almost exclusively what we call adverbs. In our example sentence, the class would be defined as those words which would fit into the position occupied by /suddenly/ or into similar positions in other sentence forms. Thus we could substitute /quietly/, /slowly/, /never/, and the like for /suddenly/ and still have a sensible sentence. So these words would fall into form class 4.

It may seem at first that these form classes are merely renamings of traditional grammatical word classes. However, a close investigation of our language indicates that there are always certain words, or certain uses of words, which are difficult to categorize. Thus we were traditionally burdened with "adjectival nouns," "gerunds," "nominative adjectives," and the like. These distinctions now become unnecessary. It has been argued by the major proponent of the form-class system, Fries, that words should be classified according to the ways in which they are used. An individual word may be used, in fact, in particular positions in sentences and not in other positions. The position in which a word may be used indicates the class or the "part of speech" the word belongs to better than any a priori set of grammatical categories. In fact, four categories will quite nicely encompass nearly all words. Admittedly, there are a few words which do not fit.

Consider in our example sentence the word /to/. There does not appear to be *any* other word which could be substituted for it. There are, of course, other prepositions, but none would fit there. None would be grammatically correct in this sentence. /To/ is somehow uniquely suited to that position, and no other word will do the job. Consider, too, the fact that: all of our form-class words can be given a definition in terms of other words. Basically, the reason they can be defined in this way is that they all refer to states of affairs, real or imagined. Any state of affairs may be said to be a collection of properties. These properties can be described in any particular order one chooses. Since /boy/ is a collection of properties, one can define /boy/ by listing those properties, e.g. young and male. Certainly a great many form-class words can be so defined.

But what about /to/? If one were faced with the task of defining /to/, perhaps one's first tendency would be to say, "Well,

/to/ means /to/." This word has no synonyms and no properties. Then how does one define it? With a little thought we would probably arrive at something like this: /To/ is a word which states a certain kind of relationship between things. It is used, that is, it functions, to convey their relationship. But what relationship? This we simply cannot say *without using the very word we are trying to define.* /To/ and similar words cannot be defined, although they have highly precise and explicit uses in the language. They are, in effect, defined completely by their functions or uses; therefore, Fries has called them *function words*.

Function words, then, are defined by the roles which they play in sentences; by the roles which they play in relating words to each other. Each function word is a precise entity in a manner in which the form-class words are not. For example, one can figure out or deduce the meaning of a strange form-class word from the contexts in which it is used. This, in fact, is how we learn many of the items in our vocabularies. But this cannot be done in the case of function words. These meanings, or functions, must be learned precisely and individually. That is, the specific environmental situations and precise grammatical uses of function words must be memorized. No deviation is permitted in their usage as it is in the case of form-class words. Consider these two examples:

/The fap grugged the zerf to his werf./
/Fap boy gave fap present zerf werf sister./

The former sentence *could* sound like a perfectly sensible string of words, except that we do not know the meaning of some of the words. But, in any case, it seems to be a sentence. The second string is not a sentence. It is a string of words, some with known meaning and some without. But the words without meaning are not function words. They do not serve to relate the real words to one another, and cannot so serve until we learn a specific meaning for them.

We need not go into the many types of function words which Fries describes, for the psychological problem here is of more interest to us than the grammatical. What are the facts here?

First of all, we see that there are two major types of words which seem to be rather distinct. There are those words which refer to states of affairs, the form-class words, and there are those words whose purpose is totally grammatical—the function words which relate form-class words to each other. Second, we see that there are vastly more different form-class words than there are function words. Third, we see that while function words apparently must be learned individually and specifically, perhaps by some rote memorization process, the form-class words can be learned either specifically, or through context, or through verbal definition. Function words must be harder to learn because of their specialized character; it is not surprising, then, that there are fewer function words than form-class words. Nor is it surprising, then, that children first learning to speak seem to have more trouble with the function words. They enter the child's vocabulary later and seem to be used more incorrectly at first than are the form-class words.

All languages appear to have some distinction analogous to the form-class–function word distinction. The "function words" in some languages may, in fact, be suffixes or other bound morphemes, as in the dative case ending of Latin which would replace the /to/ of our example. The form classes may also be represented by bound morphemes. The boundness of the morpheme is quite irrelevant to the form class-function distinction, however. The important fact is that the uses of these bound-morpheme types are like those we have discussed in distinguishing form-class words from function words. And the learning processes by which these types are acquired in different languages must also be similar. Any student of a relatively inflected language such as Latin can testify to the fact that the conjugations and declensions—most of which serve the purpose of function words—must be learned individually by repeated—and often tedious—practice. There are no synonyms for a dative or a genitive ending. You either know it or you do not; it cannot be paraphrased as a form-class word can. But, while many of the form-class words are also memorized, others are acquired by context. We can figure out what they mean by the other words in the sentence. But we cannot know how any form-class word is related to other words unless we know what purpose the word ending which serves as a "function word" entails.

As psychologists, then, we must take into account the fact that there are two types of words, words which refer and words which order other words. It is possible, for instance, that two distinct psychological mechanisms could underlie these two distinct word types. If so, we must be prepared to offer different explanations for the acquisition and functioning of the two distinct types of words. We may be asked, "How could a psychologist account for the meaning of a word?" Or, "What sort of psychological mechanisms underlie what we call meaning?" Or we might have to answer, "How do children acquire language?" or, "How do we learn the meaning of a word?" In all of these cases, the study of linguistics shows us that *no single answer may be possible*. Since a language is a system, an ordering of events, to understand a language we must understand both the events and their ordering. A language contains two types of words, the form classes which are the events, and the function words which establish the order and relationships among events.

Bibliography

Bloomfield, L. *Language*. New York, Holt, Rinehart and Winston, 1933.

Cherry, C. *On human communication*. New York, John Wiley & Sons, 1957.

de Saussure, F. *Cours de linguistique générale*. Paris, 1922. Printed in English under the title, *Course in general linguistics* (New York, McGraw-Hill, 1966).

Fries, C. C. *The structure of English*. New York, Harcourt, Brace & World, 1952.

Munn, Norman L. *Psychology: the fundamentals of human adjustment*, 5th ed. New York, Houghton Mifflin, 1966.

Potter, Simeon. *Modern linguistics*. New York, Oxford University Press, 1957.

Wittgenstein, L. *Philosophical investigations*. New York, Macmillan, 1953.

III
The Learning and Development of Language

Learning

Before continuing our discussion of language, we must first discuss and describe certain of the processes of learning as psychologists have conceived of them. Learning in general (rather than the learning of some specific thing) has long been of concern to psychologists. While much of the pioneering and so-called basic research in this area has been conducted on subhuman animals, many of these phenomena of learning seem to be generalizable to humans. And it is only the basics of learning which need concern us now. Let us point out two things by way of introduction.

First, the study of learning has been conducted in a relatively "abstract" way. Thus, the typical experiment in learning often poses some quite arbitrary problem to the animal subject. This problem may well involve something or some action which he would never meet or need in his normal environment. This is an unfortunate necessity, for if we wish to study the learning of something, and if we wish to be certain that the animal knows nothing about it prior to the experiment, then we must pose him rather unusual learning tasks. Thus it is that the learning problems often tend to be odd and arbitrary in nature.

Furthermore, the situation in which the learning takes place is often a sterile and peculiar one. In order to rule out extraneous factors and to insure that learning and learning alone is being studied, the experimental scientist must have control over the experimental environment. He must remove all of those "noisy" factors which characterize the real world and present to the subject only those variables in which he, the experimenter, is interested. The nature of experimental research requires this "refrigeration" of the subject. The results of such research yield experimental laws which are, without doubt, valid for the situations in which they are observed. But we can question the assumption that these results are in any sense *general*. That is, are the same laws and types of learning discovered applicable to a situation in which the animals are exposed to more variables, or to "noise" or distractions, or, more appropriately, to the exigencies of life in the real world? We cannot give a definitive answer to these questions. But we must keep them in mind in evaluating the adequacy of experimentally derived laws of learning and in particular when we use such laws to "explain" language learning, which is, after all, a "real world" behavior.

Second, studies of learning have not typically been concerned with the nature of the particular thing being learned. It has often been assumed that the learning of spatial-motor problems, such as the learning of a maze, is essentially similar to the learning of visual discriminations, to the learning of concepts, and the like. This may or may not be the case. Sufficient evidence to evaluate it is lacking. We should remember, however, that language, as we have defined it, is a system. It is an ordered, dependent set of events. When we talk of learning a language, we are talking both about acquiring the rules for ordering, and about acquiring events (e.g. words) of the language which are to be ordered. Moreover, much language learning takes place *after* part of the system has already been acquired. Thus, one is both learning a system, its rules and events, and learning *within* that system, since language learning continues over a considerable period of time. We must ask whether this rather peculiar situation effects the kind of learning, or the laws of learning, which pertain to it. Given experimental results which are obtained from isolated problems, or on behaviors which are not part of a system, are these results generalizable to system learning? You might automatically assume that the answer here is "No." This would be an unjustified assumption. In fact, the evidence necessary to determine the answer is lacking. But it is equally presumptuous to generalize without justification. Many psychologists would be willing to assume that the basic experimentally derived laws and types of learning are relevant to the language learning situation with no substantial changes required. Others would not. All that you, the reader, need to remember is this: we are going to talk about the basic types and phenomena of learning, and these may, in fact, have no relevance to language. That there is a lack of relevance may be doubtful, but nevertheless it is logically possible.

The first general type of learning is called *classical conditioning*. It is also known as *Pavlovian conditioning*, after the major theoretician and researcher in this area, I. P. Pavlov.* This type of learning may be conceived of as a kind of *stimulus substitution*. That is, assume that there is some sort of behavior which is always the response to a specific stimulus. We will refer to these as the *unconditioned stimulus* and *unconditioned response* and to the conjunction of the two as the *unconditioned reflex*. If we present some new stimulus which does not elicit the unconditioned response in question, along with or slightly before the unconditioned stimulus, we will get a kind of learning. After several such pairings with the unconditioned stimulus, the new, or *conditioned* (conditional), *stimulus* will be able to call out the unconditioned response without the original unconditioned stimulus.

Most of the experimental research in this area has been conducted using extremely simple responses—e.g. blood-pressure changes, salivation, or eye blink—and extremely simple stimuli. For unconditioned stimuli, one might use electric shock, food in the mouth, a puff of air to the eye, and the like. For conditioned stimuli we might use blinking lights, buzzers, taps to the skin, and so on. It has been shown, in addition, that words can be

---

* B. F. Skinner and his followers refer to this type of learning as *respondent* conditioning, since, they argue, what is learned is a specific, known response already associated with a specific known stimulus.

used both as the conditioned and unconditioned stimuli in classical conditioning studies. We will return to this below.

Perhaps the most simplistic theory of the acquisition of word meaning is based upon a classical conditioning model. In this model it is assumed that the unconditioned stimulus is the sight of some object, say a chair. The unconditioned response is whatever response we make to the object, in this case, perhaps sitting. The auditory events produced by hearing the spoken word /chair/ become the conditioned stimulus in this situation. Thus, by conditioning, the heard word /chair/ acquires the ability to call out the response which is appropriate to the object chair. This certainly may be at least part of what we mean when we say that /chair/ refers to a chair. We will not criticize this theory of meaning acquisition at this time. But let us see whether or not this kind of learning or conditioning would actually take place as we described it.

There are several restrictions we must put on the above description. First, the response which becomes conditioned to the conditioned stimulus is not actually the same as that produced by the unconditioned stimulus. This appears to be a relatively universal fact of conditioning. In general, the *conditioned response* (that response which comes to be made to the conditioned stimulus) is only a part of, or only resembles, the unconditioned response. A dog may salivate (conditioned response) to a bell (conditioned stimulus) which has been paired with meat powder (unconditioned stimulus) in his mouth, but he will not also chew and swallow as he would to the actual meat. Here the conditioned response response is but part of the original total unconditioned response.

This fact of conditioning is no drawback as far as language learning is concerned, however. In fact it is a necessity for language learning. Responses to words are not identical to the responses to the objects to which they refer. If the word responses were identical to the object responses, language could not function. We could not talk of objects when they were absent, refer to them in the negative, or even talk at all. (Imagine the chaos if everyone tried to sit down every time the word /chair/ was mentioned.) Classical conditioning, then, seems to be at least partly relevant to the problems of language acquisition—it provides a model of learning in which the learned reaction is relevant to but not identical with some original reaction, just as one's reaction to a word is relevant to but independent of states of affairs in the world.

But another aspect of language learning is that it is relatively permanent. We must question whether or not the learned results of classical conditioning are permanent enough to be a possible explanation of language learning. In point of fact, classical conditioning often appears to be a rather transitory affair. The ability of the conditioned stimulus to call out the response in the absence of the unconditioned stimulus rather rapidly fades or *extinguishes* with repeated exposures to the conditioned stimulus. Only if the unconditioned stimulus is presented occasionally in conjunction with the conditioned stimulus will the conditioned connection retain its force. The pairing of the conditioned and unconditioned stimuli is called *reinforcement*, and it has often been suggested that learning or conditioning may require reinforcement to take place and that without it the learning will rapidly fail.

It is obvious that in using the word /chair/ we do not require the occasional presence of a real chair to keep on using the word correctly, or to know its meaning. (Indeed, there are many words which refer to things which have never been, and can never be, experienced directly.) Under ordinary circumstances, words do not lose their meanings when they are not paired with their referents. We do not often forget how to use words, despite large lapses of time between uses and despite the multitude of interfering effects produced by our own particular environments. The relative fragility of classical conditioning seen in the laboratory does not seem to correspond with the robustness of language as used in the real world. In addition we should point out that classical conditioning usually takes several trials or conditioned-unconditioned stimulus pairings to prove effective. The learning of a word, on the other hand, often appears to take place on one trial. And, the more highly controlled and isolated the laboratory situation, the more rapidly conditioning takes place, but language learning appears to thrive in the bustle of the real world. It is, after all, made to function in that world.

The phenomenon of extinction, however, is not as foreign to language as we may have suggested above. Many of you may have had the experience of repeating a word over and over many times in rapid succession, and having the impression at the end that the word no longer meant anything to you. Words do, in fact, appear to lose meaning following certain kinds of repetition. This meaning loss is called *semantic satiation* by Lambert and Jakobovits (1960), who have studied this effect in some detail. It seems to be quite typical that subjects instructed to repeat a word rapidly show meaning loss for that word. This meaning loss shows up both in descriptions of the word (using the Semantic Differential technique which we will describe in the next chapter) and in the use of the word. Thus, if the connotation of a word is seen as basically "good"—as in the word /mother/—then it is seen as less "good" following repetition. Or, if number words are repeated, the subjects experience difficulty in solving simple arithmetic problems using those numbers.

In light of this apparent loss of meaning (which is, by the way, transitory itself) and in light of the typical permanence of language, what can we say about classical conditioning? In the semantic satiation studies we *seem* to have true extinction—meaning loss because of lack of reinforcement of the word. In the ordinary use of language we see no evidence of extinction even though words may be repeated quite often and even though there is no apparent reinforcement either. Clearly, part of the difficulty may lie either in a definition of reinforcement, and such a definition is something upon which psychologists find it impossible to agree, or in treating meaning as a response which can be extinguished. To make a purely semantic distinction, in real language we are *using* words, while in the laboratory, in conditioning or semantic satiation studies, we are merely repeating

them. Using words for some purpose apparently does not lead to
extinction even though reinforcement may be absent or obscure.
But why this takes place, we cannot yet say.

We have here a situation in which the laboratory results are
not directly applicable to the real-life situation. Yet this does not
deny the possible analogy between the classical-conditioning
process and the language-learning or meaning-acquisition process.
The meaning of /chair/ could, in fact, be learned by a process
somewhat like that we described above. But even if this is so, and
assuming we can solve the problem of the permanence of language learning, there are still aspects of language which cannot
be accounted for by classical conditioning. How, for example, are
we to account for the function words? These words refer to
nothing, they have no characteristic response for which they are
the stimulus, nor are they the response to some characteristic
stimulus. It would seem impossible to account for their acquisition by means of classical conditioning. But then we cannot re-
alistically expect to find single solutions for the multiple problems of language. Perhaps one of the other varieties of learning
will account for those aspects for which classical conditioning
cannot.

Operant or Instrumental Conditioning

The operant conditioning situation requires the subject's making
some response which, when performed correctly, is then reinforced or rewarded. The responses which are learned are generally of two broad types: there are the *discriminations* in which
the subject learns to make a particular response in the presence
of a particular stimulus rather than some other stimulus, and
the *operants* in which the animal learns to operate on or use
some object in his environment. As examples of discriminations,
we can point to stopping a car in the presence of a red traffic
light versus going in the presence of a green, or to making a
particular left or right turn in a hallway (or maze) to get where
one wants to go. For operants we may look at the throwing of

switches to turn on lights, turning knobs to open doors, or the pressing of a lever to get food. The latter is one of the most common experimental devices used in learning research on lower animals. It has taken the name of its inventor, B. F. Skinner, and is known as the Skinner box.

Notice the differences between these situations and those of classical conditioning. In classical conditioning, we had some stimulus which would produce the behavior in which we were interested and we simply attempted to transfer the old behavior to a new stimulus. In the operant situation, there is no such unconditioned stimulus. The red light clearly does not *make* us stop prior to learning that we should, and the light switch does not *make* us throw it prior to learning that we can turn on the lights thereby. In operant conditioning there is no way in which we can *elicit* the behavior in which we are interested. That is, we must wait until the animal does it himself, until he *emits* it, to use Skinner's terminology. We can, of course, make it more or less likely for him to emit the behavior in question, either by prior training, by controlling the environment, or by straightforward compulsion. But we still have no stimulus which we can present which will reliably produce the behavior so that we can then train it.

Since there is no initial unconditioned stimulus in operant conditioning as there is in classical conditioning, the reinforcement in the two methods is different. In the classical situation the reinforcement, the pairing of the conditioned and unconditioned stimuli, precedes the response. In the operant situation the reinforcement must follow the response. The learner must be reinforced, in other words, following the correct execution of the behavior. This is, of course, very like a real-life situation. When a person does something correctly, or something we like, we often reward him for it. And conversely when the behavior is incorrect or disliked, we may punish him for it. These examples are perfect illustrations of operant conditioning. Within the field of psychology there are divergent and vehement opinions as to the necessity and nature of reward, however. There is little agreement as to what the conditions of reward are, or of what constitutes a reward. Nor is there agreement on the issue of the necessity of reward for learning. This much, however, seems clear; without some information from the environment, without some feedback from another person or from some inanimate object, it would seem unlikely that operant conditioning could take place. One does not learn to discriminate among things unless these discriminations make a difference to him; likewise, one does not learn to operate with or on something unless his actions produce some effects or changes. To this extent reward is a logically necessary condition for learning. This is a totally untheoretical position, however, since it does not explain why reward works or what the necessary or defining conditions of reward are. But it is not a trivial position, for we will see in our study of language that a given discrimination may make a difference for some people and not for others, and that these differences will be reflected within language itself.

Once a given behavior is emitted and followed by reinforcement (used in the broadest sense of the term), further conditioning can take place. The reinforcement can be made contingent upon some feature of the environment. In other words, it will be only in the presence of, or directly following, a certain stimulus, that the behavior will be reinforced. The stimulus will be a necessary condition for reinforcement. In this situation the operant behavior is *discriminated*. A discrimination has taken place—that is, the behavior occurs only in the presence of the particular stimulus. The discrimination is acquired because the reinforcement is given only in the presence of the stimulus. As the term discrimination implies, the behavior will occur in certain situations and *not in others*, since it is reinforced only in the presence of certain stimuli. Following our discrimination training then, we arrive at the situation in which, *given the discriminated stimulus*, the animal will make the response (usually) and will then get his reinforcement.

We should note, however, that the discriminated operant is not *produced* by the stimulus. The discriminated stimulus does not *make* response appear in the way in which many unconditioned stimuli make or force the appearance of their unconditioned responses. The discriminated stimulus may be necessary, but is not a sufficient condition for the behavior to occur. The behavior will not occur when the stimulus is absent, but it will not necessarily occur when the stimulus is present either. At least one other condition must also be present; the animal must "want" the reinforcement. He must be motivated, or to be more psychological, be in a state of drive or deprivation. Here again there are theoretical issues the details of which we shall ignore, but which can be summed up in the broadest possible terms. One of the necessary conditions for the animal's doing something is that he be in the proper internal state. If he is too tired or too restless or too hungry or not hungry enough or whatever, he will not emit the behavior. The everyday way of describing this is to say the animal must want to do this particular behavior. And by *want* all we mean for the moment is that there are conditions internal to the animal which determine, in part, what he does. External stimuli alone are not sufficient to produce operant behavior, while they may perhaps be sufficient in some cases of classically conditioned behavior.

Since the relative instability of classical conditioning was one of the reasons for assuming that it could not account for all language behavior, we must now question the permanence of operant conditioning. We find that operant conditioning is more resistant to extinction than is classical in most cases. And, under certain conditions, it may be highly resistant by any standards. There appear to be two such conditions: (1) when the animal is motivated by anxiety or fear and (2) when he has been trained under conditions of *partial reinforcement*.

With respect to fear or anxiety, we find that if an animal is trained to perform some operant response to avoid the onset of pain, which are the usual experimental means of inducing fear, he will learn such a response in relatively few trials. Moreover, according to Solomon and Wynne (1954), who studied such behavior in dogs, the animals may persist in such behavior for several hundred trials without having received pain. Of course this is quite sensible. After all, the dog wishes to avoid pain and therefore does not hang around waiting to find out if the painful stimulus is there. The appropriate avoidance of pain also means avoiding the "reinforcement" which is provided by pain. Clearly, such behavior will be very resistant to extinction.

It is not obvious to what extent we can account for language learning and maintenance by means of fear or anxiety, however. There is certainly no common-sense evidence which suggests that language learning is motivated solely to avoid pain or anxiety. However, there are some theorists, of whom Dollard and Miller (1950) are perhaps the most prominent, who have suggested that most, if not all, complex adult human behavior *is* motivated by anxiety. It would appear likely that they mean to include language in this category. This is, however, a hypothesis only. There is no direct empirical evidence to support it. In view of this lack of evidence and in view of the fact that phenomenally it makes no sense, we will dismiss it.

The *partial-reinforcement effect* is one which is obtained if the animal is rewarded only on some fraction of the trials on which he makes the correct responses, rather than on every trial as in the more traditional learning process. Thus, the reinforcement may be given according to some fixed *schedule*, such as every two minutes, or on a more random schedule. It has been found (Lewis, 1960) that, in general, the smaller the proportion of reinforcements per correct trials, the more resistant the response is to extinction, although this naturally does not hold for the extreme case in which the proportion of reinforcements is zero. In other words, the less the animal gets reinforced, the less likely he is to stop performing!

There is as yet no theoretical agreement as to why this effect occurs. Numerous hypotheses have been advanced and while some appear more intuitively correct than others, none have been *shown* to be clearly true. Among those which appear to have more face validity is the *discrimination hypothesis* advanced by Bitterman (1963) and his colleagues. This hypothesis states, in effect, that the animal cannot tell when extinction begins, or when the reinforced trials stop, since he is used to having non-reinforced trials interspersed among reinforced ones. It will take him longer, then, to discover that a particular sequence of non-reinforced trials is going to continue—that is, that the experimenter means business and is really extinguishing a response. However, this hypothesis will not hold for the fixed schedule where the animal can presumably learn that he will be reinforced after every nth trial. Yet, even here he still shows the partial-reinforcement effect.

It is highly likely that there are several explanations, rather than one, for this effect. We should note here that it is unfortunately common for psychologists to try to find a cause for some particular effect. When not motivated by purely methodological considerations, this attempt appears to follow from extremely fallacious and dangerous reasoning. There is no necessary reason for assuming that each effect has one and only one cause. Indeed, there is much more reason to assume just the opposite, that any behavior may be multiply determined, that for each effect there are several possible causes, and for each cause, in all likelihood, several effects. In the case of a theory of language, it would be extremely unwise to try to find one and only one "explanation" for language, or for any given segment of language. It is highly doubtful that language could function as it does if it were not multiply determined.

To return to partial reinforcement. No matter what explanations are found to be valid, the effect itself is well validated: Responses that are partially reinforced are more permanent than those which are not. And the degree of permanence is extreme in some cases, particularly those in which there have been random reinforcements. There is little doubt that an operant response can be made relatively permanent with only a very few overt rewards to support it. As an extreme example, Skinner (1950) reports that pigeons emitted upwards of 20,000 responses (pecks at a button) for a total of only six to eight pieces of grain. And, as has been pointed out, at this rate the pigeons would starve to death in the long run since they would not be getting enough food to provide even the energy required to get the food itself. In view of this sort of evidence, it would seem reasonable to assume that at least the permanence of language learning might be accounted for by operant conditioning.

Now we must ask whether there is any evidence that language, at least in part, can be considered a type of operant behavior. The answer appears to be yes. Many investigators have demonstrated that utterances follow some of the rules of operant conditioning. Greenspoon (1955), for example, demonstrated that it was possible to condition subjects to give primarily plural nouns as responses to verbal stimuli by reinforcing only plural noun responses. In this case, the reinforcement was also verbal, consisting of the experimenter's saying /good/ or /hm-hm/ accompanied by a positive nod of the head. Verplanck (1955) and others have shown that more complete linguistic utterances can also be conditioned in this manner. Thus, sentences containing first person pronouns can be reinforced, and the speaker, as a result, talks more and more about himself. Again the reinforcement can be verbal. Some evidence indicates that partial reinforcement shows its usual effects in this so-called verbal conditioning as well. It is also relatively easy to show that extinction will take place once the reinforcement is omitted.

Indeed, there are cases in which the subjects stopped talking completely, following the omission of reinforcement for self-reference statements. This suggests that this "verbal reinforcement" provided by the nods and grunts of the experimenter is not only a reinforcer which will increase the probability of certain behaviors, but is a necessary condition for any conversation at all. Fries (1952) has classified such polite noises as the "supporters of speech." Without them, the speaker infers that no one is listening to him and stops speaking. For a quick and violent demonstration of this, try saying absolutely nothing to someone on the telephone some time. But do not do it to a friend.

One question which can be raised here is: is this really conditioning, or are the subjects merely co-operating with the experimenter and giving him the kinds of behavior he is telling them, by his nodding and "yessing," that he wants? He *is* telling them, in one sense, by means of this reinforcement. But the real question should be raised as to whether this is operant conditioning of the ordinary sort. Greenspoon reported that his subjects were unaware of both the presence of, and the nature of, the reinforcement. They were, in other words, unable to tell him that they had been reinforced, as well as what they had been reinforced for. More recent evidence by Spiegelberger (1962), however, has suggested that the extent of "conditioning" is proportional to the degree of awareness of the subject—the more awareness, the more conditioning. This would suggest that the subjects were co-operating with the experimenter, and that the supposed operant nature of utterances was purely an experimental artifact—which would undermine the entire operant conditioning theory of language acquisition. Even in the most unaware subjects, however, there still appears to be some conditioning. But then we can always ask whether we are really assessing the subjects' awareness properly. To this question we can give no final answer. All we can say is that within certain limits linguistic utterances can behave in the way in which more traditional operant behaviors behave. This suggests that parts of language, at least, could be considered operants, but it does not prove that they are. Moreover, it does not prove in any case that language is *acquired* by operant conditioning.

Let us consider this last point for a moment. We can, for example, quite easily train a subject to blink his eye in the presence of a particular sound by always following the sound by a puff of air to the eye. This would be, of course, a standard classical-conditioning procedure. Once the blink has been established as being connected to the sound, however, it would be quite possible to maintain this connection via operant conditioning: for example, by giving the subject a monetary reward each time he blinked to the sound. What was acquired by classical conditioning can be maintained, and doubtless even altered, through operant methods. Moreover, the reverse can occur as well. We could train the eye blink as a discriminated operant by reinforcing only those blinks which occurred in the presence of the sound. We could then maintain the operant by pairing air puffs to the eye with the tone. Thus while it is fair and correct to say that language could be a class of operant behaviors for some purposes, it does not follow from this that language is learned by operant conditioning.

There is, in fact, a very good reason for assuming that language could not be acquired solely by operant conditioning as it is usually conceived. To demonstrate this, all we need do is try to account for the learning of a word, say /table/. If we are speaking the language of operant conditioning, we would have to assume something like this: to the physical stimulus of a table the child makes a series of sound responses. If these resemble /table/, they will be reinforced. Thus the child learns to emit /table/ in the presence of tables. By reinforcing him only on some correct trials (partial reinforcement) we can make this learning relatively permanent. And since parents are notably sporadic reinforcers, this is quite likely to happen. But in what sense does the child know the word /table/?

We would be inclined to predict that every time the child saw a table he would utter /table/. And yet clearly he does not do this—although small children do it more than older ones do. In fact, not saying it every time is a sign that the child really knows a word when he uses it, for he uses it not as a response to an object, but as a *reference* to objects. How, from our example of operant conditioning, can the child learn to use a word as a reference? It does not appear possible that he could. He may be able to learn to *name* things, to make a verbal utterance in their presence by operant conditioning, but he cannot learn to *refer* to them in their absence by this means. We will develop this critique more fully when we discuss Skinner's theory of language behavior.

But notice that in classical conditioning, what the child may learn is to make some response to the word, a response which resembles the response to the object itself. He may not learn to say the word as a response to the physical presence of the object. Rather he would learn to make a similar response to both the word and the object. In other words, he would not learn to name, or to say the word to the object-as-stimulus. What he would learn is to react to the word "as if" the object were there.

And is this not referring? It would seem to be, in essence. Doubtless the definition of "referring" must be made clearer and more cogent, but one could argue for a tentative hypothesis that the child may learn referential meaning by a process like that of classical conditioning. And he may learn nominal meaning or naming by a process akin to operant conditioning. Whether or not this hypothesis is true, one fact is clear: neither process of learning alone will account for the acquisition of language.

STIMULI AND RESPONSES

In our discussion of the standard types of learning, we have had occasion to treat words and various other parts of language as both stimuli and responses. It appears that language can fill the positions in learning schemata which are traditionally called stimuli and responses. But both of these terms are quite loose. Unfortunately, even the most prominent psychological learning theorist, Clark Hull (1952), does not define the term "response" and only vaguely approaches a definition of "stimulus," even though he conceives of learning as an association between stimuli and responses.

We cannot attempt at this moment a really satisfactory definition of either term. In fact, such a definition is only properly made within the confines of a theory. We can present several considerations, however, which such a definition must take into account. Ordinarily, words may be considered as stimuli in at least two senses. First, as spoken, they are auditory events, describable as a complex set of pressure waves impinging upon the tympanic membrane (ear drum) in the ear. As printed events, they are a patterned set of light waves of a certain wave length impinging upon the retina or receptive layer at the rear of the eye ball. In a second sense, they are stimuli insofar as they have meaning. We conceive of ourselves as responding to the meaning of a word, not to the physical events which make up the spoken or written word.

While there was a time during which psychologists tried to treat words as only physical stimulus events, it is clear that the second common-sense view is also valid. If a word is used, for example, as the conditioned stimulus in a classical-conditioning study, it is, in fact, the meaning of the word which appears to be the "real" stimulus. Thus, Razran and following him Luria, Sokolov, and other Soviet psychologists (see Razran, 1961) have shown that generalization of conditioned responses takes place on the basis of meaning rather than phonetic resemblance. By generalization we refer to the fact that a classically conditioned response will be made not only to its original conditioned stimulus but also to other stimuli which resemble the original conditioned stimulus. Typically the closer the resemblance, the greater the generalization—that is, the more vigorously and accurately the generalized conditioned response is made. When the resemblance is too slight, naturally there will be no generalization, and the conditioned response will not be made at all to the stimulus in question.

Suppose that we have conditioned some response to a word such as /cat/. Two possibilities for generalization exist. Either the response can be made to words which *sound* similar, such as /rat/ and /hat/ and /cap/ and /cab/, or the response can generalize to words of similar meaning but different phonetic structure, such as /feline/ and /kitty/. Or, generalization can take place to both sound and meaning. In fact, the results of experimental studies on this issue are quite unambiguous. The generalization takes place according to similarity of meaning and not at all to similarity of sound, at least insofar as we are dealing with normal adults and children. In the case of feeble-minded children, however, the phenomenon reverses. The retarded child can be shown to generalize to sound patterns rather than meaning. Why this occurs we do not know. It would appear that if the retardates did *not* know the meaning of words, they could not generalize to them. Since most retardates can talk, it follows that they have some word meanings, however. Hence the fact that they do not generalize becomes difficult to understand.

If we wish to talk about words functioning as stimuli, then there are again two senses in which they are stimuli. First, they are stimuli insofar as they are auditory or visual events, events which are necessary to *perceive* the words or meaning in the first place. As stimuli associated with behaviors, or as functional stimuli, however, words are entities with meaning. It is the meaning which is the functional stimulus. Thus, the word *qua* stimulus is both an external event which gives rise to conditions necessary for perception of the word, and an internal perceived event which can effect behavior. In theorizing about language we cannot simply speak of stimuli and responses. At least a tripartite scheme is necessary in which the external events give rise to internal events (meaning), which in turn are conditioned to or control behavior. Such internal events are referred to by some theorists, of whom C. E. Osgood (1957) is the most prominent, as *mediating* responses. We shall return to this notion in the following chapter. Alternatively, we could reject the stimulus response dichotomy as being inaccurate and inadequate as usually formulated.

When we wish to speak of language behavior as a response to something, we must raise the issue of a definition of response, which runs us into an immediate problem. With the exception of the word /a/ (pronounced as /uh/) there is *no* free morpheme in English which contains only one phoneme. In fact, most utterances (for example, those in this book) contain not only many phonemes, but many morphemes and perhaps many sentences, etc. Which among these various possibilities is *the* response? The phoneme, morpheme, word, sentence, or what? Clearly each aspect of language could rationally be a response in the theoretical sense. The phoneme, being a relatively distinct, unitary act, could classify as a sort of basic or atomic response. The morpheme or word, as the smallest unit of meaning, could classify as the basic response, since we are dealing with a system in which the meaningfulness of responses is requisite. The sentence or more properly, the free utterance, may also be considered the basic response. This is the smallest unit of language which may be *said* within the system. That is, words may have meaning but simply *saying* them often may not make any sense. We must say something which makes sense, which conveys an idea or a proposition. While in some cases a single word may be a perfectly acceptable free utterance, one which can stand by itself and make sense, in other cases it may not. As the smallest unit of sense, the free utterance may have predominance as the unit of response. In some sense it is the *only* response since every linguistic behavior of an individual *must be* a free utterance. Of course we must face the uncomfortable fact that we can say things which do not make sense, things which are meaningless, incorrect, or nonsense, and that psychologically, at least, our theory of language must account for these too, since they are as much human behaviors as correct utterances are.

While these various alternative positions have been held by various competent theorists, none appears completely convincing. Neither does any appear completely wrong, for it can be shown that each theorist has been able to marshall much good evidence in favor of his definition. This suggests, of course, that perhaps language behavior can be correctly conceived as a response in several senses of that term, and that the correctness of any particular definition may depend on what sort of question one is posing about language. Indeed, we shall attempt to demonstrate that in the study of the development and original acquisition of language by the child, the unit of response shifts from time to time, and that there is no such thing as *the* response in language as a whole.

Language and the Child

It should go without saying that the first language spoken by any normal individual is learned by him during his childhood. What is less clear is exactly what must be learned. That is, will the child make the phoneme sounds necessary for speech without anything resembling learning? And if not, how are the original sounds produced by the infant? These questions probably cannot be given a definite answer: all that we can do is show what children do, in fact, do. And we can, in addition, point to some of the conditions under which they will not behave in the typical fashion.

To start with one of the latter, it is clear from the research of Spitz (1946) and others on children, and of Harlow (1959) on monkeys, that a certain amount of social contact is necessary for the normal, healthy development of the child. The child appears to need someone or something to love, and without this object he will suffer catastrophic defects. Children reared in institutional settings in which only minimum contact with adults was available became ill even to the point of death. These "unloved" children, although well fed and given all necessary medical care, showed none of the normal childish reactions. They were morose, silent, sickly, and inactive. For our discussion, the important fact is that they did not appear to make normal childish sounds and certainly did not have anything approaching the usual phonetic structure of normally reared children of that age (about six months).

Now we can make several by no means mutually exclusive interpretations of this fact. First of all, the child in the institution may not make sounds because he is not exposed to them. There are no other people about for him to imitate. This would at least account for his lack of the phoneme-like sounds of more normal children. It does not appear to account for his abnormal silence, however, since presumably there would be other noisy children in the environment who might encourage his own noise making. Moreover, the silence conflicts with the apparently normal noise making of normal deaf children. But it appears that even crying is diminished in these institutional children. We might then consider the hypothesis that some sort of generalized reinforcement of a social nature is required in order to maintain the sound-making capacity which the normal child is born with. This assumes that something which only other people can give him *keeps* him making noises although noise per se may not be reinforced. It further assumes that at some level, all noise making is a social act on the part of the child, and that sound-making instincts, if any, are not permanent. Sounds may appear spontaneously, but they are *maintained* by mechanisms more closely resembling learning. Let us now look at the normal child.

The normal child is born crying. The forcible expulsion of air from his lungs at birth, often provoked by the obstetrician's spank, vibrates the vocal cords and produces a sound. This undifferentiated sound is likened to crying although it does not resemble, either phonetically or socially, the true act of crying in the child. But it *is* a noise. We know, then, that from birth on the child is capable of sound production of at least a crude sort. We can also see that from time to time the child will spontaneously emit such noises or cries. We use the term "spontaneous" since there does not appear to be any method to this madness during the first days of life. The infant certainly does not cry to get his mother at this stage, nor does he in any sense attempt to communicate by means of crying.

Mothers in general like to assume that even the neonate cries *because* he is hungry, unhappy, wet, or the like. But there does not appear to be too much justification for this assumption. While pain does in fact seem to produce crying often enough, there is in fact relatively little pain in the infants' world. The stomach cramps produced by gas and colic are, of course, painful, as is an accidental prick with a diaper pin. Even the latter does not, however, reliably produce crying. Some infants, in fact, just seem to wake up crying. Our puzzlement by this is a function of our adult biases. We assume crying *means* something, as it of course does in the adult or older child. But one thing which the infant does not have is meaning. Crying, other than as a direct response to pain or discomfort, is simply something for him to do. It is reasonable to suppose that just as infants thrash their arms and legs about, they may also "thrash" their organs of speech about, thus producing noise. This crying, then, may be merely another form of the relatively undifferentiated activity which characterizes the waking child and which is a function of the mere fact that he is alive.

But while crying may be only something to do at first, it eventually becomes done for a reason. The child has ample opportunity to learn that crying produces certain sorts of environmental changes: mother comes, food comes, dry diapers come, and the like. Crying, then, can be learned as a response to certain internal events or wants of the child, perhaps even by operant means. This "operant" is reinforced by the satisfaction of those wants. If we wish, we can conceive of this as quite a rudimentary form of language. The cry does, in fact, resemble a *command* on the part of the child. But the resemblance is remote. The cry is not independent of the immediate environment in the way that language is; the cry is not part of a system. Moreover, while the cry may be a response to something, it does not refer to anything. It has no meaning in the sense of reference. It is really no different in quality than the grabbing response which secures the infant his rattle.

Mothers are also wont to assume that the infant has different cries for different situations. They can recognize hunger cries from pain cries and the like. We must bear in mind that this is often the mother's interpretation rather than any differentiation among the baby's cries. Thus, a cry at dinner time is interpreted as a cry for food. A cry when no cry is expected is interpreted as a cry of pain, since the mother cannot imagine anything else which might be causing the cry. Nevertheless, it is clear that the infant rapidly becomes capable of differentiating the quality of his cries. He can do this by altering both the volume and the frequency of cries. Thus a cry of pain or anger may be characterized by a series of sharp loud cries interrupted by long periods of holding the breath. Hunger cries may be a more steady, softer crying. Infants can do this, and doubtless in certain cases they do. But other sorts of sound production, which may be more meaningful or even phonemic in character, do not usually begin until the child is at least two months old.

When we wish to consider the production of phonemes, or of sounds which resemble phonemes, we must first ask what the child is capable of doing. Directly after birth, he is in fact capable of very little in the way of fine, co-ordinated muscular movement. He is, then, incapable of the very sorts of muscular activities which would be necessary for speech production. The central nervous system, and brain in particular, are in some vital ways incomplete at birth. While apparently all the nerve cells are in the brain that will ever be there, they have not yet grown to their full size. One result of this is that certain connections between nerve cells are not yet made, because the cells are not yet big enough to reach each other. Hence, certain neural circuits cannot function, and some activities are totally eliminated from the infant's potential behavioral repertoire. We have no direct evidence that such lack of neural development affects those parts of the brain necessary for speech. Indeed, we know little about what parts of the brain are necessary for speech. It would appear reasonable to assume, however, that the most complex behaviors are those most likely to be hurt by a misfunction or lack of function in the central nervous system. As a prime example of complex behavior, speech, then, is a likely candidate for disruption during infancy.

In addition to the lack of development of nerves, it has also been shown that the nerve cells in the subcortical regions (below the surface) of the brain are not completely myelinized. The *myelin* is a layer of whitish material which coats the nerve cells, particularly the axons or long wire-like conductive fibres which characterize the nerve cell. Nearly all subcortical cells are myelinized in the adult, but in the infant this layer is either missing or incomplete. The importance of this stems from the fact that the degree of myelinization of a cell relates to the rapidity with which it can conduct its impulses. Myelinized cells are faster conductors than unmyelinized ones. The myelinated brain, then, is a more efficient and rapid one than the unmyelinated brain. Since speech requires a very rapid sequential ordering of muscular movements, it is possible that the infant brain, with its incomplete myelinization, is incapable of responding this rapidly. It is of importance to note that lack of myelinization has been observed even in the six-month-old child. Even then the brain is not fully capable of its most efficient performance.

A parenthetical remark may be necessary at this point. Not all people grow at the same rate. While myelinization may be complete in some individuals at, say, six months of age, others may take several months longer. There is nothing abnormal about this. Quite the contrary, it is a rule and not an exception. Individuals quite radically and remarkably differ from one another without the differences being anything other than "normal."

The same statement holds for more behavioral things. One child may speak his first word at eight months while another waits until eighteen months. Either of these two may be unusual, but neither indicates any necessary clinical abnormality, either in the direction of precocity or of idiocy. While retarded children do, of course, speak later than those of normal intelligence, within the range of normality the correlation between the age of developing any particular behavior and intelligence is, at best, low. "Normal" is a very large range of things. Any time we mention some date at which some linguistic behavior appears, it should be understood that it might in some cases appear much earlier or much later and that no value judgments should be attached to the relative earliness or lateness.

We have attempted to show, then, that in all likelihood the child prior to several months of age is physiologically incapable of organizing his sound production into anything resembling the phoneme sequences of speech. Moreover, his sound production itself is limited. There are certain sounds which he *cannot* produce—the dentals, for example—because he does not have the necessary equipmnt. No toothless infant will be able to pronounce /tooth/ properly. Other sounds require a degree of muscular co-ordination and delicacy of which he is incapable. The /l/ sound of /lollypop/ seems to be a good example of this. Neurological considerations aside, the production of these sounds requires much more practice, they require much more skill than the production of, say, voiced vowels or lip plosives like /p/.

But what can the child actually do, and how does he do it? Jakobsen and Halle (1956) have advanced the theory that there is a definite developmental sequence in the production of phonemes. Sound production begins with expulsion of air. They see the first possible phoneme distinction arising from permitting the air to exit through an open mouth (as in /ah/) or stopping the passage of air with the lips (producing /pa/). As they put it, "The choice between /pa/ and /a/ and/or /pa/ and /ap/ may become the first carrier of meaning in the very early stages of child language." This distinction between open and closed sounds is followed, according to them, by a nasal-oral distinction and/or by a dental /t/ versus labial /p/ one. Following this come distinctions between high and low tones, and the like. They support their theory in part with the claim that persons suffering from brain damage which produces the speech disorder known as aphasia show a dissolution of language in an order which is the reverse of this hypothetical development sequence. They do not present data from children, nor, in fact, is the data from aphasics totally supportive of this theory.

Logical considerations, however, suggest that certain phonemes *must* precede others in the developmental sequence. Clearly the child must produce some sound before he can differentiate between voiced and unvoiced sounds. And he must have voiced sounds before he can differentiate between high and low vowel tones. There does not appear to be any particular reason, however, for giving precedence to the lip stop /pa/rather than, say, the palatal or glottal one as in /ga/. In fact, tradition gives precedence to the latter as "baby's first sound." Likewise, there does not appear to be any reason why the oral-nasal distinction should precede the voiced-unvoiced one, or for that matter why it should not. Within the limitations imposed by the structure of the body, and those posed by purely logical considerations, there appears to be no necessary reason for any rigid ordering of the production of phonemes.

Suffice it to say that the child eventually makes a sound which resembles a phoneme in the language of his parents. It is even possible that prior to this he has made phoneme sounds of languages not his own. It is possible to say that first sounds will not be true dentals and the like, but it is not possible to know exactly what particular phoneme *will* be the first. How the first phoneme-like sound is produced, or why it is produced, will probably remain one of the unsolved mysteries of psychology and linguistics. But what happens from there on becomes relatively easy to determine.

Parents react immediately to language-like sounds produced by the child. They imitate the child's sounds, or interpret them as words; /dada/ becomes /daddy/, and the like. It is easy to say that by doing this the parents reinforce such phonemes in the child. Not only is the utterance of particular phonemes reinforced, but the utterance of sounds in general is reinforced. It is also undoubtedly correct to say that the child, by some means or other, is able to reinforce himself for making such sounds. That is, he shows evident signs that he enjoys making all this noise. It is also true that there is a corrective process which goes on. The child apparently *tries* to imitate the speech of adults and older children. He attempts to correct his mistakes and is corrected by others, although he gives ample evidence of simply ignoring or even of not being able to hear certain crucial (to adults) sound distinctions. Thus, /lollypop/ may persist as /wowwypop/ for an extended period of time much to the exasperation of parents and the bewilderment of the child who fails to see the reason for the parental exasperation.

What we have given here is, of course, a crude picture of phoneme learning as a kind of operant-conditioning process. At some level it is unquestionably true that some sort of conditioning is actually taking place. However, it should be emphasized that we have really not explained much of anything by this description. We have not, for example, specified exactly what we mean by the term "reinforcement." The parents may on some occasion shower the child with attention and caresses for the production of some particular speech sound. At the next moment, they may ignore the same sound, or, more importantly, ignore some other sound which is part of the language but does not happen to resemble /mama/. The *obvious* social reinforcement given by parents is a very fleeting and whimsical thing. It nowhere resembles that stable, overt action which is called reinforcement in a learning experiment and which appears so crucial to correct behavior in those experiments. Yet the child learns anyway, and we are left with the still unresolved question of how.

It is not correct to say that the production of speech sounds per se is reinforcing. We have seen how the abandoned institutionalized child becomes, as does the deaf child, silent. Yet both of these start by making perfectly normal infantile sounds. They *lose* their capacity to do this. And even in the normal child, not any old sound will do. Children learn to make the sounds which their parents make. To be more accurate, they learn to make sounds which resemble those made by the parents. This immediately returns us to the parents as a reinforcing agent. Yet their reinforcement hardly appears consistent enough to permit learning of all the necessary phonemes, nor, on the other hand, is it permissive enough to permit the child to make the kinds of mistakes he often does.

If *imitation* of parental behavior is reinforcing or reinforced, our problem might be solved. This reinforcement would come both from without—from the parents themselves—*and* from within the child himself. The child must be able, somehow, to give himself the kind of pleasure or feedback which constitutes reinforcement. He must know when he is right and wish to be right in his imitations. But imitation itself raises an entirely new and mystifying set of problems. Imitation involves, of necessity, the moving of muscles in a way similar to that done by another. Then we must ask, how does the child learn that some movement is like that made by another; how does he know when his actions are correct imitations? How does he learn that his arm is the same as another's arm (1) when he cannot see his own arm as he sees another's and (2) when he does not know the meaning of either the thing or of the term /arm/. Without attempting to fully answer these questions now, we will point out this: while in fact the child appears to imitate the parents in learning to produce speech sounds, merely calling it imitation explains nothing about the learning.

There are probably two things of importance in the early mechanisms of phoneme learning. The first is learning to imitate in some crude sense of that term. The child can see others do things, manipulate the environment, feed themselves, and the like. He may, for example, see his bottle being transported by a parent, who does so by means of the behavior of his hand and arm. The child can also transport the bottle by hand and arm movement. If he is able to perceive the identity of the movement of the bottle—which he certainly will not be able to do until some time after birth—he may equate in his mind the movements of the parent with his own. The movements may be identified because they have the same *functional significance* as far as the child is concerned. Two things are seen as identical if they effect the environment in a similar manner, e.g. get the bottle to his mouth. Now it so happens that many things can be achieved in only a limited number of ways. Thus, achieving the same functional end will necessitate the same sort of behavior. But, we would hypothesize, the child interprets his world in terms of ends; things are the same if they serve the same purposes.

Thus he can learn that making noises has functional significance. A certain kind of noise will bring Mommy, another will bring Daddy; most noises will bring general approval from either parent; some noises will make his parents very upset, and the like. At this level the child is using speech sounds as quasi-operants, behaviors which change the environment to satisfy certain needs of his. The child imitates language to the extent that he attempts to achieve the same ends with it which he sees others achieving. Two sets of sounds which achieve the same end are identical to him. Thus his puzzlement at the /lollypop/–/wowwypop/ distinction. According to the above argument these are clearly the same sounds since they both produce lollypops.

Nevertheless, the imitation-to-secure-ends hypothesis is not sufficient to explain phoneme learning. For the child will learn sounds which have no functional significance and which may not even be part of his parental language. This is where the "self-reinforcement" hypothesis is usually advanced. The most frequent version runs something like this: once the child has learned that certain sounds will get him reinforced, all sounds produced by him tend to be reinforcing by generalization. Spoken sound in general becomes a reinforcement because spoken sounds so often produce and accompany objective reinforcement. Thus both hearing and producing language become learned or *secondary reinforcers*. This theory, however, suggests that the child is unable to distinguish between sounds which serve functional purposes and those which do not, and that he is further unable to distinguish between sounds which others produce and those which he himself produces, for it is only the former which will *reliably* accompany reinforcement and thus presumably become reinforcers. It is doubtful that children are either this blind or theoretically obliging.

It is more tenable to assume what seems obvious from observation: that children get pleasure from making sounds. Given this as a fact, we can attempt to understand how and under what conditions this pleasure will arise. Without being too detailed let us assume that the living organism is characterized by movement. The amount and kind of movement may vary from time to time, but the totally inert organism is a dead one. Let us further assume that continuous motion of the same kind and degree is boring and unpleasant, an assumption which seems to have some face validity. This suggests, then, that periodic changes in the amount and kind of movement will remove this boredom. However, it is doubtful that any old change will do the trick. Wildly different movements or extreme shifts in intensity of movement may quite easily become upsetting and as unpleasant or more so than the boredom itself. It will be relatively small shifts in the kind and intensity of movement that will produce the most satisfactory effects in maintaining interest and remaining in a relatively pleasant affective state.

A more sophisticated version of the above notion may be found in a theory of affect proposed by David McClelland and his associates (1953). Essentially this theory states that small changes in any state of the organism are pleasant while larger changes are not. Likewise, a steady state is unpleasant. Now let us consider the child whose waking state is characterized by a certain average level of activity. This motor activity produces changes in stimuli by feedback through the nerves of the kinesthetic sense, by visual changes as the child moves, and by auditory changes as he makes noise or approaches other noise-making objects. These stimulus changes are a direct function of the general activity level of the child. The more the activity, the greater the magnitude of stimulus change, in general. The making of sounds would, it seems, be one of the easiest possible ways of producing small changes in activity and its consequent stimulation, the very small changes required to maintain a pleasant affective state. Moreover, these sounds can be continuously changed in small degrees, thus continuously varying the state by small amounts and further maintaining the pleasure. If sound making is to serve this function, the child must have a moderate number of different sounds in his repertoire so that he can change them sufficiently often. The hypothesis suggests also that sounds will be repeated only for short periods of time without change. The child should alternate among sounds or periodically change the intensity or intonational characteristics of his sounds in order to introduce the small necessary changes in his activity state. Moreover, under certain circumstances, silence should be as reinforcing as making noise.

All in all this hypothesis gives us a picture of a child which seems to be relatively accurate. He is a child who appears to enjoy making noises. He will repeat sounds, changing them by small variations for relatively extensive periods of time. In some cases he appears to imitate the noises produced by others, but often enough all of this noise production appears to be quite spontaneous. It is pleasurable to the child in and of itself. We have, in other words, a child who is naturally equipped to make noise and whose motivational structure appears designed to reinforce this noise making. But this is not enough to produce language by itself.

Language is a social tool, and the learning of it will require social reinforcement. It is up to the parents or other elders to whom the child is exposed to select out the "correct" noises and to connect them in the proper sequence so that words are produced. But it should be clear that this training or reinforcement does not have to be of the overt, tangible sort which is usually postulated by learning theorists. If the production of a sound by the child himself is rewarding to the child, it is likely that under the same circumstances the production of that sound by someone else will also be rewarding. The dialogue between parent and child in which the child babbles and the parent imitates him provides reinforcement to the child through the relationship between the sounds produced by the parent and the child's current stimulus state. Needless to say, there is reinforcement also through parental attention and love, but the important issue is why certain sounds are reinforcing in themselves whether they are self-produced or not.

What we find, then, is that parental noise also becomes reinforcing since it, too, changes the child's current stimulus state slightly. But notice that the parents produce only a small range of noises, specifically, those which are permissible in the language. Parental noise generally reinforces the child only for those noises and sequences of noises which are *in the language*.* The reinforcement of sounds is, in effect, a dialectical relationship between the parent and the child.

If this reinforcement increases the likelihood of production of phonemes rather than non-phonetic noises, and of permissible phoneme sequences rather than non-permissible ones, as it would appear to do, then we reach the following conclusion: the child will eventually utter phoneme sequences which are part of the language, and he will do this with *apparent* spontaneity. No one consciously or conscientiously teaches him to speak, and yet speech is clearly learned. The learning takes place because the child is exposed to the language, and this alone is sufficient, given essentially normal environmental conditions.

Once the child utters his first "word," as he may do somewhere after ten months of age, the entire situation changes. This utterance will be highly and overtly rewarded by the parents, assuming that they are present at the time.† By this stage of development most sound production will take place when others are present, however, since other people provide such a consistent

* While we shall discuss this more fully later, it should be noted here that not all phoneme sequences are permissible in any language—e.g. no words begin with /thch/ in English. Thus the child is only given parental reinforcement for a certain subset of all possible phoneme sequences.

† The laws of probability suggest that for some children the utterance of their first word must take place in the absence of an audience. By most overt theories of reinforcement, this first word would thus be non-reinforced and therefore the child's language learning would be delayed. There is no evidence that such happens, which therefore argues in favor of the self-reinforcement theory of sound production.

and copious amount of reinforcement. The overt rewarding of the first word will insure its learning and eventual repetition. However, this is probably only a word in the eyes of his parents. The child at this stage can have at best a rudimentary idea of the possible usefulness of language. At one level, he may have a certain vocabulary of meaningful words, but he still must discover most of the rules for how to use them.

It is common to distinguish between what we may call *receptive vocabularies* and *use vocabularies*. In the former, the child knows the meaning of a word when it is spoken to him; that is, he will respond appropriately to a spoken word, but he will not speak or use that word himself. Thus the non-speaking child may have some receptive vocabulary. If the parent says /ball/ he may look for a ball, grab it, throw it, and the like. The word functions as a stimulus for a certain type of action. We cannot necessarily assume that the word actually refers to the object as far as the child is concerned. We cannot assume that /ball/ calls out some response appropriate to the object ball; in general the behavioral evidence suggests that /ball/ calls out behavior characteristic of the immediate absence of the ball, such as looking for it. Nevertheless, on a purely receptive level, the child has some sort of "understanding" of some words.

Once he can utter words, however, the child is in a position to learn their power. He can discover that the use of words permits him to manipulate the environment. The saying of /ball/ will secure the ball for him. The child, of course, has already learned that he can manipulate the environment through gross muscular action. He has doubtless also learned that he can imitate the actions of others and thus acquire new ways of manipulating the environment. Once he discovers that the utterance of words brings additional rewards over that of simple noise production, that words have functional significance just as actions do, then real language learning will take place. The child will then imitate words which he hears since it is apparent by his observations that they have something to do with manipulating the environment. But it must be clear that according to this reasoning, language learning requires at least three additional steps beyond the mere mechanism of sound production: (1) that the child has learned both the rewards of manipulating the environment and the functional significance of actions, (2) that he has learned to imitate the actions of others to achieve certain ends, and (3) that he is aware of the functional significance of language itself, that language can also manipulate the environment.

Our year-old child is not an inductive genius. He will not reach these three conclusions with the utterance of his first word, or his second, or his tenth. We must expect to find that the child will acquire words slowly, one after the other, until he has a vocabulary big enough to support the generalization that "all words are alike"—that they can all act as tools to effect his environment. He must acquire a sufficient number of words to understand that all words can be used to manipulate the environment. Once this generalization is made, we can expect to find the growth of vocabulary taking place with extreme rapidity since the child will attempt to learn all that he can of this new tool. The facts seem to support this generalization; vocabulary growth, used vocabulary that is, takes place slowly over the first months following language development. At some point, the vocabulary increases by tremendous strides. During this period it may not be uncommon for a child to acquire eight or ten new words per day. Smith (1941) reports the following figures for the size of the average child's vocabulary at varying ages:

Age (in months)	Words in Vocabulary
12	3
15	19
18	22
21	118
24	272

A comparison of the growth in vocabulary size from 12 to 18 months with the growth from 18 to 24 months of age indicates the phenomenon we are trying to account for. The increase during the latter period was about thirteen times as large as at the earlier age.

We assume, then, that once the child discovers the usefulness of language, he will attempt to learn it as rapidly as he can, but that this discovery will take some time. By no means do we wish to imply that this discovery is a rational or conscious one. It is certainly not framed in the pseudo-syllogistic form in which it has been presented here. After all, the child does not yet have the language which he would require to be able to reason as we have done. But it is reasonable to assume that at a completely conscious level the child wants to learn to speak. The acquisition and utilization of this desire is not conscious, however. The child simply wants to speak: he is not aware of the reasons for this want.

We have a child with a vocabulary of words which are presumably learned because of their functional significance or their "reinforcement-securing" properties. But what is the nature of this vocabulary? Are these words in the sense that we as adults use the term; and do they have meaning in the same way or of the same kind that adults have for the same phonetic sequences? To these questions we must first reply with a generality: *adults are not children.* Keeping this generality in mind will probably save much confusion.

To begin with, words to children are not items coldly listed in dictionaries, as they may be to adults. Words are not things, nor are they parts of sentences, to children. They are, as we have suggested, tools for manipulating the environment. When the child says /ball/, it must be recalled that for him this is a free utterance. It is, in other words, some sort of sentence or proposition. He is not simply emitting a vocabulary item; he is attempting to achieve some end. He is saying, /Give me the ball./, or /Catch the ball./, or perhaps somewhat later in his development, /This is a ball/. /Ball/, then, serves as a stimulus to effect the behavior of others, who, in turn, will change the environment in some desired manner. In addition to this /ball/ may be a response to the object, a name, if you will. This name learning will take place only if there is reinforcement or some sort of approval for saying /ball/ in the presence of balls. Not all nouns, then, will necessarily be names. Some may have only manipulative functional significance. Other parts of speech will not be names at all.

But one thing is clear; under the above conditions /ball/ will not refer to balls in a manner such that the child will talk about balls in their absence or in the abstract; it is still a response to the immediate stimulus of a ball. At this level, which is a crucial one for language, words do *not* have meaning as they do for adults, and we can say that the child does not fully have a language. He will only be fully linguistic when his words can acquire an abstract referential function.

The word is a simple sentence for the child; it is both a social stimulus and a naming response. Furthermore, the word has an element of concreteness to the child which it does not have for the adult. Piaget (1955) has described this by saying that for the child, the word is *part of* the object or is, at least, *not distinguishable* from its referent object in the mind of the child. To the adult, by way of contrast, the word *refers* to an object, but it is usually distinguishable from that object in his mind. To try to clarify this distinction, let us return again to the ways in which children use words as tools to manipulate the environment.

The child learns that saying a word will achieve some end in a manner which is essentially equivalent to the way in which other kinds of behaviors achieve ends. Thus saying /ball/ can be equivalent to going and getting the ball since both will result in having the ball. Our very simple notions about imitation suggest that means are equated if ends are similar. The word /ball/, then, is an interaction with an object which, to the child, is seen as identical with certain overt interactions with the ball, because they both achieve similar results. These interactions, the verbal and the other, are indistinguishable or at least totally interchangeable to him. Saying things and doing things are seen as the same by the child. Perhaps in certain conditions, even saying things and having things are the same. Whatever the mechanism, the child practices a kind of *word magic* wherein he appears to expect that the saying of a word will produce certain concrete environmental changes; he expects to have total control over the people and things in his world by means of his use of words. Saying /ball/ is perhaps as good as (results in) having the ball. The word and the deed are totally intermingled in the experience of the world. Thus Piaget uses the term *concrete* to refer to the child's use of words: his use is totally tied to and inseparable from the environment of physical objects. Words are not used abstractly or in the absence of certain environmental conditions. They are not used in an adult manner.

Eventually it becomes apparent to all parties concerned that the one word sentences which the child utters are not sufficient for purposes of communication. In other words, the child finds that his new tools, words, do not always perform accurately. Their functional significance rests on flimsy assumptions. /Ball/ may produce the wrong ball or the wrong action with the ball. /Daddy/ may produce Daddy, but it does not guarantee that he will perform as desired. There are, in fact, very few single words which are unambiguous.* But strings of words are much less ambiguous. Parents are generally co-operative about clearing up the ambiguities in children's language. They may say, "Red ball, not the green ball," or the like when a clear ambiguity in the use of a word arises. So when such explanations are offered during the period of rapid vocabulary growth, we can reasonably expect that the child will learn sequences of words, whether they be phrases or complete (if mangled) sentences. As in the case of single words, the learning of word sequences will be reinforced by their functional significance, by the fact that they produce desirable environmental changes. In general, the reinforcement resulting from using these phrases will be greater and more reliable than from the more ambiguous single words. This mo-

---

* One class of words which are unambiguous, from the child's viewpoint, are those known as obscenities. It is a constant source of amazement to some parents how one slight slip into locker-room language will be seized upon immediately by the child and used indiscriminately in the presence of inappropriate audiences. But if you realize that for the child, these words are unambiguous, the puzzle is solved. The child uses the word, any word, to change his environment, and the use of a taboo expression does this very nicely indeed. It produces great consternation, upset, and, as a result, attention from his audience. Taboo words do this infallibly at first. Considering the child's functional approach to language, this makes such words seem exceptionally desirable for some time. No other words have this apparently infallible quality.

tivation by concrete results leads to a restriction in the kind of sequences learned and used. Basically it seems that nearly all the early words used have functional significance in isolation. The child may learn to say /red ball go table/ in which each word taken by itself, can be used to achieve a certain end. He is not likely to learn to say /the red ball . . ./ since /the/ by itself will accomplish nothing.

This suggests a characteristic of the child's first multiword sentences; they are lacking the function words, particularly the articles, prepositions, and verb auxiliaries. Their first sentences are made up almost entirely of form-class words. Exceptions to this may arise in either of two cases: (1) the case of the learning of some stock phrase—a child might learn to say /box of cookies/ but be unable to use /of/ in any other appropriate sentence—and (2) in the case of the social-function words. Thus Fries (1952) categorizes words such as /hello/ and /please/ as function words. But unlike function words, these have clear environmental effects. They are socially manipulative tools. For example, a child who learns /hi/ as an early word, will almost certainly be rewarded by an excessive burst of affectionate attention from most adult audiences. But these are exceptions to a generality, namely that the child's speech is to an extent ungrammatical by adult standards. The specific locus of the ungrammaticality is in the lack of function words.

The child's sentences are quite grammatical, however, in other respects, notably in the case of word order. It is a fact little noticed, but important, that English-speaking children typically follow the subject-verb-object ordering of words in their sentences. It is necessary that they do so, of course, because no adult would understand them if they did not. And since language is so highly imitative, it is not surprising that they do so. Moreover, they will be reinforced for it through the functional success of their speech. What is surprising is the apparent ease with which sentence ordering is mastered and generalized. For it is at this stage that we first encounter one of the great puzzles of language, namely that it is possible for a speaker to generate sentences previously unuttered by him.

The child does this from the very first. He says things which he has never heard before, things which, from his point of view, are new creations. Some are ungrammatical and some are not. Yet these linguistic creations are characteristic of all speakers of the language. Their occurrence is not restricted to geniuses. Even a below-average child produces them. And despite the ubiquitous nature of this fact, we know little or nothing about it. It would seem that the child learned general principles or rules of word ordering. Indeed, it would seem that if he is to use the language at all he must learn such rules, for they are one of the defining characteristics of any language. Even a single-word utterance, in fact, is an utterance which conforms to a rule. It is in this sense grammatical. He does not learn all such rules immediately upon the utterance of his first sentence, however. Probably he must learn many sentences before he can generalize and induce certain grammatical rules from the specific sentences he knows. Yet the facts are that he rapidly learns a relatively complex, although not adult, grammar, that he uses this grammar fluently, and that he does all this with a staggering degree of nonchalance. There are laboratory studies which demonstrate that children can be sensitive to word ordering, and that they can learn to use words in similar sentence positions or contexts to the ones in which they originally learned the words (Braine, 1963). But these experiments only demonstrate a phenomenon which we know must exist. They do nothing to clarify our understanding of how such learning takes place.

Let us for the moment leave the question of how grammatical learning takes place and deal simply with the fact that with the onset of language usage the child simultaneously acquires a grammar. But this original simple grammar soon proves itself to be inefficient and inaccurate. When sentences need to become longer and longer, function words are necessary to organize them. Sentences containing only form-class words become incomprehensible and eventually seem to be only lists of words, particularly if they are very long. Moreover, such simple sentences are often functionally ambiguous. /Red ball go table/ may, to the confused parent, mean either that the child wants his red ball to go on the table, or under the table, or that there is a red ball on the table or under the table and that the child wants it, or even perhaps that some-time in the past the red ball and the table got together somehow. Parental confusion does not lead to child reinforcement. Hence, new learning is required, again solely to satisfy the requirements of using the language to effect the environment—in order for the child to insure his getting what he wants.

This new learning often involves the learning of function words, which does, in fact, take place relatively late in the vocabulary-learning sequence. Late in the second year is probably the best guess as to the average starting time for function-word learning. And the picture we must have of this learning is further complicated by the fact that function-word learning may be of a different kind than the learning of form-class words. Form-class words are acquired by means of their effects on the environment. Their use is learned by means of these effects. To some extent they may also be learned through sentence position. The child may be able, say, to detect the fact that first words often refer to objects, while second words often seem to deal with human or object behaviors. But function words have no simple achievement effects. They must, as we suggested in the previous chapter, be learned individually and precisely. The child must learn (not necessarily consciously) the specific ways in which function words are used. The reinforcement for such learning will still be the fact that he can manipulate the environment verbally. But the function word, unlike the form-class word, is useless except in conjunction with other words. The difficulty and the indirectness of application of such learning suggests that it will take place more slowly and with a greater degree of error than is the case with form-class words. This hypothesis appears to be correct. Much of the "correction of grammar" which parents must do is in connection with the use of function words, particularly in the cases of verb tense, ending, and auxiliary. But despite its slowness, the learning does take place.

Aside from the fact that the child becomes gradually more and more grammatical (by adult standards), we find several other effects as well. We discover that the acquisition of new grammatical rules radically changes the entire nature of language. With the advent of the multiword sentence the child acquires the capacity to use language in a *referential* sense which was denied him previously. This is particularly so when the function words are added to his vocabulary and the rules of their use incorporated into his grammar. To take a simple example, the child may now use the past tense or the future tense. In both cases he is using language concerning something which is not present. The future tense can be said to be even more abstract than the past, since language is being used concerning something which may, in fact, not ever happen. These grammatical rules for using words in utterances thus permit abstractness in a way that is not inherent in words themselves. One might argue, of course, that the child has ideas of the past and future and the like prior to his acquiring the language to express them. If one means "concept" by "ideas," this argument does not appear defensible; rather, it would appear that one would logically have to acquire the concept first by means of the language—otherwise how would one acquire it? Nevertheless, there remains the residue of an issue concerning whether thought is abstract and the child expresses this abstractness through his language, or whether the thought becomes more abstract as the language is acquired.

A single-word sentence may be uttered by the child in the absence of the object to which the word refers. But almost without exception, such a use seems to have the intent of producing the object. There does not appear to be anything in the child's language akin to the statement /I played with the ball this morning./ prior to the stage at which the child's grammar permits the expression of past time. The child does not *refer to* or *mention* balls until this time, although he desires and uses them. Only with the onset of more adult grammar, particularly with that provided by the acquisition of function words, does language become truly referential and truly abstract.

Children do not appear to refer to abstract *classes* of objects, for example, prior to this time. Using language to refer to classes, e.g. balls in general, generally requires that the speaker *predicate* something about the class, e.g. balls are round. Such predication cannot take place without the appropriate grammatical rules' being acquired. Conversely, the availability of the grammatical rules *permits* the conception of classes of objects by virtue of the possibilities for abstractness which it grants, permits the predication of general characteristics typical of all class members, and in general lays the foundations for logical and creative thought. The child can now deal with *objects in general* as well as with objects not present, and via language he can "experiment" with those objects. He can place them in relation to other objects or properties, all without the physical entities being there at all.

This sudden growth of intellectual capacities which can appear only with the development of a complex grammatical language, can do nothing but change the child's whole world of experience. This change is not sudden, of course, since the development of grammar is not sudden. But it is profound and radical nonetheless. The world of the child, his experience within his environment, can be seen and reacted to quite differently. Moreover, the child can experiment with different forms of experience; he can hypothesize states of affairs by means of language. He can begin to become an adult with all the vices and virtues implied by that term. But, more importantly, he can now be said to have a language in the fullest sense of that term; one which seems to have all of the identifying characteristics which we specified earlier. The only other linguistic additions remaining are the addition of vocabulary items and the acquisition of a greater sensitivity to the language habits of the particular culture in which the child lives. Only literacy remains to provide another radical change in the child's approach to the world, and that is still generally more than a year in the future.

All of the above discussion suggests that the child's use of language, irrespective of its grammatical complexity, is self centered. That is, language is used primarily to achieve certain ends or desires of the child. Even more developed grammatical language is learned to facilitate such acquisitions and the experimentation with language is equally oriented toward the child's own immediate desires and views. To use Piaget's term, the language of the child at this age is egocentric. His verbalizations concern his own problems and interests. No real "conversation" takes place at this level unless the other party is willing to devote himself entirely to the interests of the child. The "conversations" of two young children of, say, three to four years of age illustrate this egocentrism perfectly. Each will talk, one beginning as the other finishes, but the subject matter of the two speeches may be totally different. Thus, one may hear something like this: /I have a red shovel./ /Yes, but I have pretty hair/. The /yes, but/ often appears to be the most common figure of speech at this age.

Notice, however, that despite the egocentrism of this pair of utterances, they still constitute a real social interaction. Piaget, it often seems, emphasizes the semantic egocentricity of the *topic* of conversation and neglects the real social contacts which are made, despite the egocentricity in the conversation itself. These children are keeping in touch with one another even though they apparently refuse to consider each other's verbalized needs. Two such children will continue to interact verbally although they may never come any closer than this to arriving at a mutually agreeable topic of conversation. It is important to keep in mind that even though an individual may have the freedom to ignore everyone else's utterances and to determine everything he says by his own needs, language is, from its origins, inescapably a social tool. It was learned to influence others. Its form is such that it can influence others in nearly any conceivable manner in which one might want to influence another. The social nature of language determines that word meanings and grammatical rules must be standardized, at least within tolerable limits. No one who uses a language, no matter what its particular use, may escape these limitations imposed by language's social heritage. And no use of language can ever be anything but somewhat social, even if one is "only talking to oneself."

The egocentric nature of his topics of conversation disappears as the child grows older, of course. There are doubtless wide individual differences with respect to when it disappears. In part these differences may be due to the social environment of the child, how many age peers he must interact with, when he starts school, and the like. For many people, the development of language essentially stops at this point, say around five or six years of age. Only vocabulary and an adult style are added, but these do not change the functions of language or the intellectual capacities given by language. However, some proportion of *Homo sapiens* learn a new skill at this time, a skill called writing.

Literacy is a topic which has been rarely treated by theoretical psychologists, even by those interested in language. The structure of language, it is correctly stated, is a function of the phonetic composition and grammatical rules of the language. These are not effected by writing. Writing is a mere convention. Whether one chooses an alphabet, syllabary or ideaographic script seems arbitrary. Whether the alphabet is completely phonetic or not seems a matter of historical accident. None of these decisions had any real effect on the language. To the psychologist, reading is often seen as merely a matter of pairing certain visual patterns with certain auditory ones, and writing only a matter of learning to reproduce those visual patterns by means of certain motor activities. Conceived at this level, reading and writing have little real theoretical importance. The extreme difficulties which one often sees in children learning to read or write are explained either as emotional in origin or as induced through faulty training in pattern recognition.* All in all, it is assumed that by a certain age the child has the physiological capacity to associate the proper sounds with the proper sights, and that given the appropriate reinforcement conditions, he will do so.

Let us ignore, for the moment, whether or not this simple conception is true, and ask instead what the acquisition of literacy is likely to do to the child's experience of the world. Here we should first state a general assumption: we are maintaining the position that language and meaning cannot be meaningfully divorced from other types of behavior and experience. Not all psychologists would agree with this. We shall attempt to defend the

---

* There are, of course, genuine cases of organic reading and writing deficiencies, primarily due to injuries to the central nervous system which prohibit or make the acquisition of reading extraordinarily difficult. These do not invalidate the argument and will be discussed in Chapter 8.

position more fully later. At any rate we have seen that the child acts as though his use of language is behavior which is functionally equivalent to non-linguistic behavior—as though it is a tool with which to mold the world. Objects and names of objects are in some sense equivalent or part and parcel of one another to the child. The name of an object is *seen* as part of the object, indicating a lack of separation of what we might call *perception* and *meaning*. Gradually this lack of differentiation has been eradicated as the use of language becomes more abstract and less dependent upon contemporary perceived states of affairs. Yet, considerable traces of this primitive experienced unity between the name and the named remain. Children are vitally concerned with knowing the names of things; they find considerable humor in the misuse of names, as though for example, a table could be anything other than /table/. They persist in being mystified by the fact that utterances do not immediately result in the deeds to which they refer.

All this is also characteristic of many so-called primitive societies. There too we often find the practice of "word magic." In some extreme cases, objects may have two names, one public and the other private, a possession only of members of certain classes within the society. To them, to possess the name of a thing is to have power over that thing. God would not disclose his name to Moses, since to do so would have given Moses power over Him—an unthinkable situation. It is true that in these senses the language of primitive societies is child-like. But it is undoubtedly more accurate to say that it is pre-literate instead.

Writing does a peculiar thing. It freezes and isolates words. When a word is written, one can say, "Here is a table and here is /table/." Lo and behold, the word and the object are not alike at all; they are not part of one another; they are not functionally equivalent, at least in this form; the word is one *thing* and the object quite another *thing*. Writing permits, then, a dissolution between word and object. It indicates clearly that the word has no more power over the object than any other independent object does, and it may even come to indicate that the object has no power over the word. Anything can be said without any necessary connections between word and world—in either direction.

Anthropology gives evidence which supports this notion in a number of interesting ways. We find, for example, that practically no pre-literate societies have fiction in any form. Their tales and songs may appear fictional and fantastic to a literate, civilized man, but to the pre-literate primitive man they are not. These tales are history, recorded perhaps, in a stylized form, but factual history nevertheless. One cannot play games of fantasy with words in a primitive society, since the word and its object of reference are so closely connected.

To write fiction is to *create* a world, to the civilized man. To some primitive pre-literate men to write fiction is to *lie*, to change the world. The power which words have over objects prohibits anything but their factual or religious use. Further, we see that in partially literate societies, it is without fail the powerful classes which are literate. Writing, in fact, may convey this power since the literate man is in permanent possession of the words which have power over the objective world of the non-literate. He can, in fact, hold the word on paper and, hence, hold its power in his hand—a fact which must be tremendously impressive in a non-literate population. This has led Claude Lévi-Strauss (1961) to suggest that the origins of writing may have come about through the desire for social power.

We have tried to show that writing permits the realization of the true abstractness of language and, moreover, its true arbitrariness. Words and objects can be seen as really separate, and it can be seen that their relationship is contingent. Thus, to the literate child, the word may be one thing and the object quite another thing. Notice the paradox: while on the one hand the word is loosened from its referent, it is at the same time made concrete, because it can itself be represented as an objct. Because of writing we can see words as things themselves. Any word at all is a thing to a literate man. Thus, perhaps all words come to have equal reality and equal concreteness. Since words are all alike at this level, it is hardly surprising that we find them treated as alike on other levels. So we find doctrines which assume that all words must refer to something, since some words do. From this develops notions of the essence of the word or name. And we find that nonsense can be treated with as much reverence as sense, since there are words for both. We find that philosophers can talk of /nothing/ as though it were indeed a thing, a paradox almost inconceivable in a culture which could not objectify /nothing/ by writing. And finally, since all words are merely things, they cannot be easily differentiated in terms of value or worth. From this may develop the notion of value freedom or moral relativism.

All these statements are the conscious reflections of an adult in the process of writing a book on language. The child learning to write does not think to himself this way. Nevertheless, in learning to read and write he is required to treat words differently than before, to treat them as abstract things (if such a thing is possible). But these words have been for several years an integral part of his experience of the world. *To treat them differently is to change this experience*, to change experience perhaps in radical and profound ways, depending of course on the particular child's past history. Is it any wonder, then, that the acquisition of literacy poses an occasional pedagogic problem? Is it not conceivable that a child might resist this changing of the world as he knows it, that he might find such a change fearful if not actually dangerous? Given the possibility of such reactions on the part of the child, it is hardly surprising that the educator and psychologist who have taken no notice of such possibilities find themselves mystified in the presence of the unwilling reader.

We find, in the acquisition of literacy, the last great moment in the development of language. While certain theoretical issues have been discussed here, and while the entire issue has been presented from a particular theoretical point of view, we still cannot say that we really *understand* the functionings of language from a psychological point of view. It would appear that we must discuss more fully psychologists' approaches to at least some critical problems of language, of which meaning is probably the most obvious. The adequacy of any psychological theory of meaning must be evaluated in light of the aspects of development which have been outlined in this chapter, however.

Bibliography

Bitterman, M. E., Fedderson, W. E., and Tyler, D. W. Secondary reinforcement and the discrimination hypothesis. *Amer. J. Psychol.*, 1953, 66, 456-64.

Braine, M. D. S. On learning the grammatical order of words. *Psychol. Rev.*, 1963, 70, 323-48.

Dollard, J., and Miller, N. *Personality and psychotherapy*. New York, McGraw-Hill, 1950.

Fries, C. C. *The structure of English*. New York, Harcourt, Brace & World, 1952.

Greenspoon, J. The reinforcing effect of two spoken sounds on the frequency of two responses. *Amer. J. Psychol.*, 1956, 68, 409-16.

Harlow, H. F., and Zimmerman, R. R. Affectional responses in the infant monkey. *Science*, 1959, 130, 421-32.

Hull, C. L. *A behavior system*. New Haven, Yale University Press, 1952.

Jakobsen, R., and Halle, M. *Fundamentals of language*. The Hague, Mouton, 1956.

Lambert, W. E., and Jakobovits, L. A. Verbal satiation and changes in the intensity of meaning. *J. exp. Psychol.*, 1960, 60, 376-83.

Lévi-Strauss, C. *Tristes tropiques*. New York, Criterion Books, 1961.

Lewis, D. J. Partial reinforcement: a selective review of the literature since 1950. *Psychol. Bull.*, 1960, 57, 1-28.

McClelland, D., Atkinson, J., Clark, R., and Lowell, E. *The achievement motive*. New York, Appleton-Century-Crofts, 1953.

Osgood, C. E., Suci, G., and Tannenbaum, P. *The measurement of meaning*. Urbana, University of Illinois Press, 1957.

Piaget, J. *The language and thought of the child*. Meridian Books, New York, 1955.

Razran, G. The observable unconscious and the inferable conscious in current Soviet psychology: interoceptive conditioning, semantic conditioning and the orienting reflex. *Psychol. Rev.*, 1961, 68, 81-147.

Skinner, B. F. Are theories of learning necessary? *Psychol. Rev.*, 1950, 57, 193-216.

Smith, M. K. Measurement of the size of general English vocabulary through the elementary grades and high school. *Genet. Psychol. Monogr.*, 1941, 24, 311-45.

Solomon, R. L., and Wynne, L. C. Traumatic avoidance learning: the principles of anxiety conservation and partial irreversibility. *Psychol. Rev.*, 1954, 61, 353-85.

Spiegelberger, C. D. The role of awareness in verbal conditioning. In C. W. Eriksen (Ed.) *Behavior and awareness*. Durham, Duke University Press, 1962.

Spitz, R. A. Anaclitic depression. *The psychoanalytic study of the child*, Vol. 2. New York, International University Press, 1946, pp. 313-42.

Verplanck, W. S. The operant, from rat to man: an introduction to some recent experiments in human behavior. *Transactions* of the N. Y. Academy of Science XVII, Series II, 1955, 594-601.

IV
Meaning:
Two Stimulus-response
Theories

It might seem proper to define the term "meaning" before we present and criticize theories which attempt to account for it. However, it will become clear that such a definition is impossible except in connection with a theory. There is no such thing as *the* definition of meaning. There are, however, certain facts for which a theory of meaning must account—facts concerning the referential and naming functions of words, for example. Meaning cannot be considered independently of language as a whole, for it is, after all, a characteristic of the total functioning system of language. A theory of meaning must be a theory of language as a whole. At the most immediate level, then, we have our own use of language as a set of data which must be accounted for by a psychological theory of meaning and language. To the extent that it cannot account for our behavior, the theory and any definition of meaning it suggests are suspect.

If a given theorist does not specifically mention meaning, that does not imply necessarily that his theory is incorrect. If a theory can fully account for the *facts* of language, it is a correct theory. And such a correct account may not necessarily require the use of the specific term "meaning." A careful analysis of language may indicate that the concept of meaning is a spurious one; just as the world appears flat to the earthbound observer, so the "meaning" which he sees in his own language may be an illusion produced by his restricted vision. Thus, for example, Wittgenstein (1953) suggests that we abandon the concept of meaning as being misleading, and study instead the way language is used. We will return to this idea later, but meanwhile we must establish one methodological rule: we will not insist upon the use of any particular concept to understand language. Let us look at the set of behaviors called linguistic and ask of a theory whether or not it can account for those behaviors; but let us ask this with no bias as to how the account is to be phrased.

Skinner's Operant Theory of Verbal Behavior

The first theorist we will discuss is B. F. Skinner, a prominent psychological theorist of learning who has advanced a theory of language, or, to use his terms, of verbal behavior. Skinner (1938) has been noted for his insistence upon several psychological rubrics which he intends to generalize to his considerations of language. Among the most important of these are the following.

(1) Psychology is the study of behavior. The psychologist needs to speak only of behavior and of objective facts in general. He should shun the use of "invisible," intangible, non-denotable concepts. To him such concepts might be "mind" or "consciousness" since these seem to be not directly observable by the scientist's senses. Such concepts are, at best, only inferences from behavior, and therefore add nothing to a simple statement of what the behavior is. We may, of course, speak in our theorizing of *any* observable, public type of event, such as stimuli. It follows from this that meaning may well fall into the class of the non-denotables, and if so, that Skinner (1957) will not speak of meaning in this theory.

(2) A satisfactory psychological theory will be achieved when the psychologist is able to *predict* and *control behavior*. To the extent that the psychologist knows under what conditions a particular behavior will be observed, and can manipulate the conditions such that the behavior will, in fact, occur, he may be said to have a correct theory. The term "understanding" is a senseless

one if we mean by it anything other than a specification of those conditions under which a particular event will occur. Actual control of behavior may, of course, be impossible or extremely difficult for purely pragmatic reasons; the situation may be too complex to control. But one can still specify the requisite conditions for the behavior in question.

We cannot pass this notion by without some remarks concerning both Skinner and his notions about the nature of theory. It is important to know that Skinner (1950) has been adamantly opposed to theories in the traditional sense of the term; that is, he is opposed to the use of unobservable entities within an organism such as mind or consciousness as explanations of the organism's behavior. This opposition seems to stem from two beliefs: first, that such concepts are subjective, not directly observable, and hence not scientific, by definition; and, second, that they are superfluous since such concepts are all defined by observable stimuli and observable behavior. Therefore, why add a third concept when two will do the trick? He also feels, apparently, that psychology is not ready for theory. Theory should come when we have enough data to theorize about. Given the data, the theory should then be more or less self-evident. Skinner's critics often reply that without some implicit theory, Skinner never would have been able to do any rsearch, since without a theory he would not have known what questions to pose. Such a criticism is too glib to be taken seriously. If one means a formal, deductive system, à la Newton's mechanics, as Skinner clearly meant when he spoke of theory, then one in fact does not need a theory to do research.

Regarding the necessity of the term "understanding" and of the merits of prediction and control as the aim of science, we have more serious difficulties. It is unquestionably true that understanding, in the fullest sense of that term, should allow at least the logical possibility of prediction and control. That is, if one cannot even conceive of predicting and controlling an event, then one clearly does not understand that event in any scientific sense. Thus, I may not be able to turn a star into a nova (an exploded star), for the primary reasons that I cannot get to the star and I cannot manipulate the necessary variables since they are too "bulky." But if I cannot *stipulate the conditions* under which a nova *could be* produced, I simply do not understand novae. Thus, some form of prediction and control is a logically necessary concomitant of true understanding. But it does not follow that prediction and control equal understanding. Skinner feels that there is nothing more to understanding than prediction and control. Common sense would appear to deny that this is the case. But what else does understanding require, in fact? One missing component appears to be this: logical necessity.

Let us suppose, for example, that given x, y will occur. From the occurrence of x we can successfully predict the occurrence of y. And if we can produce or manipulate x, we can control the occurrence of y. But, clearly, we can ask: why does y follow x? What are the reasons for this connection? These questions may appear subjective and unscientific. So we can rephrase them: what are the conditions under which it is logically necessary that y follow x? It would appear that this establishment of logical necessity is what we mean by scientific understanding; it is the establishment of the logic of events, not just the specification of causes and their effects. A non-theorist, such as Skinner, cannot and does not specify such logical grounds. He therefore does not truly understand, and, moreover, he is not fulfilling his job as a scientist.

Finally, we should note that Skinner apparently believes strongly in the actual control of behavior. Some years ago, he wrote a utopian novel (1948) in which he hypothesized that a benevolent psychologist might re-make people into a more desirable form; that their behavior and personality was in fact malleable and controllable by knowledgeable others. The strength of his belief in the social power of psychology is attested to by the fact that Skinner is actually attempting to found such a utopia. Not only the logic, but the *practice* of control, is possible, according to him, and humanity's only hope is to see that such control does not fall into the wrong hands.

(3) The purpose of psychology is to describe the lawful relations between stimuli and responses, according to Skinner, and his theory of language is a description of the particular subclass

of such laws that language entails. Skinner gives both the term "stimulus" and the term "response" *operational*, observable definitions. A response is any behavior that can be shown to follow the laws of conditioning, and a stimulus is any part of the environment to which a response may be conditioned. There is an apparent circularity here. All responses (but not all behaviors) must be conditioned (or conditionable) since if they are not, they are not responses, by definition. Likewise, all conditioning must be stimulus-response learning since something which does not follow the laws of conditioning can be neither a stimulus nor a response. In fairness to Skinner, we should point out that definitions such as this have a validity which may be obscured by their tautological character. Not everything which happens in the organism's environment is what we would want to call a stimulus. Stimuli are things which effect the organism in certain ways, and responses are kinds of behavior which have certain definable properties; for Skinner these properties are that they follow the laws of conditioning. Both stimuli and responses are what they are because they function in the ways that they do. Since the effect that a stimulus has upon an organism must be behavioral at some level—it might be neurological "behavior" only—stimuli cannot be identified independently of behavior. Since responses are what they are—behaviors which are caused by certain variables among which are stimuli—it follows that responses, too, cannot be identified completely independently of stimuli. It is considerations such as these which made Skinner choose the particular type of definition which he did.

We still have not indicated what a *law* is. According to Skinner, the characteristics of a lawful relationship, which is what psychology is supposed to describe, are that it is both orderly and continuous. For him lawful relationships are those which have no sudden changes or breaks in them. Graphically, such relationships would be represented by continuous lines, lines with smooth curves and with few, if any, changes in direction. It is difficult, if not impossible, to fathom the reasons for Skinner's insistence on this definition of lawfulness. Most scientists would find this nonsensical. It succeeds in completely eliminating certain kinds of behavior, and certain attributes of behavior from consideration by the "scientific" psychologist. I would argue strongly that any statement that claims that "such-and-such behavior is out of the bounds of psychology" is an incorrect statement.

The acceptance of such a definition of the nature of psychological law is going to have a profound influence on the kinds of problems studied by a psychologist. Skinner will naturally concern himself only with those kinds or attributes of behavior which show this type of lawfulness. And such a restriction of interest cannot help but give him a distorted picture of psychological laws. By considering only that which is simply ordered, one can arrive at a simple set of laws, but a set of laws which can be shown to be almost totally irrelevant to the more complexly ordered facts of real life.

We find, then, that Skinner in fact restricts his investigations almost entirely to the effects of *schedules of reinforcement* on the rate of response in an operant-conditioning paradigm. We described in the preceding chapter what is meant by a schedule of reinforcement, namely the way in which partial reinforcement is delivered to the animal. Rate of response, or probability of response as Skinner sometimes refers to it, is equally simple. It refers to the number of occurrences of a particular response per unit time; the more occurrences, the higher the rate. Such relationships are lawful by Skinner's definition, but the restricted range of such laws is obvious even to Skinner.

Rate of response can be studied only in a situation in which a response can be made repetitively; and such situations arise rarely outside of the laboratory. Hence, instead of speaking of rate, Skinner will often speak of the probability of a response, or the likelihood with which a given response will occur on a given occasion. Strictly speaking, response probability would be the number of times a response did actually occur divided by the number of times in which it was possible that the response would occur. But notice: on any single given occasion, *response probability is indeterminate*. On any given occasion, either the response occurs or it does not. One cannot tell the difference between a high probability response and a low probability response if they both occur, or if they both do not occur. Response probability can be a meaningful scientific concept only when one is looking at a long series of repetitions of occasions on which the response might occur. In any particular situation, probability has little relevance.

Thus we find that on occasion Skinner will talk about the strength of a response, by which he refers to the vigor with which a response is made. Such a variable can be measured on a single trial with ease. But we find ourselves in a difficulty. While Skinner assures us that rate of response, response probability, and response vigor are all aspects of the same thing—namely, how well the response has been conditioned or how much it has been reinforced—there is in fact no concrete evidence to support this contention. Indeed, it is quite possible to show that rats can be conditioned to respond slowly and/or weakly to a given stimulus, but at the same time that they can make this slow, weak response with high probability. Almost any permutation and combination of these variables is possible; any aspect of a response can be increased or decreased by means of the appropriate reinforcement. If there is *a* law describing the relationship between these behavioral variables and reinforcement, and if these concepts of behavior all follow the same law, then we should suspect that the whole relationship is artifactual; it has been produced by the fact that a particular sort of behavior was studied in a particular sort of experimental situation. There is, in other words, no universality to these laws.*

Bearing in mind this brief presentation of Skinner's philosophy of psychology, and bearing in mind its defects, we can proceed to a consideration of Skinner's theory of language. Needless to say, he considers language to be learned, from beginning to end, according to the laws of operant conditioning. To begin with, sound production and, following that, the production of certain phonemes are both operantly conditioned. As we indicated earlier, in order to assume such learning it is necessary to assume that

* A much more sophisticated discussion of these issues can be found in an excellent review of Skinner's "Verbal Behavior" by Noam Chomsky (1959).

somehow the child is able to reinforce himself, since the parents are neither reliable nor sophisticated enough to do the job well; even partial reinforcement by them cannot make up for this lack, not alone at any rate. Skinner is not unaware of the evident pleasure which children seem to derive from making sounds. He therefore constructs his theory in such a manner that verbalizations both by the self and by others become reinforcements per se; they are secondary or learned reinforcements, to use typical s-r terminology. One could criticize Skinner's handling of this problem. Accounting for reinforcement has never been one of Skinner's strong points, but we will not follow up this criticism since the theory and its difficulties in accounting for the facts of language are much more instructive.

Given the fact that the child makes sounds, we must now account for his learning of language. To do this, we must first have some idea of what language is, of what facts we are trying to account for. It is at this point that Skinner's genius becomes apparent. He is, regrettably, the only modern theorist of note in psychology who has attempted to consider carefully the facts which he is trying to explain. He alone has seen that not all linguistic utterances are the same, that different utterances serve different functions, and that there may be a *classification* of language with somewhat different principles operating for each class. We must, he would argue, first develop a *typology* of language, where that typology will follow sound psychological and developmental principles and evidence. We can see from simple observation that the child's language begins with brief utterances which have the nature of commands or demands. From there the child becomes more abstract or descriptive in his use of language. The child becomes less dependent on environmental determinants of language and responds more to other people's, and his own, verbalizations. He acquires grammar, and perhaps later on, that indefinable thing which is called style. It is to Skinner's credit that he is willing to consider all of these aspects of language and, moreover, that he considers all language as relevant data. A proper psychological theory of language must account for everything from the first utterance of the child to the most abstract verbalizations of the poet, scientist, or mathematician.

It is interesting to see that from a behavioristic approach one can reach the same conclusion as was reached by much more linguistically oriented theorists. Since behavior is the important fact to psychology, a psychological theory of language is a theory of verbal behavior. Verbal behavior is something which occurs in units or chunks; an utterance starts at some particular time and finishes at another time. All verbal behavior is made up of these utterances; hence, it follows that the utterance should be the basic unit of verbal behavior. Words are not the proper basic unit. A word has "no psychological reality" until relatively late in the development of language; that is, the child is not aware that his utterances may consist of several words. Utterances— sentences, if you will—are the first verbal behaviors, and a theory of verbal behavior must treat them as basic. The child starts by behaving, by using language. The fact that some verbalizations have common or similar parts allows him to *develop* the concept of a word, but only after he has already learned the language. The sentence, then, is the basic unit of verbal behavior to Skinner, just as the sentence or proposition was the basic unit to theorists of another orientation such as Jackson (1878), the neurophysiologist, and Goldstein (1948), the physiological psychologist, both of whom would have no sympathy for behaviorism. To understand Skinnerian theory, then, we must first understand the typology of utterances.

THE FUNCTIONAL TYPOLOGY OF UTTERANCES

The Mand: The term "mand" is derived from "command" and "demand," and utterances of this type are those first learned by the child. To use Skinner's terminology, the mand is a class of operant behaviors which are conditioned to the deprivation states of the individual, which constitute essentially internal stimulus states. They are reinforced by satisfaction of those deprivation states. Typically these reinforcements will be provided by other people. Thus, demands which seek assistance from others and questions which seek verbal information from others are both instances of mands.

Before criticizing this notion, let us outline its obvious virtues: demands, commands, and questions do have certain functional similarities which cannot be ignored. They are each oriented toward influencing or effecting the behavior of others. And they are each designed to get that other person to do something or provide something for the speaker. Rhetorical questions and the like do not refute this contention; as Skinner would rightly point out, they are not really questions or mands. It is also apparently true that the child's first utterances seem to be of this general type; his verbalizations are meant to get the parent to do something for him: they have a functional significance.

But we must ask whether it is possible to describe language, even of this subclass, within the terminology of operant conditioning as proposed by Skinner. To answer this, we must consider the two crucial terms of his definition of "mand": *deprivation* and *reinforcement*. The notion of deprivation stems from research on rats and other lower organisms where it is typically found that learning or performance is superior when the experimental animals have been deprived of something such as food or water and when they are allowed to satisfy their needs upon successful completion of the learning problem. The use of the term "deprivation" in this sort of research is quite justifiable. Something has been, in fact, removed from the animals. And in the common cases of food and water deprivation, the thing deprived is of vital importance; without it the animals will die. The technical and ordinary uses of "deprivation" are, in fact, the same in this case. They both imply that something has been removed from the animal which he normally would and should have.

But what is the meaning of deprivation in the case of a mand? Suppose a child says /ball!/ in a manner that clearly indicates to the listener that someone is supposed to get him a ball. The child will no doubt only say this when he does not have the ball. But can he be said to be deprived of the ball in any meaningful sense? He might, for instance, demand the ball after not playing

with it for a week or, instead, after having just thrown it from
his play pen. Surely, he must be more deprived of the ball in the
former case than in the latter, if we are to use "deprivation" in
anything like its technical sense, wherein deprivation increases
as a function of time. Yet, it is probably more likely that he will
demand the ball in the latter case, after having just gotten rid of
it. In many cases the most likely condition under which children will mand things is that of seeing other children playing
with them. If this is deprivation, it seems not to be deprivation
in the technical sense, for in the technical sense deprivation is
something which increases with time, not with "noticing" a lack.

As Chomsky (1959) has pointed out, what Skinner apparently
means by deprivation is simply this: the child *wants* something,
so he asks for it. But to implicitly equate *wanting* something with
deprivation, as Skinner does, is both false and misleading. It is
quite possible to want something because one already has it and
one wants more of it. While this is a lack of something, the lack
comes about only when one already has it. This is certainly
not the usual Skinnerian sense of the term "deprivation." It is
equally possible to be deprived of something and not want it, as
testified by the actions of people on hunger strikes, for example.
What is perhaps more important is that the use of this idea
gives the theory a totally misleading façade of technical rigor,
because in fact the term "deprivation" is used erroneously.
Verbal behavior is equated with rat behavior by virtue of the
fact that the same words are used to describe both. But at this
level of analysis there is no evidence for the validity of this equation. Deprivation may be used as an explanatory concept with
the rat because the deprivation is defined independently of the
person who is deprived. It is defined in terms of the time since
the last encounter with a certain class of things, e.g. food. *Wanting* is not defined in this way. The only way to know whether
a person wants something is to ask him; the fact of his stating a
want is evidence for that want and is, in general, the only easy
way we have of knowing about that want. It is logically and
scientifically indefensible to explain a behavior by itself; stating
a want cannot be explained by the want for which the statement

is the only evidence. There must, by definition, always be a want for each statement of a want, since the statement is the only way of recognizing the want. Thus we reach triviality: a relationship which is true by definition is not an explanatory one.

Skinner has failed to *explain* the existence and action of mands on this very basic, logical level. His problem lies in a very subtle misuse of "deprivation"; he shifts unintentionally from a technical laboratory use to a non-technical, everyday use. It would appear that much the same criticism can be raised against the use of "reinforcement." One cannot define a reinforcement as something which satisfies a deprivation if the concept of deprivation itself has no real significance. But even if one deals on the level of wants, there is still a problem. It is no doubt true that if a person gets what he wants after manding it, his behavior will be different than if he does not get it. But some peculiar issues can arise all too easily.

Consider a child is saying /I want a lollypop/. If we give him the lollypop, he will clearly be reinforced on any level of interpretation. The result will be that he ceases to verbalize this mand since his deprivation or want is alleviated. The next time he wants a lollypop he will presumably be more likely to say it since his manding was successful the first time. This we will not question at the moment. If he does not get the lollypop, it is a little bit more difficult to predict exactly what will happen. He may go on repeating the same mand since the deprivation is still present. Or he may stop immediately since the mand is being extinguished by the lack of reinforcement. Sooner or later, at least, he will stop manding the lollypop since reinforcement is lacking. Presumably, given enough such non-reinforcement and extinction, the child will stop manding lollypops altogether. There may be some hesitation at accepting this conclusion in view of the persistence of children. One child of the author's acquaintance spent two years in the relatively continuous but unsuccessful manding of a two-wheeler bike. She eventually got the bike, of course, but during this time the manding showed no signs of extinction. Perhaps manding itself can be reinforcing, but for the moment we can ignore this issue.

So far we have discussed the obvious possibilities: either the child gets the lollypop or he does not. But life is not always obvious. Suppose the child says, /I want a lollypop./, to which his mother replies, /You can't have one, but here is a cookie instead/. It is easy to imagine the child being quite satisfied with this arrangement and giving ample evidence of being reinforced by the cookie. This example poses a considerable theoretical problem for Skinner. If our understanding of the theory is correct, Skinner would have to predict that the cookie would reinforce any behavior which secured the cookie and that the child would thus be conditioned to say, /I want a lollypop/ every time he wanted a cookie. To Skinner, a reinforcement is a reinforcement; they are all functionally identical. Likewise, all operants are alike in that they are effected identically by reinforcement. Either the cookie is a reinforcement—in which case it will strengthen the operant /I want a lollypop/—or it is not, in which case the child should not have accepted it and should have continued manding the lollypop.

Any ordinary person would say at this point, "But what the child really meant was that he wanted a sweet, or something to eat, or something like that." This is clearly true, but there are no provisions for that sort of statement in Skinner's theory. Skinner (1957) refuses point-blank to talk of meaning.

We seek "causes" of behavior which have an acceptable scientific status and which, with luck, will be susceptible to measurement and manipulation. To say that these are "all that is meant by" ideas or meanings is to misrepresent the traditional *practice*. We must find the functional relations which govern the verbal behavior to be explained; to call such relations "expression" or "communication" is to run the danger of introducing extraneous and misleading properties and events. The only solution is to reject the traditional formulation of verbal behavior in terms of meaning (p. 10). . . . The result is simply the probability that the speaker will emit a response of a given form in the presence of a stimulus having specified properties under certain broad conditions of deprivation or aversive stimulation. *So far as the speaker is concerned*, this is the relation of reference or meaning (p. 115).

It is clear, then, that according to Skinner, the child could not be reinforced because of what he "really meant," nor could what he "really meant" get reinforced, since there is no such thing. Only behaviors can be reinforced. All we have is the fact that a response is uttered. If it is uttered and it is reinforced, then its probability of occurence will be increased. The conclusion is clear: linguistic mistakes which are followed by reinforcement will be perpetuated. Speech becomes accurate only insofar as accurate statements are reinforced accordingly. But reinforcement is much more vague and general in real life, much too vague to account for the specificity of language if reinforcement effects only what is actually said. If we are willing to consider that there may be an intention or meaning that lies behind what is said, or even, perhaps a family of potential utterances of which the particular utterance is one example, then we might come closer to understanding language. But Skinner is not willing to do this, and so even at the simple level of mands we must judge him to have failed. We will describe the other categories of his linguistic typology, however, since they raise other problems which deserve discussion.

The Tact: The term "tact" derives from "tactual" or "contact" and suggests a verbal touching of the world. The tact is usually a description or a declarative sentence. It is, according to Skinner, an operant which is conditioned to some more-or-less subtle feature of the environment (stimulus) and which is rewarded by social approval of some sort. While the mand was conditioned to an internal event, deprivation, the tact is conditioned to something more external. Once again, the nature of this stimulus and of the reinforcement must be discussed.

There are certainly some kinds of utterances which appear to be more or less likely occurrences depending on external stimulation and other similar circumstances. What is spoken of, in other words, is dependent in some general sense on the context in which the speaking takes place. One is more likely, perhaps, to speak of tables when tables are present than when they are not; one is more likely to speak of religious matters in a church than in a pool room; one is more likely to be egocentric in speech in a psychiatrist's office or in a barroom than in a classroom. At this level, utterances are conditioned to or contingent upon the circumstances or stimuli which are present. But this conditioning is not causal, nor are the stimuli in any sense simple. The power of Skinner's position is that he seems prepared to deal with both of these facts.

A *discriminated stimulus,* according to Skinner, is the *occasion for a response,* not the cause of it. This stimulus is a necessary but not a sufficient cause for the response. There is, therefore, nothing surprising about the fact that, for example, a table is present but the utterance /That is a table./ does not occur. This state of affairs in no way invalidates the contention that /That is a table./ is conditioned to tables. If the presence of tables is not *sufficient* to produce the utterance, then there must also be other conditions required. In part these other conditions may be motivational, and in part they may require other stimuli. It would seem that the utterance /That is a table./ would not be made if there were no tables; neither would it be made if there was no one to hear it. Thus the presence of another person becomes part of the stimulus which controls the utterance. We could clearly extend this line of reasoning until the stimulus becomes quite complex indeed. The stimuli to which tacts are conditioned are discriminated stimuli in this sense.

The full complexity which the definition of a stimulus requires can probably be illustrated by two versions of an utterance: /That is a dining-room table./ and /That is a round table/. The stimulus which controls /dining-room table/ must contain determinants in objects which are not part of the table itself but are part of the general surroundings, e.g. dining rooms. Exactly how one defines a dining room in stimulus language is not easy to see, but let us suppose for the moment that it can be done. An additional problem arises when dining-room tables are not in dining rooms. The stimulus must then be some property which dining-room tables have in common but which is not possessed by other sorts of tables. But one immediately becomes puzzled, for the first property which suggests itself as common to all dining-room tables is that people sit around them and eat at them. But how can the quality of being able to be sat around and the quality of being able to be eaten at be represented in a stimulus?

To approach this problem from a somewhat different direction, let us consider the "round-table" problem. Roundness seems to be a perfectly overt and objective property of certain *objects*, and indeed it is. *But it is not a property of stimuli.* If, by "stimulus," we refer to a particular kind of pattern of energy striking a receptor organ, which would seem to be a common and legitimate use of that term, then stimuli from round objects are more often than not, not round. A round object will produce a round image on the eye only when it is: (1) directly in front of the viewer, (2) situated with its center on a line which passes through the center of each eye, and (3) perpendicular in both directions to this line. This is often called "frontal-parallel position" and it is clearly a very restricted set of conditions which are very rarely met in viewing round tables. Now it is perfectly correct to say that ordinarily the table *looks* round to the viewer, or that he *perceives* that it is round. But then one is no longer talking about stimuli. It would appear that when Skinner is talking about stimuli, he is referring either to the objects themselves (which contradicts his definition of a stimulus) or to perceptions.

But if he is talking about perceptions, his theory has lost the presumably objective status which the term stimulus grants. Stimuli become subjective things, perceptions, rather than objective energy patterns. To say that we call something round because it looks round is not an explanation of the same sort as an explanation which says that we use /round/ when the stimulus has such and such properties. Indeed, it is no explanation at all, for it allows me to "explain" the use of /table/ by saying that it looks like a table, of /dining-room table/ by the fact that it looks like a dining-room table, and the like. To escape this problem, we must either postulate a theory of perception, which essentially pushes the problem one step away, rather than solving it, or return to a strict definition of stimulus. Skinner, unfortunately, does neither.

If this argument is not sufficient to condemn Skinner's stimulus approach to tacts, let us consider two other examples: /This was a table./ (said while pointing to a pile of chopped-up wood) and /This could be a table./ (pointing to a pile of lumber). By his own admission, when he speaks of utterances being under the control of stimuli, Skinner is attempting to handle the problem of what is commonly called *reference*. Words or utterances refer to things. Sometimes the "things" to which they refer may be other words, as one might argue is the case with /atom/ or /God/; in neither of these cases is there an object to which anyone can point, but it is possible to conveniently avoid the reference problem by saying that the objects of reference of these nouns are other words. Skinner makes use of this device, but it would appear not to be sufficient to handle the problems posed by the past and future tenses.

If one is going to use the language of referring to *things*, it would seem that past utterances could refer only to memories, and future utterances only to potentialities (whatever they are). A stimulus theory meets the same problems. What is the stimulus property, be it ever so subtle, that controls /table/ in these two utterances? We cannot answer. Moreover, we cannot find it to be within the realm of plausibility to assume that these two utterances have had the opportunity to be conditioned to the particular stimuli which are present. It is a rare individual who speculates about the construction of tables; but it is an equally rare person who could not do so if he wished. Then how do such speculative utterances become conditioned? Skinner may be able to account for the "creative" or novel aspects of language. We shall discuss this later. But however he does this, either /table/ is conditioned to tables or it is not. If it is, then somehow we must account for the fact that neither the speaker nor the listener would react to either of these two utterances as though a table were present. (Needless to say we cannot permit the absence of an object to be a stimulus.) If it is not conditioned to tables, then we must answer this: how does /table/ refer to tables? If it is not conditioned to the objects, what is it conditioned to? Skinner fails us here too.

The Intraverbal: The intraverbal is a class of utterances, or parts of utterances, which are conditioned to verbal stimuli. A number of quite different sorts of phenomena can be included here. The so-called free association is one. The term "free association" refers to the fact that certain words remind one of other words, or that a person can give a single-word response to a single-word stimulus if so required. Here we have a clear example of a verbal stimulus provoking a verbal response. Alliteration (the calling out of certain sound patterns by other sound patterns or the repetition of these sound patterns in utterances) is a second example. Here the phonetic character of one word becomes the stimulus for the phonetic character of a second. Clearly some people, notably poets, learn this technique better than other people. It is here that we begin to see Skinner deal with the problem of style in language. A third example would be translation, in which a word in one language is (presumably) a response to a word in another.

It is both reasonable and accurate of Skinner to isolate this category of verbal behaviors. These behaviors and perhaps some others do have the characteristic of being entirely, or in very large measure, determined by verbal considerations. One is dealing here with sounds, or with verbal units as such, with little or no reference to questions of meaning and the like. One can wonder whether or not Skinner has actually given a correct account of these phenomena; for instance, we get a picture of translation as a word-for-word substitution from one language to the other. Translation of this order would produce nonsense in most languages, if for no other reason than that the word orders themselves are different from language to language. But we will offer no extended discussion of the intraverbal since the next and final category in the verbal typology offers much more important issues for discussion.

The Autoclitic: The autoclitic is a part of an utterance, or sometimes a complete utterance, which modifies or changes the character of some other utterance. That is, the autoclitic in some
way either changes the listener's response to a given utterance
or signifies that a person is going to respond differently than usual
to a particular utterance. Examples of autoclitics are numerous:
/I see that. . . ./, /I believe that. . . ./, /He said," . . ."/, /yes/,
/no/, /not/, /please/, /may I. . . ./, and the like are all autoclitics. Some serve to make a listener behave differently, some
serve to get the speaker more reinforcement, some "cancel" utterances, and some indicate acceptance of them. All modify reactions to the utterance. And all are essentially grammatical devices. The realm of the autoclitic is essentially the realm of
grammar to Skinner, for he would classify the agreement of number between the subject and the verb of a sentence as an autoclitic device, as he would many other purely grammatical rules.
Verb auxiliaries, active verbs, and passive verbs, and the like are
all autoclitics. Since the autoclitic is apparently supposed to account for much of grammar, we must evaluate it on this level.
While Skinner is, of course, primarily concerned with the functions of language—getting rewards, etc.—he cannot ignore the
fact that language functions the way it does because it follows
certain rules. It has a grammar, and the fact that behavior corresponds to these grammatical rules necessitates that we understand how this is possible.

Consider the sentence (tact, in Skinner's terms) /The table is
red/. We have here at least two grammatical principles which
any theory of language must be prepared to explain: the use of
the article, and the ordering of the subject and predicate of the
sentence. Let us consider the article first. How is the use of /the/
determined? Following the usual argument of Skinner's position,
/the/ must be under the control of some stimuli and must be
reinforced in some manner. The reinforcement is not the most
critical issue here, so we will ignore it. We can just take it for
granted that the use of /the/ gets the speaker something he
would not otherwise have gotten. But what about the stimulus?

If we assume that this sentence is the first one uttered in a conversation, which it easily could be, and if we consider the fact that /the/ is the first word in the sentence, then clearly /the/ cannot be controlled simply by present or even recent *verbal* stimuli. /The/ is not an intraverbal, in Skinner's sense. So what other stimuli might be involved? /The/ is used in reference to *specific* items; that is, it is the *definite article* in contrast to /a/ which is indefinite. But certainly the presence of a specific table is not a necessary stimulus for this utterance, since the table referred to by this utterance could easily be thousands of miles from the speaker, or even totally non-existent.

If we try instead to account for some use of the indefinite article, we will have even more difficulty. The indefinite article is used when the particularity of the item is irrelevant. /A table/ refers to any old table; anything which is a member of the class or family of objects called tables. Even if we suppose that it is possible to give an objective definition to the class of objects called tables, e.g. they all have flat tops, or the like, we still are missing something. To be Skinnerian, we must determine what the stimulus is that controls *talking* about *specific* objects, rather than talking about *classes* of objects. This is what Skinner must tell us if he is to account for the use of /a/ and /the/. Talking of classes is not something which can be easily accounted for by considering present stimuli, since classes are never present. At best, all we see at any moment is one or more *members* or examples of a class, never the class itself. In fact, class membership is something which is *imposed* upon objects by people; it is therefore in some sense subjective by definition. We cannot even conceive of a class of objects without saying something about events which are internal to people. The "stimulus" for a class, then, is not something external, but is something at least in part internal to a person, if such a thing can indeed be called a stimulus. The only internal stimuli which Skinner permits, however, are those arising from deprivation, and deprivation is not an issue here, for we are dealing with tacts.

It would appear that to understand the use of the articles, we would need to ask and get an answer to one of the following questions: what do you want to talk about, to what do you want to refer, or what do you mean? /The/ is used in reference to one sort of thing and /a/ in reference to another sort. In both cases, the determinant can be seen only as something which is *characteristic of the speaker* himself; more simply, we would say that the speaker tries to convey some idea. He says what he means. It is better to use technical terms at this point; the use of articles is apparently under the control of events which are not stimuli in the sense in which Skinner uses the term; these events are neither external nor deprivation states. Attempting to understand this sort of grammatical device by some form of "objective stimuli" such as that which Skinner attempts is doomed to failure.

But what about the ordering of words? It is clearly tempting to try to account for the fact that verbs follow nouns in tacts by assuming that verbs are responses conditioned to nouns. The difficulty with this interpretation becomes obvious as soon as we raise the question of how to recognize whether a word is a noun. Is there, in fact, any attribute of a word which signifies its nounness, other than the way in which it is used? To account for ordering in an objective theory, we must have an objective characteristic of nouns to which we may condition the verbs. Within limits there *are* such objective characteristics. For example, in general, words ending in /ism/ and /tion/are nouns. Such identifying endings could act as conditioned stimuli for other words; they could control the emission of verbs, perhaps.

But not all nouns have such distinguishing characteristics. /Table/, for example, bears a striking resemblance to /crumble/ and other verbs. And, in fact, /table/ is a perfectly good verb itself (to table a motion). It is difficult to see what aspects of this word could possibly be distinctive stimuli to which verbs could be conditioned, at least if we insist on treating the word as though it were a physical stimulus object. Perhaps, then, we might conceive of the relevant stimulus attribute as the position of the word in the utterance. Nouns generally come relatively early in sentences and verbs later. Perhaps nouns are primarily conditioned to the second position in a sentence and verbs to the third, or some such thing.

The notion that word position orders word ordering is not a foolish one unless carried to the extreme of saying that this is all there is to grammar. It has been shown experimentally that children are capable of learning where a word is to be used in a sentence (Braine, 1963) so that they will typically use, for instance, certain words at the end and others at the beginning of sentences, even though they do not know the meanings of these words. Furthermore, it is possible that different word orders could even be conditioned to "external" stimuli. Thus the presence of deprivation states which usually cause us to mand things could be the conditioned stimuli for the order which is typical of mands: verb followed by noun. The ordering of passive and active sentences could be determined by environmental considerations: if the objective recipient of the action is stated first, then the passive order must be used, and the like. One would still have some difficulties in accounting for why the recipient of the action was stated first, particularly in conditions in which there is no real objective referent to the sentence present at all. But one could still argue that word order is not completely independent of objective conditions and that it is possible that certain of these conditions could be the stimuli which elicit the order.

But our problem is still not solved. Granted that nouns precede verbs in tacts, it is not correct to say that nouns come in the second position and verbs in the third, or any similar statement. Consider the following:

/Tables are red./
/The table is red./
/The old table is red./
/The big, old table is red./
/Big, old tables are red./

One could go on like this indefinitely. The only commonality here is that subjects precede predicates, but the objective ordinal position of the verb is almost infinitely variable.

In other words, we reach the following state: for the verb to be conditioned to follow the noun, we need some objective stimulus to control this conditioning. Position is not stable enough to do the job accurately. Thus the objective stimulus must be something inherent in the noun itself. But we have already shown that there is nothing about many nouns which indicates that they are nouns. Nothing objective, that is. The only thing that identifies nouns is how they are used in sentences, or *to what they refer*. That is, if we are willing to talk about what a word means and if we are willing to assume that there may be some systematic differences between noun meanings and verb meanings, then, and only then, can we hope to account for word ordering by conditioning principles.

We are working here under the assumption that word-ordering rules must be acquired, and hence that some form of conditioning description could be relevant to them. This, of course, uses the term "conditioning" (those processes by which one learns) as synonymous with "learning." On this point there is no disagreement between Skinner and us. But it is equally clear that no theory which attempts to exclude meaning can account for the construction of an utterance. Since Skinner refuses to discuss meaning, his theory must be judged to be invalid. This does not mean that Skinner is all wrong nor does it mean that stimulus-response theories are necessarily invalid. What we must do now is turn to a stimulus-response theory which assumes the relevance of the concept of meaning and see what insights into the psychology of language this can provide.

Osgood's Mediation Theory of Meaning

Charles Osgood and his colleagues (1957), working within the framework of stimulus-response associationism as developed by C. L. Hull (1942, 1952), have attempted to develop a theory of meaning. They feel that meaning is the most critical problem which a theory of language must face and therefore attempt to deal with it first. As we shall see, their researches have little direct relevance to any of the other problems of language. In fact, both their theory and research are based upon the assumption that meaning can be treated independently of language as a whole. The success of their endeavors depends upon the validity of this very crucial assumption.

But to begin with, Osgood assumes that meaning is something which is acquired, and, moreover, that it is acquired by some method of conditioning. We tend to think of conditioning as something which is relevant to overt behaviors or responses. However, it is equally possible to think of the conditioning of less directly observable responses; for example, changes in heart rate or blood pressure. Indeed, it has been shown that it is possible to condition the activity of the central nervous system itself, so that the presentation of a conditioned stimulus elicits, for example, a particular pattern of central neural activity. The fact that such central-nervous-system conditioning can take place clearly suggests the possibility of acquiring meaning by conditioning procedures, without at the same time requiring that the meaning be some overt behavior. The equating of meaning with behavior and its controlling stimuli is, of course, the assumption which caused Skinner most of his trouble.

According to Osgood, we should consider meaning to be a *mediator*. That is, the meaning of any stimulus, be it a word or something else, is some internal event which comes between that stimulus and overt behavior. It mediates the connection between the stimulus and the response in the sense that the stimulus does not directly cause the response. Rather the stimulus gives rise to the central mediator which in turn gives rise to the response. Thus, responses are not made directly to properties of the stimulus but only to the mediators aroused by the stimuli. This notion permits us to account for the fact that two different stimuli can give rise to the same response, presumably because they are elicitors of the same mediator. We could say in this case, if we wished, that these two stimuli meant the same thing, or had the same meaning. It is not farfetched to think of meaning as something which stands between the word *qua* stimulus as heard or seen by a subject and his response to the word, where the response could be nearly anything at all.

Now we must ask what sort of conditioning process might produce these mediators? Clark Hull laid the foundation for the

answer which Osgood accepts. In order to understand the manner in which laboratory animals learn problems, such as the
solution of a maze by a rat, Hull found it necessary to assume
that they have some "anticipation" of the goal (1937). There
are, he said, three sorts of stimuli which control any given response: stimuli from external objects in the environment, stimuli
produced by deprivation states (the feeling of hunger, etc.), and
stimuli produced by immediately prior responses made by the
animal himself which stimuli arise from his own proprioceptive
and kinesthetic sensory nerves. It is characteristic of deprivation
stimuli that they alone *persist* throughout any given trial of
problem solution. At the end of the trial, they will be reduced
or partially removed by the reward given in the goal. The goal
itself is characterized by a particular response which is consum-
matory in nature; the animal does something, eats or drinks,
typically, which reduces his deprivation state. Because the goal,
which must be conceived as a stimulus, always accompanies immediate reinforcement, i.e. reduction in deprivation, the response
made in it becomes conditioned to any available stimuli more
strongly than any other response made in solving the problem.
All the other responses are temporally further removed from the
reward than is the goal response, and hence are conditioned less
strongly.

Thus the goal response, says Hull, is strongly connected to all
stimuli, including of course the persistent deprivation or drive
stimuli. Now what happens if we put the animal back at the
beginning of the maze after a suitable period of deprivation?
Since there is a strong association between the deprivation stimuli and the goal responses, it would seem likely that the animal
would make the goal response. But of course there is no goal
object present, and he would seem to be rather foolish to sit
there at the beginning of the maze and eat when there is no
food around. So clearly he does not. Rather, according to Hull,
he makes a response which is some *part* or *fraction* of the goal
response. These fractional responses have the character that (1)
they are part of the goal response, but (2) they can be made in
the absence of the goal without interrupting other ongoing be-

haviors, such as running the maze. Since these fractional responses will now be made prior to reaching the goal, they in some sense anticipate it, and they become the theoretical device by which Hull accounts for the apparent goal-directed nature of problem-solving behavior.

How Hull used this device need not concern us here. Suffice it to say he has postulated a kind of learning where the behavior learned is not overt or readily observable and where the behavior serves to mediate more overt acts—in this case, running the maze. The mediating and directing aspects come about through the medium of proprioception or kinesthesis. That is, any behavior involves muscular or glandular movement. And any such movement activates the receptors which exist in any muscle. These receptors send messages to the central nervous system "about" the movement. Each and every response, then, produces stimuli, and the fractional goal responses are no exception to this. Thus, while the fractional goal response is a response, it also produces stimuli to which other responses may be conditioned. It can, then, stand between or mediate some overt stimulus and overt response, which themselves are not directly connected but become connected by virtue of this mediating response.

Osgood generalizes this notion to account for meaning. Let us suppose that a spoken word is heard by a subject (child) in conjunction with his seeing an object. We have here the pairing of two stimuli and the laws of classical conditioning would lead us to suppose that one stimulus would acquire the power to call out the response typical of the other—that is, the unconditioned response. Thus by classical conditioning, the response to the object can now be elicited by the word. Logically, of course, there would seem to be no reason why the opposite could not also occur, namely that the object should come to call out some "conditioned" response produced by the hearing of the word. Osgood chooses to ignore this possibility, apparently under the mistaken supposition that it would be contrary to his theory. Actually it makes perfectly good sense, both psychologically and commonsensically, as we shall see later.

But the word is not the object and rather ludicrous results

would occur if one sat down to the word /chair/ rather than in the objective chair. Thus, Osgood assumes, what actually gets conditioned is some *fraction* of the response to the chair, a fraction which can be made *independently* of the presence of the actual object. As a response, this fractional response produces its own stimuli. Thus the fractional response both (1) is a response to something (the spoken word) and (2) can become the stimulus for other responses. This fractional response is identified as meaning by Osgood. As such we see that it possesses one of the attributes of meaning as we generally think of it—meaning as caused, or as a response to something, able to cause or stimulate other activities in turn. Things have meaning and we react to the meaning of things, to use more common language.

But what is the nature of this mediating response which Osgood identifies with meaning? In what sense is it a response, first of all? Clearly we are not to take the term "response" too literally. The mediating response is not necessarily a muscular or glandular movement, as was the fractional goal response to Hull. It apparently can be simply a neural event, according to Osgood. It is a response only in a conceptual sense; that is, it is a response because it can be conditioned to stimuli. Likewise, it is a stimulus because it can control responses, not because it is in any way connected with the activities of sense receptors or sensory cortical areas. But even as a neural event, it is also some fraction of the response to the object. We must determine, of course, what fraction it could be. We must decide what part of the response to an object could be made in the absence of that object. One possibility is emotion. The emotions proper to an object could be made in the absence of that object in a way that the overt reactions to the object could not. But Osgood will not be satisfied by speculation on this problem. In order to identify the nature of the mediating response, we must attempt to describe or measure it. We must, therefore, tackle the problem of the measurement of meaning, which he and his associates proceed to do.

How are we to measure meaning? Since measurement is a precise form of description, why not try asking subjects to *describe* words and see if these descriptions yield results which we would wish to identify as meaning. There are a number of possible ways in which an experimentally oriented psychologist may ask subjects to describe something for him. Whatever technique he chooses, it will have to have first of all the characteristics of *reliability*. That is, the results yielded by the measuring technique must be repeatable. The objectivity and usefulness of the measurements is a function of this reliability. It will be necessary, therefore, to control the descriptions given by the subjects in some way, to eliminate as much as possible any purely idiosyncratic, subjective factors and fluctuations which would lead to unreliability of the descriptions of meaning. To the extent that the subject is free to give any description that comes to mind, he may give somewhat different descriptions of the same event on different occasions. These descriptions, since they differ, will not be completely reliable. But, on the other hand, restricting the descriptions to eliminate these fluctuations runs the risk of not obtaining fully accurate and exhaustive descriptions. And to the extent that the descriptions are not complete, we may be missing some critical aspect of meaning. These considerations should be borne in mind in evaluating Osgood's methods.

Osgood chose to have words described by means of rating scales. Each scale was defined as lying between two points which were determined by *antonymic adjectives*. A further restriction was that each scale was divided into seven segments which were presumably equal in extent—an assumption which has never been fully validated. Thus, the description of any word might take place as follows: The subject is given a number of seven-point scales, each defined by two antonymic adjectives such as good-bad, hard-soft, weak-strong, active-passive, and the like. The seven points on the scale are identified by modifying adverbs; thus for the good-bad scale, the seven points would be (1) very good, (2) quite good, (3) slightly good, (4) neutral, or neither good nor bad, or equally good and bad,* (5) slightly bad, (6)

---

* It seems obvious that these three designations do not mean the same thing. Yet sometimes they appear to be used interchangeably by Osgood and other researchers in this area. The ambiguities inherent here could have important implications for his results.

quite bad, and (7) very bad. The same seven qualifying points are used for all scales, that is, for all pairs of antonyms. The subject is instructed to indicate the appropriate rating of each stimulus word on each scale. He is not given the opportunity to leave a scale unused if he feels it is irrelevant.

What we obtain, then, is a large collection of ratings of several words on several scales by several subjects. Somehow these ratings must be consolidated to give a picture or summary description of the meaning of each word. The method by which this consolidation is performed is known as factor analysis. Factor analysis is a method for determining which of the scales are rated similarly to each other. The method will yield *clusters* or *factors* of scales. All scales within each factor will be reacted to similarly to each other—that is, for the average word and average subject. At this point one may object to the concept of an "average word" or even of an "average subject" as being meaningless. Neglecting the fact that the statistical techniques require this assumption, one is still often on perfectly safe and sensible ground in making it. However, it is doubtful that this is one of those safe cases. We shall return to this issue later. To continue, the assumption is that if several scales are used in a similar fashion and, hence, fall in the same factor, when they are in effect measuring the same thing. By looking at the particular scales which belong to particular factors one decides, arbitrarily, what it is that that factor is measuring.

As a result of performing this sort of analysis, Osgood and his associates isolated three factors which were statistically large enough to be judged of psychological importance. The first, and statistically most important, of these factors contained scales such as good-bad, beautiful-ugly, and pleasant-unpleasant. It was therefore identified as an *evaluative* factor or dimension. The second factor contained scales such as active-passive and fast-slow and was identified as an *activity* dimension. The third factor, which was about equal in importance to the second, contained scales such as weak-strong, masculine-feminine, and hard-soft and was identified as a *potency* factor. According to Osgood, then, these are three dimensions of meaning. This is not an exhaustive list, perhaps, but at least it does help to define meaning, presumably.

Osgood and his associates have referred to the rating-scale technique by which one measures these three factors as the *semantic differential* since it is a method whereby one can differentiate or discriminate objectively among the meanings or semantic nature of words. Each word can be described as falling at a particular point on each dimension. The meaning of a word can be graphically described, then, by treating it as a specific point in a three-dimensional space and defining each dimension of this space by one of the three factors of meaning. This abstract space within which one can pinpoint words and, by doing so, objectify their meaning is called the *semantic space*. One can conceive, then, of a new sort of dictionary which consists only of a set of points in space. Each point is a word and those points which are close to each other are more similar in their meaning than points which are more distant from each other. One can use the semantic differential, then, to assign words to their appropriate position in the semantic space. It should be pointed out that there is no such thing as *the* semantic differential. Any set of scales which measure each of the three factors or dimensions of semantic space constitutes a semantic differential, irrespective of what specific scales are used.

There is a certain ambiguity in Osgood's theory. It is not clear whether the three factors are to be conceived of as three *dimensions* descriptive of the mediating response which we call meaning, or whether there are *three mediating responses* for each word, one for evaluation, one for activity, and one for potency. Apparently Osgood originally considered the former to be correct but has more recently shifted to the latter interpretation. The advantages of one interpretation over the other are not immediately obvious.

It is a well-established fact that these three factors are highly replicable. Osgood and his colleagues and students have by now performed many factor analyses using many different scales and many different words. In all cases the same three factors have appeared, and they have appeared essentially in the same order and to the same degree of importance. Some studies yield more than three factors, but these additional factors have not received sufficient empirical use to interest us here. Osgood has also shown that the same factors may be obtained in languages other than English. He has conducted studies in most of the major European (Indo-European) languages and many of the major tongues of the Orient and in all cases has arrived at the same three factors, with the evaluative factor always first in importance. Furthermore, he has reported data which show that the factors are obtainable on ratings of non-verbal material. Pictures, radar screen patterns, and the like have been rated, and they yield the same three factors. There is little doubt that Osgood has a genuine, reliable phenomenon here. The only question is this: is it really what we would want to call meaning?

Before attacking this crucial issue, let us complete the picture of Osgood's theory. Osgood attempts to approach the issue of grammar through the study of what happens in the grammatical process of modification. That is, a noun such as /table/ has a particular meaning, as does an adjective such as /old/. The phrase /old table/ also has a meaning which is not independent of the meanings of the words making it up. Neither is the meaning identical, however, to those single-word meanings. A mediating response theory of meaning would seem to suggest that the mediating response to a two-word phrase should be predictable from the mediating responses to each of the single words. Moreover, it should be some simple predictive rule that works since there is a limited number of ways in which one can conceive of combining responses.

The particular model with which Osgood chooses to predict the effects of grammatical modification is called the *congruity hypothesis*, and is represented by the following formula:

$$D_{PH} = \frac{/D_N/}{/D_N/ + /D_A/} D_N + \frac{/D_A/}{/D_N/ + /D_A/} D_A$$

In this formula, the D's represent the distances from the neutral point on the seven-point rating scale of the adjective (D_A) and noun (D_N) respectively. The symbol D_{PH} represents the predicted rating of the phrase on that scale. These predictions are made scale by scale, or at least factor by factor. By custom, Osgood represents distances which are toward the good, active, and strong ends of the three dimensions as positive in sign, while those toward the bad, weak, and passive ends are negative in sign. The straight verticle lines which bracket some of the terms direct one to ignore the sign for a particular term. These brackets indicate that the numbers enclosed are *absolute numbers*; that is, these numbers are to be treated as though positive.

From Osgood's point of view, the important thing about this equation is that it does *not* predict that the rating of a two-word phrase will be a simple average of, or compromise between, the adjective rating and the noun rating. Rather, the word, be it the adjective or the noun, which is the most distant from the neutral point will have the most weight in determining the rating of the phrase. Thus, in the case in which one word is rated as neutral (o) while another is at some other non-neutral position on the scale in question, the congruity model predicts that the phrase rating will be identical to that of the word which has a non-neutral rating. If two words are rated identically, the phrase will have the same rating as the words. Thus two "goods" do not make a "better" in this model. In the case in which the two words are given opposite ratings equally distant from zero, the phrase rating will be zero or neutral. In all other cases, the phrase rating will be most similar to the rating of the word with the higher D value. To repeat, the solutions of this equation are calculated separately for each scale or for each factor.

Osgood, Suci, and Tannenbaum present evidence which demonstrates that this model has a reasonable degree of success in predicting the ratings of phrases from the ratings of their component nouns and adjectives. These data indicate that while the predictions are not completely accurate, the phrase ratings are closer to the predictions of this model than they are to predictions made by a simple averaging process. While this is perhaps not all that one might wish, evidence certainly provides partial support for the model or at least for the rationale underlying the model.

There are, however, at least two empirical difficulties, which Osgood himself is careful to point out. First with regard to the congruity hypothesis, there is a phenomenon which Osgood has nicely referred to as the *sticky negative*. The congruity hypothesis would predict that a very good word paired with a "very bad" one would be rated at or near the neutral point of the scale. In fact, however, these phrases tend to be rated at or near the "very bad" end of the scale. A strong negative evaluation appears to take "all the weight" in the phrase; it sticks, to use Osgood's metaphor. Thus, a /*treacherous doctor*/ despite the virtues of his profession (to the average rater) remains treacherous, and is therefore rated as bad. Likewise a /*sincere prostitute*/ remains evil by virtue of her calling. One can get a good deal of amusement out of meditating on examples such as these and debating the concept of meaning in light of them. All that we need to point out now, however, is that these results are *contrary* to the congruity hypothesis. And, moreover, they are clearly not merely statistical aberrations; they constitute a genuine phenomenon of meaning. They are things for which the congruity hypothesis should be able to account but for which it does not.

The second difficulty appears in the use of the semantic differential itself. Osgood (1962) refers to this problem as *concept-scale interaction*. It can be illustrated as follows: given a sample of Democrats rating political names and concepts, we might find that /Adlai Stevenson/ was rated as strong and as masculine. /Eleanor Roosevelt/ would, on the other hand, be rated as strong and feminine. The difficulty here arises because according to theory, or at least according to factor-analysis results, strong-weak and masculine-feminine are measuring the same thing and they should, therefore, behave identically. Strong things should always go with masculine, and weak with feminine. Now, of course, statistical considerations allow us to expect small differences between scales purportedly measuring the same dimension, but these differences should be random and due to chance. It is obvious that this difference is due not to chance but to the nature of the concepts—to what they mean, if you will.

It would appear, then, that strong-weak and masculine-feminine do not really measure the same thing, at least not under all conditions. Osgood's difficulty arises from an attempt to establish that we may combine them into a *single factor* and call it potency. We are apparently dealing here with a "dimension" which at some level has been *produced* by the very statistical techniques chosen for the analysis of the data. Specifically, we could argue that the factors are *produced* by the factor analysis and not by any considerations of what really happens. What we have here is a set of data which clearly calls into question the concept of clear-cut dimensions of meaning.

It is time now to ask whether or not the semantic differential is really measuring meaning. Two kinds of negative arguments can be advanced, one empirical and one theoretical. Let us consider the empirical one first. If we consider the positions assigned to words and concepts in the semantic space defined by the three factors of meaning, we find that there are some peculiar bedfellows there. For example, /table/ and /chair/ would be located in similar positions and therefore would be judged as having similar meaning. Yet they most clearly and unambiguously do not mean the same thing. One could, of course, argue that both are instances of the same concept /furniture/ and that is why they can be said to have similar meaning. But, then, by definition /good/ and /bad/ are both instances of the concept of /evaluation/ and they are not rated similarly. Furthermore we find a psychiatric patient rating /myself/ and /evil/ similarly, or a Democratic rating /Adlai Stevenson/ and /good/ as similar. By no stretch of the imagination could we say that these pairs mean the same thing, if we use meaning in any ordinary sense of that word.

It would appear then, that Osgood's semantic differential is not measuring ordinary meaning. Osgood has acknowledged this and claims that what he is measuring is affective, emotional, or "connotative" meaning. In logic the word "connotation" is used to refer to the defining attributes of a class, in contrast to "denotation," which refers to examplars of the class. Osgood is not using the term in this sense. Rather, he means by "connotation" a meaning which is essentially private, idiosyncratic, and emotional. The semantic differential, then, measures meaning in the sense that it measures one's feelings about the word or phrase rated. This is all very well and good and constitutes an issue of considerable psychological importance. But for one interested in language it is rather disconcerting. For we find that in fact the semantic differential does not measure meaning, if by "meaning" we refer to reference, denotation, logical connotation, or any similar concept. And it tells us, therefore, very little about language.

The theoretical or conceptual difficulty with the semantic differential is this: it has never been clear exactly what the theoretical connection is between the mediating response theory of meaning and the semantic differential. If we are going to conceive of meaning as a mediating response, where that response is covert, microscopic, and perhaps even confined solely to the central nervous system, there is a definite sense in which measuring it is a ludicrous idea. Short of using physiological techniques which we do not even have yet, measuring such a mediator would be impossible. When looked at this way, it is clear that the concept of the semantic differential in no way follows from the concept of a mediating response theory of meaning. And, therefore it is correct to say that the validity or invalidity of the semantic differential as a tool, has no bearing on the truth or falsity of the mediating response concept of meaning.

Now what Osgood really wanted to do was to find some way of describing words so that he could make inferences about the meaning of these words from the descriptions. Moreover, he hoped to phrase these inferences in mediating response language. But it must be clear, first of all, that we are in no sense measuring meaning, if by this we refer to central mediating responses; we are *inferring* meaning from a set of measurements of something else, namely how subjects respond to words in a particular situation. It is clear then, that the adequacy of our inferences about meaning will be determined by the adequacy of the responses which we ask subjects to make to the words in question. Here, by his own admission, Osgood has proved to be inadequate. We find that the only sort of meaning we can possibly make inferences about is emotional meaning. And even here the vagaries of the semantic differential might make us have doubts about our inferences. But even with the greatest degree of charity toward the methodology, emotional meaning is the only meaning we can say that we are measuring.

So where do we go from here? Is it possible, for instance, to develop an objective measurement of meaning, as Osgood attempted to do? Restricting ourselves to emotional meaning, let us ask whether the semantic differential could be successful at this type of measurement. To measure the meaning of a word, it would appear to be necessary to get some subject to use the word. But to make the measurement objective, it will be necessary to restrict and control the situation in which the word is used. Only by doing this can we assume that successive measurements mean the same thing, and that they are not influenced by factors other than meaning. Osgood attempts to control the situation by having the subject "use" the word in the context of a fixed number of predetermined rating scales.

The difficulties with this approach should be obvious. First of all, in the interests of precision, an arbitrary context within which the word is to be used must be established. But the very arbitrariness of the context makes the measurements potentially meaningless. Most words are not used in such a contrived laboratory context. If the meaning of a word has any relation to the way in which it is *typically* used, as it should if meaning is to be worth studying, then studying the use of words in atypical contexts may well tell us little about meaning.

The subject who must rate the word is put into a quandary. The context provided by the rating scales is often irrelevant to his normal usage of the word. How is he to use the scale intentional-unintentional on concepts such as /fire/, /mother/, /table/, /democracy/, and /black/? Here we reach the crux of the problem; the semantic differential does not really control or standardize the context in which a word is used. Rather it requires each individual rater to provide his own context. This in itself is no drawback since such idiosyncratic differences in word usage are of psychological interest. The difficulty arises in that we have no way of determining or knowing the context within which any given individual has rated a word. While the ratings are not independent of the meaning of the word, we cannot, in fact, make any conclusive inferences from them to some internal process called meaning since we do not know what other variables and conditions were affecting the ratings. And, moreover, we have good reason to suspect that these "other conditions" vary considerably from individual to individual—while meaning, owing to the social nature of language, will not.

This argument suggests strongly that it is in fact impossible to develop an objective measurement of meaning by any of the techniques typically espoused by psychologists. All of them involve producing arbitrary contexts within which the measurement takes place. But the facts of language suggest that any such arbitrariness will automatically invalidate the measurements. Words are not used arbitrarily in practice. At some level of analysis, it may be said that words are "conditioned" to stimuli as Skinner argued. And when words are removed from these stimuli, they cease to perform their normal functions. In particular, words are rarely used in isolation. Words are used in sentences made up of other words. While single-word utterances are used on occasion, these are more often than not replies to other utterances. Hence, the single-word utterance is used in a verbal environment. This verbal environment contributes to the significance of a particular word; through it we determine which particular meaning of a word we are using. No word has *a* meaning; each has many meanings, and the particular meaning of interest is selected out by the context, verbal and otherwise, in which the word is used. It is senseless to attempt to get a context-free measurement of meaning. It is senseless to attempt to measure meaning within a *particular* context, for that will only tell you about that context and not about any of the hosts of other possible contexts.

This leaves us in the position of saying that if we want to assess the meaning of a word, we should look at how it is used. And not just at some *one* particular use, but at *all* possible uses. This is of course the position that Skinner would take, except that he would add, "since what you call meaning is the total sum of all uses of the word, no more and no less, why bother to talk about meaning at all?" To this, Osgood (and the author) would reply that there are certain internal psychological processes which determine the use of a word which must be studied if one is to get an adequate psychological understanding of language. We choose to call these processes meaning. Whatever one calls them, it is incorrect to assume that only objective stimuli and objective responses can be the basis for an adequate understanding of language.

But then does the notion of a mediating response provide us with the appropriate conceptual tool for understanding meaning? I fear that one's immediate response to Osgood's theorizing (if one is not a psychologist, that is) tends to be, "But that is not what I mean by 'meaning.'" Two problems immediately suggest themselves. First of all, how do we account for the use of a word? Why is it that I call the thing in front of me a typewriter? Mediating response theory might be capable of accounting for my being able to refer to an object by name—that is, by assuming that the word called out part of the response appropriate to the object itself. That response is the mediating response. If I as a speaker can call out the correct mediator in you, the listener, you will know how to respond. In that sense /typewriter/ can be said to refer to typewriters, since it calls out parts of the response appropriate to typewriters. But why do I call it /typewriter/ when I see it? Osgood does not account for the processes by which something is called by name. He has the word as a stimulus to which a response appropriate to an object is conditioned. He does *not* have the spoken word conditioned as a response to the object and, in fact, cannot do so. Conditioning theory, as he uses it, prohibits something's being an external stimulus and a response to that stimulus at the same time, although the mediating response concept does blur the stimulus-response distinction considerably. But words seem to have that very property. To the extent that he cannot account for words, being both stimuli and responses, Osgood cannot account for meaning.

Second of all, we run into difficulties when we try to understand the learning of meanings of new words, particularly when this learning is done verbally. Osgood has provisions for the learning of meanings of words from other words. Here a new word acquires part of the mediator of the old known word which serves as the unconditioned stimulus in the paradigm. But suppose we define a word negatively, as is often done. Suppose you do not know what /cortical grey/ means, and I tell you that it is that experience which results when no light is striking the retina of the eye. Now I am sure you all know exactly what /cortical grey/ means. But exactly what conditioning took place? Clearly, this term could not be conditioned to the mediators of /light/ since this would produce exactly the opposite meaning which is intended. Therefore it must be conditioned to the combined mediators of /no light/. But what sort of response can be given to no light—where no light is, after all, not a stimulus?

We have a difficulty here. I do not believe that it is an insoluble difficulty for mediating response theories. It is clear that Osgood has not solved it, however. Indeed, he has not even seriously considered it. Later we shall attempt to sketch the outlines of a more adequate sort of mediation theory of meaning, for the approach has too many obvious merits for us to abandon it. Osgood, after all, has made no serious attempt to develop the position to its fullest, for, unlike Skinner, he has never attempted to look at language in use.

Comparisons of these two theorists are interesting. They each approached a different aspect of language, Skinner the question of when an utterance is made and Osgood the question of what an utterance refers to. One is struck by the possibility (although a doubtful one) that some judicious combination of the two might produce a very fruitful theory of language. As it stands now, Osgood's method of study involved an attempt to take language into the laboratory, while Skinner attempted to impose laboratory results on language as used in the world. The results appear to be that both achieved an unreal picture of language, each for his own reasons. In general, Skinner seems to have offered the more stimulating theory since it deals more fully with the actual problems and issues of language. Its solutions are clearly inadequate, and in many cases clearly wrong. Yet, because of his selection of data, one can go far indeed while speculating about why Skinner is wrong. Osgood has a theoretical conception which may turn out to be a forerunner of a much more correct one. Yet the restricted and arbitrary nature of much of his research prohibits the gaining of anything really significant from speculation on his failures and successes. In either case, it is clear that we must progress beyond the *traditional* stimulus-response models if we are to give a psychological account of language.

Bibliography

Braine, M. D. S. On learning the grammatical order of words. *Psychol. Rev.*, 1963, 70, 323-48.

Chomsky, N. Verbal behavior by B. F. Skinner. *Language*, 1959, 35, 26-58.

Goldstein, K. *Language and language disturbances*. New York, Grune & Stratton, 1948.

Hull, C. L. Mind, mechanism and adaptive behavior. *Psychol. Rev.*, 1957, 44, 1-32.

Hull, C. L. *The principles of behavior*. New York, Appleton-Century-Crofts, 1942.

Hull, C. L. *A behavior system*. New Haven, Yale University Press, 1952.

Jackson, H. Affection of speech from disease of the brain. *Brain*, 1878, 1, 304.

Osgood, C. E. Studies on the generality of the affective meaning system. *Amer. Psychologist*, 1962, 17, 10-28.

Osgood, C. E., Suci, G. and Tannenbaum, P. *The measurement of meaning*. Urbana, University of Illinois Press, 1957.

Skinner, B. F. *The behavior of organisms*. New York, Appleton-Century-Crofts, 1938.

Skinner, B. F. *Walden two*. New York, Macmillan, 1948.

Skinner, B. F. Are theories of behavior necessary? *Psychol. Rev.*, 1950, 57, 193-216.

Skinner, B. F. *Verbal behavior*. New York, Appleton-Century-Crofts, 1957.

Wittgenstein, L. *Philosophical investigations*. New York, Macmillan, 1953.

V
Language Statistics
and Word Use

We have come to a tentative conclusion, based on our considerations of Osgood's works, that a laboratory-experiment study of language produces a distorted and perhaps even inaccurate picture of language. An alternative approach would be to look at language in its natural habitat and to study language usage under conditions as close to normal as possible. If we are to speak accurately of the meaning of a word we must first see how the word is actually used. We will eventually have to face the issue of whether word meaning and word usage are synonymous. But for the moment we must look at language.

The scientific study of language, even when that study takes place naturalistically, is going to require methods for describing the phenomena observed. The scientific tradition immediately suggests that such a description utilize the tools of mathematics or of numbers in general. In fact, we shall see that certain mathematical statistical tools appear to be singularly appropriate for the description of language. This appropriateness stems not only from the relative objectivity of the techniques but from the fact that their use suggests important insights about the nature of language.

To take an example, suppose we are interested in the word /table/. And suppose further that we want to find out how often in telephone utterances /table/ is used. We will find that if we consider a large sample of such telephone utterances, there will be a very large number of different words which occur. (We are not here interested in what *could* occur, only in what actually does occur.) Moreover, we see that of these words, some occur relatively more often than do others. We can assume for the moment that out of a large number of observations of words used in telephone utterances, /table/ will occur several times. We can now express the occurrence of /table/ as a proportion; that is, we can divide the number of times it occurred by the total number of words we observed. In such a case we might find that /table/ occurred in telephone utterances five times out of a million, or .000005 times. This proportion we could, of course, compare with proportions similarly gathered on, say, newspaper utterances or on face-to-face utterances. This would then tell us something about the different situations in which /table/ was used.

Now, in all likelihood when we gathered these utterances which we tabulated, we did so by one of the typical methods of scientific observation in the social sciences. Namely, we selected the utterances *randomly*. All that the term "random" refers to in this sort of situation is that the observer did nothing to influence what utterances he observed. He did not select among utterances after he observed them but rather took all that came his way. Likewise, he did nothing to predetermine the nature of the utterances in any manner other than that described in his particular research design, e.g. he may have decided to look only at utterances which had more than four words, but among these four-word utterances there was random determination of which particular ones he observed.

If we are willing to grant the assumption that the utterances were observed randomly, then we can translate the proportion which we calculated above into a *probability*. A probability is the proportion, or relative frequency of times, something will occur among a large number of random or chance occurrences. We can say then, that we have a probability of five in a million of observing /table/ in telephone utterances, if we observe a random collection of such utterances. You must keep in mind that this is a completely accurate, justifiable, and even useful way of describing language.

The use of the concept of probability does not mean, however, that the processes actually determining the use of a particular word in a particular situation are random or chance processes. There are probably specific and determinant causes for the occurrence of a particular word in a particular situation. All that the probability means is that *observing* the word is a random or chance event—a statement which must be true by the very nature of how we make our observations. We may speak legitimately of the probability of observing a word or the probability of a word occurring in a given situation when such situations are randomly observed. But can we talk about the probability of *using* a word?

It is a common assumption of psychologists, and Skinner is an excellent example of a psychologist who makes this assumption, that the probabilities of observing an event represent some internal psychological probabilities of using or producing the event observed. Such an assumption implies that inside you, the speaker, are a set of probabilities or probabilistic mechanisms which determine the relative frequencies with which you use words. Moreover, such theorists would have to assume that these hypothetical, individual probabilities conform to those observed on a macroscopic scale in the utterances made by a large sample of people. But the fact that words can be assigned, legitimately, a probability of being observed does not mean that the concept of "probability of using a word" on some psychological level is a legitimate one, or even a useful one. Nor does it necessarily mean that it is illegitimate. In fact, the notion of a probabilistic psychological theory is one which cannot be justified or refuted on the basis of response probabilities based on *large samples* of observations, since by definition such theories deal with an individual's internal probability mechanisms. Thus, while probability is a useful descriptive tool for masses of observations, its use as a theoretical concept, as a supposedly internal psychological mechanism, must be justified in and of itself.

Let us now proceed to a discussion of some of the statistical descriptions of language which have been made to see what, if anything, such gross descriptions can tell us about the psychological processes underlying language and meaning.

ZIPF'S LAW

The best known of the statistical descriptions of language was given by G. K. Zipf (1949), who attempted to demonstrate the validity of a law of least effort by means of these statistics. The power of Zipf's position comes from two sources: first that he was able to derive and predict the nature of his observations from theoretical considerations, and second that his data have a regularity and reliability that is compelling to all, whether or not one agrees with the theory.

The best-known part of "Zipf's law" is shown in the relationship between the frequency with which a word is used, and the rank of its frequency of usage. That is, suppose we take all the words which appear in some piece of text such as James Joyce's *Ulysses*, as Zipf did. We will count the number of times each particular word was used and arrange the words in order of decreasing frequency: the word used most frequently comes first with a rank of one, the next most frequent comes second with a rank of two, etc. We now make a plot of the rank against the actual frequency with which the word was used, and we find that this plot is an almost perfect straight line when drawn on logarithmic graph paper.* In fact, no matter from which source we count words, this straight-line relationship between log frequency and frequency rank will be observed. Now what does this "law" indicate?

It shows that in any text, there are a relatively few words which are used extremely often and a very large number of words which are used relatively infrequently. As Zipf indicates with further data, the most frequent words tend to be shorter than the more infrequent words. Moreover, the more frequent words tend to have more meanings (as listed in the dictionary) than the more

---

* There will obviously be some sort of relationship between the frequency and the rank of the frequency and this relationship must be negative; that is, the high ranks have low frequencies and the low ranks high frequencies—by definition. The relationship is linear, but there is no reason to assume that it must be linear simply from a consideration of the "numbers" alone.

infrequent words. To Zipf, all of this tends to suggest a law of least effort in language. That is, presumably the speaker of the language tends to try to make do with as few words as possible. Moreover, he should try to make the words he uses as short as possible, hence presumably easier to say. He should try to lump as much meaning as possible in as few items as possible, and use these few items as much as possible. In point of fact according to Zipf's data, this *is* what people do with their language. Whether they do it to conserve energy or not is another matter.

If we look at the words which are used with the greatest frequency, we find that they tend to be short words. And most of these short words fall into the class which we have called function words. That is, they are the words which serve to order and relate form class or substantive words in a sentence. The function words *must* be used if an utterance is to be comprehensible. It is not surprising, then, to find that they are used with relatively high frequency. But what about the substantive words? Zipf's data suggests that language usage is restricted to a few words, each of which has a relatively large number of meanings. This suggests that in some sense ordinary words are *ambiguous* in their meanings and that, in fact, *the more ambiguous they are, the more likely we are to use them*. Presumably the context in which they are used clarifies this ambiguity. Yet this clearly contradicts our common-sense view of language, which assumes that each word means something clear and distinct, and which suggests that we strive for such clarity and distinctiveness. One could easily wonder how language could function as a communicating device, how it could refer to things, indeed how it could have meaning at all if there were no clarity in meaning. But according to Zipf, the greater the ambiguity, the more likely we are to use the word, which clearly suggests that the more ambiguous it is, the more meaningful it is. We must try to account for this apparent paradox. To do so, we will have to introduce another statistical technique.

INFORMATION THEORY

Information measurement is a technique which was developed by engineers (Shannon and Weaver, 1949) in order to describe certain events which take place in electrical communication systems—computers, telephones, and the like. It is a technique which has had immediate appeal to many psychologists and does, in fact, seem to have particular relevance to some problems of language. You should be aware, however, that the term "theory" is not entirely accurate here. Information theory is not a psychological theory in the sense that one can make predictions about behavior or mental events from it directly. Rather, it is a mathematical system which can be used to *describe* certain attributes of behaviors or mental events, and from these descriptions it sometimes appears possible to make accurate predictions. When events are described by information theory they seem, at times, to be more understandable than they were before. But the usefulness of information theory depends entirely on choosing the right sorts of things to describe with it.

To begin our discussion of information theory we must have a definition of information. Let us consider some examples which we would or would not consider to be informative in some sense. One can argue, correctly, that both of the following statements are not informative at all:

/The sun will set tonight./
/The earth is flat./

In the former case this lack of information stems from the fact that the sun *always* sets at night. The sentence in question tells us nothing we did not already know; it is trivial. If we had said instead /we will be able to see the sunset tonight/ this statement might be considered informative since it is not always predictable or obvious that one will be able to see a sunset on a particular evening. The statement that the earth is flat is uninformative (for an educated adult) because it is beyond doubt. We know without question that the statement is not true. But it is not its truth or falsity that is the issue; it is the fact that the statement does not relate to anything about which there was any doubt.*

Thus /The light in the kitchen is burnt out./ is an informative statement, and it is informative whether or not it is true or false. It *could be* either true or false quite easily, and that is exactly why it *is* informative. The sentence in question clears up some issue about which there could be doubt. And it is the ability to reduce doubt that is the defining characteristic of information. In information theory we use the term "uncertainty" instead of "doubt." *Information is anything which will reduce or remove uncertainty.* In any situation in which there is complete certainty, there is no information. This holds whether or not it is correct certainty, and whether it is certainty that something is or certainty that something is not the case. No communication could possibly tell us anything about something when everything is already known about that thing. Since certainty implies complete knowledge, no communication can give information when there is no uncertainty.

But once there is uncertainty, then there is the possibility that information may be transmitted. Uncertainty can be removed. If we could measure the uncertainty in a situation, then we could have an estimate of the amount of potential information which could be transmitted in that situation. Or, if we could measure the amount of uncertainty reduced in a given situation, since a given communication need not necessarily reduce all uncertainty, we would know how much information had been transmitted. If we are to measure information, then, one must be able to measure uncertainty.

The measurement of uncertainty returns us to the issue of statistics and probabilities. We have already defined the situation of total certainty as (1) one in which there is either *no*

---

* This illustration obviously does not hold for children and for certain other people. Its lack of information is the case only for educated adults. This does not invalidate the argument. But it does show that there is *no* such thing as *the* information value of an utterance—any more than there is *the* meaning of a word.

probability or possibility that something will happen or (2) one in which it will *always* happen. These would be represented as probabilities of zero (p=o.o) and one (p=1.o) respectively. But what, on the other hand, is the situation of *maximal uncertainty?* To illustrate this, let us consider a sequence of two events, call them a and b for convenience, and let us assume that we are trying to predict whether a or b will occur on each particular occasion. Now, if a always occurs ($p_a = 1.o$) or if it never occurs ($p_a = o.o$) then, as above, there is no uncertainty. There will only be uncertainty if a occurs some of the time and does not occur at other times. Now let us suppose that a occurs on the vast majority of the occasions, but that b also occurs sometimes, albeit rarely. Clearly there is some uncertainty in this situation; b always *could* occur this time. But there is still not much uncertainty, for if we predict that a will occur, the vast majority of our predictions will be right. If we make b occur more and more frequently, it should be reasonably clear that the uncertainty in the situation will increase, until uncertainty reaches its maximum when a and b occur equally often; that is, uncertainty will be maximum when $p_a = p_b = .5$. Here, no matter whether you guess a or b, you will be wrong half the time. In any other set of probabilities you can always expect to be right more than half the time. Uncertainty, then, can be expressed as a function of the probability or relative frequency with which events occur.

There are, of course, situations which appear to complicate this illustration. You can easily find a sequence of events in which a and b occur equally often, with equal probabilities, but in which there is no uncertainty. The following are examples:

ababababababababab
abbaabbaabbaabba

In both of these sequences one can always accurately predict whether an a or a b will occur if one knows something about the sequence in which the a's and b's are occurring. While a and b do occur equally often, the probabilities of a following b and of b following a (in the first example) are unity. These *transitional probabilities* have no uncertainty then, and thus there is little or no information in the sequence as a whole. The mathematics of information theory is quite capable of handling this issue. We raise it here simply to demonstrate that information is maximal when $p_a = p_b$ only under the following conditions: (1) one knows nothing about the specific preceding events in the sequence or (2) there is no connection or dependency between preceding and succeeding events; that is, when the probability of a following b equals the probability of a following a, and the like.

We still have not really arrived at a solution for measuring the uncertainty in a sequence of events. At this stage of our descriptions it is possible that you might feel as follows: highly probable events are certain and highly improbable events are uncertain; hence, simply dealing with the probabilities will describe uncertainty. But this reasoning would make totally improbable events totally uncertain, which we have tried to argue is not the case. Let us take an example to try to clarify the issue. Suppose you tried to guess each day whether or not there would be an eclipse of the sun. Clearly those days on which there was no eclipse would be very uninformative since there is very little uncertainty in the situation. It is highly likely that there will be no eclipse, and the fact that there is none reduces very little uncertainty. But what about those rare occasions on which there is an eclipse? The occurrence of an eclipse would clearly be a very striking, even memorable, occasion. But that an event is unlikely does not mean it is uncertain. And the fact that it is emotionally laden does not make it informative either. Eclipses are quite certain events, certain in the sense that we know that they will not occur. But more importantly than this, the very fact of their rarity insures that in the long run they will contribute very little uncertainty to a sequence of events. Something which practically never occurs cannot be something which produces uncertainty, for its rarity insures that it never has the opportunity to produce uncertainty.

So we arrive at the following conclusion: uncertainty is a function of the probability with which an event occurs. Uncertainty will be low for very probable and for very improbable events and will be maximal for events of intermediate probability. But let us go one step further. Let us define a *unit* of information which we shall call a *bit:* one bit of information is given when the un-certainty (remember that information is a function of uncer-tainty) produced by two equally probable events ($p_a = p_b = .5$) is reduced. To take a specific example, any particular flip of a coin, where the probability of a head equals the probability of a tail, gives us one bit of information. It can be shown that the equation (Equation 1) $H = -\Sigma p \log_2 p$ meets all our require-ments for a mathematical definition of information.*

You should know certain things about this equation, but with-out going deeply into the mathematical considerations. We find in it the use of the unusual logarithm to the *base two* ($\log_2$). Two justifications can be given for the use of this device. First of all, we must realize that in information theory we are dealing with mutually exclusive alternatives. In determining a probability we ask only whether something did or did not occur; we demand a "yes" or "no" answer. Since there are only two possible answers, we use a numerical system based on counting by twos, which is what the base 2 signifies.

Second, a more complex and traditional example is this: let us suppose that we have to pick between two alternatives, a and b, one of which is "correct." In this situation, one guess will tell us the correct answer, whether or not the guess itself is correct. Thus if we guess a and we are correct, we know the answer. If we guess a and it is wrong we know b must be the answer, since it is the only other possibility. Either way, one guess will allow correct selection between two alternatives. Now suppose there are four alternatives:

$$a_1 \quad b_1$$
$$a_2 \quad b_2$$

* This equation directs us to calculate the possibility p for each event we are measuring with the assumption that all available p's will total to unity ($\Sigma p = 1.0$)—that is, when we count *all* events. We then are to take $\log_2 p$ and multiply this by p itself, and do this for all p's. We are then to sum (Σ) these products for all p's. The total is the information, H. The stray negative sign merely cancels out the one which results from the fact that logarithms of fractions (all p's are fractional) are negative numbers.

In this situation two guesses will give us the answer. Suppose b_2 is the correct alternative. Then if we guess "it's an a" and are told "no," we will know that it must be a b. If we then guess "it's b_1" and are again told "no," we will know that the correct alternative must be b_2. Two guesses will always correctly identify one of four equally likely alternatives, whether or not those particular guesses are correct. If we have eight possibilities:

$$a_1' \quad a_1'' \quad b_1' \quad b_1''$$
$$a_2' \quad a_2'' \quad b_2' \quad b_2''$$

we will find that three guesses will give us the correct answer, the first to identify, say, whether it is an a or a b, the second to identify whether it is a "1" or a "2," and the third to identify whether it is a $'$ or a $''$. You might demonstrate for yourself that four guesses could identify the correct alternative out of sixteen.

We can summarize these illustrations in an equation: number of alternatives equals two raised to a power equal to the number of guesses ($n = 2^H$). Mathematically, this reduces to (Equation 2) $H = \log_2 n$, another definition of information. Equation 2 gives the amount of information in a situation in which there are n different alternatives, each of which has an equal probability of occurrence. It is, in other words, the *maximum* possible uncertainty or information in any situation. Our Equation 1 will give the same results if we make all the p values which we sum equal. But this first equation will also allow us to calculate the information in situations in which the probabilities of events are not equal, hence it is a more useful and general equation.

We now have methods for measuring or quantifying the amount of uncertainty in a situation. The amount of information *possible* in the situation is equal to the amount of uncertainty measured but, of course, less than the maximum possible information may be *transmitted* in any particular situation. In such a case, the uncertainty will not be reduced to zero but will remain at some finite value which is smaller than that at which it started.

We may also determine in any situation something which we

may call the *relative uncertainty*. This value is the ratio of present uncertainty to the maximum possible uncertainty which could exist in the situation. It is obtained by taking the results of applying Equation 1 to the situation, and dividing by the results of Equation 2, which assumes that all events are equally probable. We must show exactly what happens in using this ratio. The amount of information in any situation is a function (1) of the number of possible alternatives (n) in that situation and (2) of the probabilities (p) of the alternatives. As the number of alternatives increases, and as the probabilities become more equal, uncertainty or information will increase. *Relative uncertainty* will always be between *zero* and *one;* it will be zero in the case in which there is no uncertainty at all (there is only one event which has a probability of 1.0); it will be unity in the case in which all of the available alternatives are equally probable. In this latter case, there will be no greater likelihood of the occurrence of one event over another; hence, the situation is maximally unpredictable or uncertain. In any intermediate situation, in which there are several possible events, some of which are more probable than others, the values of relative uncertainty will be somewhere between zero and one. As the probabilities become more and more equal, relative uncertainty will approach unity as an upper limit.

Now all this has to do with numbers, but we have yet to see what it has to do with language. We have already argued that the concept of probability is one which is appropriate to the description of linguistic events. Such probabilities can clearly be entered into the equations which make up information theory; by so doing we would obtain some sort of measure of information. But exactly what would we be describing by such procedures and what would the descriptions tell us about language?

Let us start our answer by indicating some of the ways in which it is possible to use information theory to describe language. (1) We could, for example, count the words in a piece of text of considerable length, as Zipf did. Each of the n words used would have a given frequency of occurrence which could be expressed as a probability, and these probabilities could be entered into the information equation. The result would be a description of the uncertainty of the vocabulary of the text. Various texts would presumably differ in their uncertainty, with those of greater uncertainty (a) having larger vocabularies and/or (b) using their words with relatively equal frequency. If we were interested only in the relative frequency with which the vocabulary items were used, we could use the relative information statistic. Such a measure could conceivably measure something like the difficulty of the text—those texts with less relative uncertainty could be comprehended with a smaller vocabulary. We are here, of course, summarizing the results which could be read from a graphic presentation such as that employed by Zipf.

(2) Another possibility would be to take some sentence and remove one of the words from it. We could then require a large sample of subjects to guess what the missing word was. They would, in all probability, make several different guesses, some of which would be more common than others. We could then compute the probabilities of the various guesses and by means of them calculate the uncertainty of that particular position in that particular sentence. If we did this for all the separate positions in the sentence, we could then add the uncertainties of the positions and get an estimate of the uncertainty of the sentence as a whole. This would be an alternative method, then, of measuring the uncertainty of a piece of text. It would give a result which would unquestionably be different than that given by the preceding word-count method, for it would be measuring something quite different. The preceding method measured the vocabulary uncertainty by ascertaining the probabilities of the words actually used. In this sentence method, we are measuring uncertainty by trying to get values for the probabilities of all words which could *possibly* be used, not just the ones which actually were used. It is as if one were measuring the uncertainty of a particular *kind* of sentence or text, rather than of a specific particular sentence or text. But this should be clear: there are several different ways of measuring something which might be loosely called "the uncertainty or information of a sentence." Such measures are clearly different one from another. And, in

fact, there is no such thing as measuring *the* uncertainty of a sentence.

(3) We could take a word and administer it to a group of subjects, giving them the instructions to respond to this word with the first different word they think of. This is one of the free association methods which we shall discuss more fully later. A large group of subjects will give many different associations, some of which will be given by more than one subject. We can, of course, then calculate the probabilities of the several associations and use these probabilities to calculate the uncertainty of the distribution of associations. This uncertainty might be said to be the uncertainty of the stimulus word, since it reflects the uncertainty of the distribution of responses given to the word; it reflects the difficulty or uncertainty of predicting a response to that word. On the other hand, the preceding sentence guessing method can also be said to measure the uncertainty of a word. It shows how much uncertainty will be reduced by using a particular word in a particular position in a particular sentence. As in the prior example, we have several things which could reasonably be called measures of the uncertainty of a word. None of these are identical numerically; all are conceptually different. Again there is no such thing as *the* uncertainty of a word.

It should be clear by now that information theory can be used in many ways, some of which may be relevant to particular psychological problems and some of which will not be relevant. At this level, information theory is not correct or incorrect; it may simply be used in better or worse ways. On the other hand, we must realize that language in its normal use has something to do with the conveying of information. Therefore we might expect that information theory should be relevant on some much more basic conceptual level. Ordinarily, we would assume that the meaning of a word and the sense of the sentence convey the information being related. Now if meaning and information are conceptually related, as this suggests, we must ask, "what does information theory have to tell us about meaning?"

Information theory, as we have seen, attempts to quantify various *amounts* of information, rather than *kinds* of information. It is a *quantitative* rather than a *qualitative* theory. Meaning, on the other hand, is generally regarded as qualitative rather than quantitative. We would customarily ask *what* something means, not *how much* it means; in information theory we would ask how much information there is, not what information. To the extent, then, that there is a relationship between information theory and meaning it would necessarily imply that there are also quantitative aspects of meaning. If the information conveyed by a word is a direct function of its meaning and if information varies in quantity, then the possibility arises that meaning may also vary in quantity. The question then becomes: how are we to conceive of the *amount of meaning* possessed by a word? We shall return to this shortly.

The second suggestion about the nature of meaning which we can derive from information theory is this: since all information requires uncertainty, if information is a direct function of meaning, then meaning too may have some uncertainty or ambiguity. This seems opposed to our everyday conceptions of meaning, however. Hence, if it is true, it must be demonstrated in some detail. Nevertheless the implication is clear that to the extent that a word carries information, it must also deal with uncertainty, for without that uncertainty there could be no information. We must discuss both of these issues jointly and to do so we must first look at the ways in which words are used.

Word Usage

Let us restate a few basic facts. First, *an essential characteristic of language is that it is used* and used, moreover, in social situations. To the extent that language does not permit communication between speakers, it is not just bad language, it is not language at all. This point was well recognized by Skinner (1957), who rejected the term "language" in favor of "verbal behavior," which is a set of operants reinforced by, i.e. influencing, the behavior of others. Needless to say, to the extent that language is not used, it cannot do anything. Second, it should be clear that there are no one-to-one correspondences with any obvious features of the environment, either physical or verbal, which can be said to determine any particular utterances or parts of utterances. It is usually correct to say that a word is "generally used" in such and such a circumstance, but it is *never* correct to say that it is always used in that manner. Words are not independent of their contexts, but they are not restricted to them either. If such restrictions were permitted, there would be certain things which could not be said for the simple reason that the use of the necessary words would not generalize to or be permissible in certain new contexts. Such a situation does not appear to be an accurate description of language. Every speaker is constantly uttering new utterances, and it can be shown that the possible number of utterances in a language is infinite (Chomsky, 1964).

Now then, what do we mean when we say that a word has meaning? It is time for us to come face to face with this question. Perhaps we might also ask "what is meaning?," although this is probably not the same question as the first. Either way, we must come to grips with the concept of meaning.

Perhaps the most obvious answer to the first question, "what do we mean when we say a word has meaning?," is that the word refers to things or states of affairs, or names them. But there are some grave difficulties with this, in addition to the fact that it is probably just begging the question. That is, to accept it we would have to define *reference* and *naming* and that would get us into difficulties too. But let us, for the moment, be naïve and treat this answer as a straightforward one. /Table/ is clearly a word which refers to things and names things. We can ignore for the moment that it refers to a class of objects. It is certainly a word which has meaning, if any word does. If we ask someone what the word means he would tell us: /Table/ refers to a kind of furniture; it is an object, generally with a large flat surface for putting things on; there are many kinds of tables: coffee tables, dining-room tables, pool tables, and the like. Moreover, he could say that that is a table over there; he could give us an example of one. We could go on indefinitely. Now consider /Robert Francis Terwilliger/. This "word" clearly refers to an object which at this moment is seated at a typewriter. It is, by common acceptance, the name of that object. Now let us ask, what does /Robert Francis Terwilliger/ mean? The silence is deafening; there does not seem to be any answer to this question, which, unfortunately, suggests that this proper name may not mean anything at all.

Numerous contemporary linguists and philosophers would agree with the implications of the above argument. Proper names, they would say, do not have meaning. In some sense, they are not words at all. Certainly there is little resemblance between the way /table/ functions in the language and the way in which some proper name functions (Ziff, 1960). Yet it must be clear that proper names do refer to and name objects just as much, perhaps even more, than ordinary words do.

This problem of naming and referring has another difficulty. It is easy enough to claim that /table/ refers to this, that, and the other object. Yet this is not strictly true. /Table/ refers to *any old table*—to a class of objects, if you will, of which these particular objects happen to be examples. /Table/ and other words can be used to mention specific things not because they are oriented toward specifics, but precisely because they are not. They work because they can function in a large number of conceivable situations and because they are not determined by any specific one. Proper names are restricted to specific situations. There is only one /Robert Francis Terwilliger/; the use of this name has no generality at all. As we shall see, that is why it has no meaning.*

Perhaps another illustration is in order. If we switch from the consideration of nouns to other form classes, we immediately run into more difficulties with the problem of reference. To what

* By now, after some deliberation, you have probably decided that proper names do have meaning. After all, you may well have some general conceptions or stereotypes about /Robert/'s and the like. But this illustrates the point. /Robert/ only has meaning if you use it in many situations, if you know several Robert's. If it were a true proper name—the property of one and only one specific thing—it would have no meaning. Also, consider whether the fact that /Robert/ *suggests* things to you is what you want to call *meaning*. I suspect it is not.

does /slowly/ refer, or of what is it a name? One might be tempted to give some definition in terms of stimulus properties, perhaps concerning the time interval during which certain stimulus changes took place. But then we must consider that /slowly/ can refer to both jet planes and turtles. What do the two situations to which the word can refer have in common? There appear to be only two possible solutions to this problem. Either the word does not refer to anything, or it refers to some concept or idea which is internal to the speaker or is at least non-environmental. External or denotative reference simply will not account for the facts of language or for the problem of meaning.

Let us now consider the possibility that the meaning of a word is some sort of idea or concept. This possibility will, I am sure, suggest itself to many as being obviously true. But there is a serious question as to whether or not it will do the job. The theory has one logical drawback—namely, that it can explain everything. No matter what word we dredge up, if we ask what its meaning is or to what it refers, we can say "the idea or concept of x." All words can be accounted for in this manner, since all that one is really doing here is saying that the word has meaning, and *that* we know already. We cannot explain the meaning of a word by postulating undefined ideas to which it refers; to do so is to merely restate the fact that it has meaning. To use the notion of meaning as being equivalent to concepts or ideas, we must offer some explanation or account of the concepts themselves. We must be able to state how they are the way that they are, how they got that way, what properties they have, and the like, both on a structural and on a functional level. We must, in other words, postulate a theory of the mind to explain the ideas before we can use the ideas to explain meaning. In all likelihood we will have to do exactly that. But before we do, let us consider the possibility that words do not refer to anything at all—that they do not have meaning in this ordinary sense of that term.

There is an extremely important school in modern philosophy— that of linguistic analysis—which defends the position that the concept of meaning is irrelevant to our understanding of language. Part of the linguistic analysts' rejection of the notion of meaning is similar to the argument given above, that there is nothing objective to which a word can refer. What the word means is not objective. Yet, they correctly point out, words are used, and used successfully, in objective physical situations. So while the meaning of a term cannot be objective, the word can be used "objectively," that is, correctly. The term "use," they would argue, is the critical one here.

People use words. This is the nature of language. There is no word which cannot in some sense be defined by enumerating those conditions under which the word is used. Thus /slowly/ can be defined by saying that for jet planes I will use it whenever the speed is under 300 mph. and for turtles whenever it is under 300 inches per hour. In fact, they would argue, if one stops to look at the situation dispassionately, one would see that all of definition or the specification of meaning, as "meaning" is generally used, is really a specifying of the conditions under which it is proper to *use* the word. The correct meaning of a word, and the correct definition of "meaning," is *those conditions under which the word may be used (correctly)*—or so the linguistic analysts claim.

There are an awful lot of "corrects" in that definition, and unfortunately the whole issue of correctness beclouds the "analysts'" argument. It would seem that if someone knows what the correct usage of a word is—that is, if he can use it correctly —then he must know something which we might want to call the meaning of the word. It would appear difficult, if not downright impossible, to differentiate semantically correct from semantically incorrect word usage without some sort of standard. And what could this standard be except that which is commonly known as meaning?

Language analysts are well known for their criticisms of various schools of philosophy on semantic grounds. They would claim that philosophers often misuse words, and that if one realizes how they are misusing their terms, the philosophical problems generated by these scholars will disappear. It must be pointed out that up to a point, this sort of criticism is not only legitimate but correct. Philosophers use ordinary words. They must, since they are as bound by their language as the ordinary man is. However, they do not use ordinary words in ordinary ways.

Now we would customarily say that ordinary words probably mean something different in philosophical systems than they do in everyday life. If we wish to argue that *one* of these meanings is correct and another is not, then we must have some absolute view of what the correct meaning or usage is. But such an absolute would be something independent of the actual usage of a word, and since the analysts wish to restrict their discussion of language to the actual uses of words in ordinary language (they are the behaviorists of philosophy) it would appear that any such absolute standards would be judged by them to be meaningless by definition. Clearly, then, to the extent that they rely on absolutes for judging the correctness of language, they are being self-contradictory. If they do not use such absolutes, it is not clear what they do use.

Moreover, the analysts contend that certain things cannot be said in a language. While this contention may have some validity at a rather advanced logical level, it does not appear to be true at the level of the "ordinary philosophy" we are discussing. This contention is based upon the idea that there are correct and incorrect ways of using the language. There are certain statements which the analysts criticize as being misuses of language, as attempts to say that which cannot be said, and they feel that all of these statements are *false*. But they confuse falsity with incorrect language usage. There is no doubt that some statements are true and others false, but on this level of analysis there is considerable doubt as to whether there are correct and incorrect uses of language. On a linguistic level, their sentences seem grammatically correct. Rather it seems that there are different ways of using the words and sentences of a language. To equate usage with meaning is to say there is not *a* meaning, but many meanings, for a word or a sentence.

Now one thing is clear: as long as we stay within the province of linguistic analysis, whether we agree with the position or not, we will find that we do not need to speak of some object of reference in connection with the concept of meaning. Meaning can be equated with or defined as word usage whether or not one accepts the other dogmas of linguistic analysis. In fact it seems that some sort of definition involving usage is the only sensible one which we can make. But what sort of definition?

We saw that in connection with the notion of reference as a definer of meaning, that it was necessary to assume that words referred to classes of objects rather than to specific ones. The fact is that language is not bound to a specific context, but can be used by the speaker in contexts which are quite new to him, and which have no obvious physical similarities to those he has experienced in the past. This fact of language must be accounted for by a theory of meaning. If we wish to use some "reference" theory, to account for this novelty we will have to postulate the ideas or concepts which are within the individual speaker and to which the word referred. This has certain logical difficulties, since it all too easily leads to the problem of a world of Platonic ideas, a postulation which would appear to be scientifically barren. Moreover, it is not clear what sort of psychological process or mechanism would correspond to such ideas.

If we deal with word usage, we still have somewhat the same problem. The meaning of a word cannot simply be a catalogue of all the times and contexts in which it has been used. It must also include all those circumstances in which the word *might* possibly be used. But the notion of a set of possible or potential uses seems to be no more substantive or objective than a concept or an idea. Yet we must have such a set, since tomorrow I might use a word in a way different from any in which I had previously used it. And it would be rather foolish to assume that the word did not "mean" that particular usage until after I had used it. For I would not have used it unless it were appropriate to use it—that is, unless it already meant or referred to the situation at hand. Again we must reiterate: if we are to define meaning as the uses of a word, we must not simply speak of actual, but also of potential, uses, and these potential uses are apparently no more objective than, and perhaps little different from, concepts or ideas.

We cannot at this time deal fully with the psychological problems which the usage-concept of meaning calls forth. We will try to find in the next chapter some psychological process or mechanism by which we can discover a "possible use" without at the same time assuming that the word has actually been used that way in the past. For the moment we can say that thinking in terms of potential behaviors is not uncommon to psychologists. The concept of "attitude" is often defined as a readiness to respond in a particular fashion, and the concept of "habit" is often given a similar definition. In the next chapter we shall attempt to give full development to the idea that meaning can be accounted for by a theory of response readiness, but for the moment we can leave this topic with the simple statement that it seems promising.

We have arrived, meanwhile, at a tentative definition of meaning: *the meaning of a word is the possible uses to which it can be put.* We can probably translate this as: the meaning of a word is the possible contexts in which it can be used. These two definitions are equivalent since different uses would have to be identified by different contexts: hence, denoting the use is identical to denoting the context in which it is used. Such a definition is not one which is foreign to linguists. Bloomfield's (1933) definition of language approaches this when he says that meaning is the stimulus situations which give rise to the word, and the responses made to the word. More recently the context notion has been fully developed by, for example, Ziff (1960) under the name of the *distributional theory* of meaning. But linguists would not be satisfied with the definition as we have phrased it, for it does in fact neglect one critical aspect of meaning.

Consider the use of any common word; let us take /table/ and /black/ as examples. When we call something a table, we are saying that it is a member of a particular class of objects. When we call something black we are saying that it has a property of a certain sort, a property which can, of course, belong to other objects. In both cases we are isolating, verbally, some particular state of affairs or "concept." By such isolation we are implying that there are certain other things which are *not* this sort of state of affairs. Black things are black, they are not white or red or any other color. Tables are tables and not chairs or lamps or anything else. Language classifies and categorizes; and categories imply that some things belong to them and some do not. Language functions, in other words, by making *discriminations*. The use of any word *implies* a whole set of discriminations, indeed it implies an entire vocabulary which is *not* being used at the time.

Consider /Get me that thing over there/. If such an utterance comes out of the blue, it will be almost impossible to say what is meant or to know what the speaker wants. /Thing/ does not discriminate among the many possible objects which are /over there/, which in turn does not really discriminate among locations. We would typically respond to this statement by saying /What do you mean?/. In fact, the original command was meaningless, and it was meaningless precisely because it did not select out or discriminate among aspects of the totality of present states of affairs. Meaning is, by necessity and by definition, discriminative. Words, therefore, will be used to make discriminations, and these discriminations constitute the meaning of the word, because they state where the word can and cannot be used. But a discrimination involves separating things into two categories, those to which the word "belongs" and those to which it does not. To return to the original argument: the meaning of a word is defined by those contexts in which it can be used *and* by those contexts in which it *cannot* be used. So meaning involves what a thing is not, too.

To be even more general, let us add that the meaning of a word involves *when* it is not used—in addition to *where* it is and is not used. For it is a characteristic of language that it has no one-to-one correspondences. In any particular given situation, a word may be used on one occasion and not on another. There are contexts in the world (and in sentences) in which it is *likely* that a word will occur, contexts in which it is *unlikely, but possible,* that it will occur, and contexts in which it *will probably never occur.* But there are no contexts in which it will always occur—not if it is to remain a functioning word. There are, in fact, two ways in which a word may easily become meaningless and, hence, not a word at all in a functioning, discriminative language. The first way is for the word to be permissible in all conceivable contexts. In such a situation its use would clearly not discriminate between contexts. By meaning everything, it would mean nothing at all. The second would be for the word to occur always in a particular context. In such a case the word would contribute nothing to our understanding; since the context is always there, the use of the word would not *single out* a particular occurrence of the context. It would not discriminate *temporally* among contexts and would therefore be meaningless.

We have now come full circle back to information theory, for we can see that this definition of meaning is one which corresponds perfectly with the theoretical definition of information. Information theory states that information exists only when there is uncertainty, and that information can vary in amount. The contextual theory of meaning says the same things, and more. To have meaning a word must be used in several contexts, and never be used universally in any one context. It is possible then to conceive of one word's having *more meaning* than another because the first is used in more contexts than the second. Or if we wish to stick even closer to information theory, one word can mean more (have more information) than another because the first has equal probabilities of occurrence in its possible contexts, while the probabilities of occurrence for the second word in its possible contexts are more unequal. Either way one wishes to quantify it, it is not only legitimate, but even necessary, to conceive of meaning varying in amount as well as in kind. Needless to say, it is the particular contexts in which a word may be used which determine the "kind" or "quality" of the meaning of a particular word, while their number and probability determine the quantity of meaning. Information theory ignores the former since it is non-qualitative while the contextual definition of meaning starts from it.

We see that having meaning depends upon a word having *several different contexts of uses,* and that the word not be used in *every* occurrence of any particular context. Probably proper

names come as close as any other utterances to being restricted
in their uses in one context. And proper names, as we have tried
to illustrate, do not seem to have meaning in any ordinary sense
of that term. They do not, in fact, discriminate in the sense of
conceptualizing or identifying a class of objects. While a proper
name singles out a specific individual being, it does not do so
on the basis of any specific characteristics of that being. It would
be impossible to identify another Robert Terwilliger on the basis
of having seen this one. Indeed, it is absurd to even talk about
another Robert Terwilliger. A proper name, to be proper, must
be restricted in its use to the context of the individual for whom
it is the proper name. And therefore it, of necessity, loses (or
never acquires) meaning.

Now, if to have meaning words must be used in several contexts, and if they cannot be used with a probability of 1.0 in any
particular context—that is, on every occurrence of that context—
then according to information-theory terminology, for a word to
have meaning, it must have certain uncertainty—in this case
uncertainty of use. There must be uncertainty in the use of the
word both in order for it to convey information, and in order for
it to have meaning. It is a defining characteristic of language that
it may or may not be used in any particular situation, and that
words may be used here, or there, or not at all at any particular
time. Language is by definition, then, uncertain.

Two things would appear to be suggested by this. The first is
that if language is not determined by any particular, concrete,
objective situation, and thus if a word may occur in fact in many
situations, it may also be used *incorrectly*. Wittgenstein (1953)
has said that in order for a word to have meaning it must be
possible to use it wrongly. This possibility follows from the probabilistic nature of language. One has the possibility of using a
word in one context (with one sense) as one should use it in
another (with a different sense), of using the word when one
should not, or of not using it when one should. All of the mistakes are explicable if one assumes that words do not have single
meanings and that their use is not completely predictable at any
time. This is an important conclusion for the psychological

theorist. It tells him two things: first, that he must construct his theory so that it is possible for the person to make linguistic errors within it and second, that these errors cannot be explained after the fact. To illustrate what we mean by the latter, consider any ordinary perceptual illusion in which the subject makes a visual error. These errors are usually attributed to special circumstances in which the otherwise correct visual processes are distorted or do not function. But there is no distortion or lack of function in language per se when one makes a linguistic error; rather such errors show that the language is functioning properly. Any theory of language which explains linguistic errors solely as the result of special circumstances is clearly wrong since such an explanation does not comprehend the nature of language properly. Thus we would have to conclude, for example, that Freud's (1951) theory that linguistic errors arise only from repressions and the like is incorrect. This is so not because repressions do not produce errors but because repressions are but one of the types of things which produces errors. The nature of language itself requires the possibility of error.

Secondly, we see that for language to function it must have a certain amount of uncertainty, but it cannot, of course, have complete uncertainty. To be completely uncertain, it would have to be possible to use any word in any context whatsoever. But this would imply that the word did not discriminate among contexts, and hence it would not be functioning as a proper word. While a word must be able to be used in *several* contexts in order to have meaning, it cannot be used in *all* contexts. It must have contexts in which it can be used and contexts in which it cannot be used as we suggested above. Thus, even though meaning is linked with uncertainty, it is possible to say that there are regularities in the use of words. These regularities allow us to specify when the word is likely to be used, and when it is likely that it will not be used. Attempts to specify such regularities by listing selected, appropriate uses of a word, can be found in the Oxford English Dictionary, for example.

There is a strong temptation now to say that there are semantic *rules* for the use of words. Whether one accepts this will

depend on how one uses the word "rule." If by a rule we mean
something which *always* occurs, then clearly the statement is
false and must always be if we are dealing with words. More
likely we would use the term "rule" in the following way:
people follow rules in the use of words. By this statement we
mean one of several things. For instance, this statement refers
to the fact that there are regularities in the physical contexts in
which words are used and that, moreover, different individuals
tend to exhibit the same regularities. This will, of course, be a
necessity if language is to function as a communication device.
This use of the term "rule" adds nothing to the above statement
using the term "regularity."

But the use of the term "rule" leads us into other potential
difficulties. We rejected the notion that meaning could be defined as that idea to which the word refers, at least in part, because of the indeterminancy of these ideas. Where they are and
what psychological processes correspond to them are difficult
to comprehend. Moreover, we might point out, when the normal
person speaks he is rarely *conscious* of the ideas or concepts behind his words determining their selection and use. Speaking is
done too rapidly for that. One simply talks: one is not aware of
"meanings"—not directly aware that one's words have meanings
or references or aware of any relationship between a word and
something it stands for. In this sense ideas have little phenomenological validity. The person is simply aware of what he is
talking about—not about any metaphysical entity or relationship. The psychological processes by which language is generated
in a particular speech act do not always include having an idea
and then framing it in words—at least not in the vast majority
of cases. Language is used, and it is used particularly. That is, it
has specific functions. Language may be a means to an end. However, it is not correct to say that on any conscious subjective
level awareness of these ends always determines the means within
the ordinary everyday use of language. This simply does not
happen. Again, often enough one just talks.

Now it would appear that this fate would apply to the rule
concept also. For the most part the speaker of the language does

not at any conscious level follow rules, either those relating to physical context or syntatic context, when he uses the language. He simply uses it, and his uses of it are regular. There is no doubt but that the psychologist must be able to account for this regularity. But to do this it would not appear necessary to assume that the speaker learns a set of rules, particularly if we mean consciously learns, when he learns the language. It is difficult to conceptualize just how such a rule would be expressed as a psychological process, just as it is difficult to conceptualize an idea as a psychological process. In both cases one is trying to account for something which *happens*—an ongoing act called linguistic—by some psychic *thing*. At some level we will eventually probably have to do exactly this. But it does appear that postulating some psychological "rules" which one "follows" in using language does not clarify much. In fact, all that such a statement is saying is that language behavior *exhibits* regularities. It is not really *accounting* for those regularities.

Lest anyone think that we are begging the issue, I will simply state that accounting for regularities in behavior is not an easy psychological problem. We will return to it in the chapter on grammar, for it is here that we can see some of the most regular of language's regularities. At the moment we can end with this brief summary: It appears that the most fruitful approach to the problem of meaning is the study of how words are used. We assume that by the concept of meaning we refer to the possible uses of a word. We can see then that to have meaning at all, there must be some uncertainty in the use of words. It becomes possible, then, to quantify certain aspects of meaning by the use of information theory. A proper psychological theory of meaning will have to account for these characteristics of language which we have described above.

Bibliography

Bloomfield, L. *Language*. New York, Holt, Rinehart and Winston, 1933.

Chomsky, N. *Syntactic structures*. The Hague, Mouton, 1964.

Freud, S. *Psychopathology of everyday life*. New York, Mentor Books, 1951.

Shannon, C. E., and Weaver, W. *A mathematical theory of communication*. Urbana, University of Illinois Press, 1949.

Skinner, B. F. *Verbal behavior*. New York, Appleton-Century-Crofts, 1957.

Wittgenstein, L. *Philosophical investigations*. New York, Macmillan, 1953.

Ziff, P. *Semantic analysis*. Ithaca, Cornell University Press, 1960.

Zipf, G. K. *Human behavior and the principle of least effort*. Addison-Wesley, Cambridge, 1949.

VI
Meaning:
Associations and Dispositions

We have arrived at a position which states that meaning is related to the contexts within which a word is used. The term "use" is a vague one, however. Up to this point we have implied that uttering the word was using it, which indeed it is. But spoken or written words are not only behaviors on the part of individual speakers of the language; they are also stimuli for behaviors as well. So we must expand the definition of "use" to include the ways in which an individual may react to a word when it is spoken to him by another or by himself. If we equate meaning with the contexts in which a word is used and with the reactions made to the word (calling both of these "use" for the sake of simplicity) we arrive at a definition close to that given by Bloomfield (1933). He defined meaning as the stimuli giving rise to the word and the responses made to it. We have arrived at a similar definition but one within the more precise contexts of modern linguistics and of information theory. If we are going to turn this definition into anything more *psychologically* meaningful, we are going to have to be more specific about two things: stimulus (or context) and reaction (or response). Let us consider responses first.

Approaching the problem of meaning by considering the responses to a word is a psychologically ancient tradition. Experimental psychologists from the time of Wundt and Ebbinghaus have considered meaning to be a function of associations. One thing had meaning only if it was associated with something else; the nature of the meaning depended on the particular associations, and the amount of meaning depended on the multiplicity of associations involved. In general, these early theorists used the term "association" in a more or less technical sense. That is, associations were defined within their theory and, in general, were considered to be associations between ideas or between sensations. The desire for more precise experimental investigation of psychological problems led to a corresponding desire to be able to measure the number and the kinds of associations. In other words, some *operational definition* of associations was needed.

One of the original attempts in this direction was made by Glaze (1928) who presented subjects with stimuli and simply asked the subjects whether or not they thought of anything when they saw each stimulus. The stimuli were then graded in terms of the proportion of subjects who reported having such associations. In this case the stimuli were nonsense syllables—that is, meaningless three-letter sequences of a consonant-vowel-consonant form. These nonsense syllables were used on the assumption that if meaning were simply a matter of the number of associations to a thing, then psychologists could study the effects of meaning without recourse to real words or to parts of a real language (Ebbinghaus, 1913). Hence, to the extent that one could demonstrate that, say, the ease of learning a list of nonsense syllables was a function of their "association value," to that extent one had demonstrated that meaning was important in memorization.

The tradition of studying meaning by means of linguistically meaningless material is not at all uncommon in psychology. It stems in part from a desire to be precise and in part from an attempt to compare relatively meaningless material with truly meaningful material. This attempt at comparison obviously has some legitimacy, but unfortunately tells one very little about the nature of meaning or about the influences of the amount or kind of meaning present. The desire for precision is a natural one for a scientist and it seems to many psychologists that one can be a good deal more precise about a nonsense syllable than one can about a word, at least for certain purposes. A word is a horribly slippery and elusive creature; it defies pigeonholing. Meaning and uncertainty are mutual phenomena. So we see that the desire for absolute quantification, for measurement of fixed characteristics with no range of error, is totally incompatible with the study of meaning. That is, to the extent that measurements are precise and unequivocal about verbal stimuli, to that extent we can assume that these stimuli are not part of a language, since meaning necessitates uncertainty and error.

This is an unfortunate conclusion for it throws a shadow of doubt on a great deal of psychological work. We find, for example, that the relationship between associations and learning is by no means a universally accepted conclusion. Underwood and Schulz (1960) spent considerable effort in determining that most of the supposed effects of association value were actually a result of the fact that some nonsense syllables were easier to pronounce than others. To the extent that one is interested in the memorization of nonsense syllables, this is clearly an important piece of work. If one is interested in language, however, it is clearly of no value whatsoever. One would not be able to generalize such a conclusion to language. If such a conclusion is valid about language, then it would have to be demonstrated on language.

We must also realize that something's having an association with another thing is not identical with its having meaning unless one is using "meaning" in a non-linguistic sense. Stimuli may *suggest* things to you without meaning what they suggest. Thus /Paris/ may suggest barges on the Seine, but it certainly does not mean that. Yet this is an association to /Paris/. Language, as you will recall, is a system of behaviors and potential behaviors. The uses of a word are uses within such a system. Nonsense syllables, since they do not fall within a system, cannot be equated with words. Associations to things which are not part of a system clearly need not have the same significance as associations to things which are part of a system. Theorists concerned with associations have sometimes noted with greater or lesser surprise, and have sometimes ignored the fact, that some non-sense syllables have more associations than do some words. By theory this would mean that the nonsense syllable was more meaningful, or had more meaning than the word. Such a con-clusion is so untenable that either it invalidates the association-istic definition of meaning or it suggests that not all associations are identical. Let us assume the latter for the moment and work under the assumption that associations to words do not have the same significance that associations to non-linguistic stimuli do. To defend this, we must seek to determine what an association is. Let us look, then, at associations to words to see what they are like.

MEASURING ASSOCIATIONS

There are two basic ways of measuring the associations to words. The earlier method, expounded by Kent and Rosanoff (1910) among others, is probably regarded as *the* method by those not trained in experimental psychology. In this situation, the subject is presented with a stimulus word and asked to respond with the first word he thinks of. His response and, in some cases, the time it takes him to respond are recorded. This method has been pre-sented as being of some diagnostic value in the psychotherapeutic situation. Here presumably the patient will show "bizarre" as-sociations or abnormally delayed associations to words connected with his particular areas of psychological disturbance. We need not concern ourselves with the supposed diagnostic validity of this method other than to say it has not been conclusively estab-lished even after some sixty years of work.

Our concern here is with what the associations look like. Prob-ably the clearest picture comes from considering the associations given by a large sample of subjects to a large list of stimulus words. We find first of all that most often there are one or two very common responses to the stimulus word (i.e. responses given by a large proportion of the responding subjects), a larger number of less common ones, and a very large number of responses given by only one or a very few subjects. The degree of commonness of the most common responses varies from word to word but in some cases may exceed 80 per cent. In other words, it is not unusual for a vast majority of the subjects to agree upon the association given. As one might surmise, words vary in their distributions of associations—some words reliably elicit more associations than others, some words reliably have associations more equal in their frequency of occurrence than those of others, etc.

It is much more difficult to be precise about the qualitative nature of the associations given. We find that the more common associations are sometimes antonyms of the stimulus (white-black), sometimes synonyms (beautiful-pretty), sometimes a descriptive property (snow-cold), sometimes indicate class membership (table-furniture), and so on. To some extent it is possible to divide associations into two categories: those which reflect or respond to the referential characteristics of the word, and those which reflect its uses in utterances. In the latter case, we might find as associations words which would customarily follow the stimulus word in a sentence. This type of association seems to be relatively more common in children than in adults, however. To those who have looked at free associations, a third category seems to suggest itself—associations which for want of a better term are idiosyncratic. Thus some associations seem to reflect the mood or value judgments of the subjects while still others reflect determinants which are totally out of the ken of the experimental psychologist. Among the latter class are cases in which the subject will respond with some proper name to a common stimulus word (table-Harry). What produces this connection we cannot know without interviewing the subject. But whatever it is, it is not an association which is relevant to the common social uses of language, for to function as a part of a language, its uses cannot be idiosyncratic.

Before generalizing from these findings, let us look at the other association method. In this method the subject is given a stimulus word and asked to give as many associations to it as he can within a given period of time—say, one minute. In one common use of this method, the results are presented in terms of the average number of associations given by the average subject. Noble (1952) refers to this as the *meaningfulness* of the stimulus, a conception which appears comparable to what we have called the amount of meaning. Such a lumping of responses, of course, ignores a good deal of the actual data. A word could have a meaningfulness of 8, say, if all subjects gave eight responses, or if half gave four and the other half twelve. Or, each subject could give the same eight responses, or each could give a different eight responses from any other subject. We ignore, in other words, all aspects of the individual differences in associations. Nevertheless the method has obvious merits as a simple description of the quantity of associations, or meaningfulness.

This method has one possible methodological drawback in that it is difficult to be sure that the subject is always really responding to the stimulus word. It is easily possible that in fact the subject is giving first an association to the stimulus word, and then an association to his first association, etc. This process is referred to as chaining of associations. Association chaining is probably an effect of little importance if one is interested only in the quantity of associations as, say, a variable in a learning experiment. If we wish to make any statements about the meaning of the stimulus from the associations, however, then any such artifact becomes of considerable importance. While methods have been devised to attempt to limit this sort of chaining, such as printing the stimulus word followed by a blank space many times over so that the subject must read the stimulus before he gives each association, no such method can absolutely guarantee its total elimination. What we find, in fact, in dealing with associations is much the same problem we found with the semantic differential: when a word is presented out of context, the subject provides his own, which, in this case, may be his last response in the situation.

It is customary to speak of "free-association" methods, which may be the biggest misnomer in psychology. Association methods are indeed "free," if by this we mean that the stimuli are removed from any normal context in which they might be ordinarily used.

But they are by no means free of contextual effects; indeed, the original Kent-Rosanoff approach to associations as indicators of personality variables indicates that they saw the associations as determined by a context, but a context which was essentially idiosyncratic. When we face the subject with an association task, we are asking him to *use* the word to which he must "associate." But we are not restricting how he is to use it; he must supply his own context. Those contexts chosen by subjects range, as we have seen from readily understandable linguistic ones to almost incomprehensible idiosyncratic ones. The method, then, is to some extent unavoidably indeterminate, just as the semantic differential is. This does not deny, of course, that one can get some information about the word from "free" associations.

But in the case of the semantic differential we were faced with an attempt to measure *the* meaning of a word—or at least the meaning for a particular subject. The lack of power of the semantic differential stems largely from the fact that words do not have single meanings, but rather multiple ones. Only by virtue of the fact that they are used in *many* contexts do words acquire meaning. The fact that semantic-differential ratings are vague, imprecise, and indeterminate is not a criticism of the method, for any measurement of language must have these characteristics. The difficulty here is that the type of use provided for the words, i.e. the ratings, was arbitrary and unrealistic. They often have no relationship to the ways in which words are ordinarily used. So the rater is not only required to provide his own context within which to "use" the word, but he is permitted to use it only in ways which may seem arbitrary and decidedly unusual to him. The semantic differential, then, may provide at best a dubious measure of meaning.

The association methods while equally permissive with respect to context, permit the subject to "use" the word, or respond to it, in any way he chooses—providing, of course, that the response is another single word. The responses obtained, then, could conceivably be more relevant to the actual use of the word than would semantic-differential ratings. In fact, it would seem that a subject might tend to use the word in a way in which he was accustomed to using it, providing, of course, that the instructions for the association task permitted or encouraged this. If so, then the associations obtained in so-called free-association studies may well reflect or be related to the actual use of the stimulus words.

The association methods have been severely criticized by Osgood (1961), among others, since on one level, it appears quite obvious that associations cannot be the meaning of a word. As Osgood points out, if we equate the meaning of associations with meaning of the stimulus word, then it is clear that /white/ would have to mean /black/, since the latter is a common associate of the former. An associational theory of meaning, however, does not have to equate the meaning of the association with the meaning of the stimulus. What it says is that the associations reflect the *uses* of the stimulus word. Again this does not say that the uses of the associations are the uses of the stimuli, that /black/ is used the same as /white/ is. If, on the other hand, we say that meaning is involved in use, particularly in uses which involve *discriminations* among classes of events, then it is clear that /black/ is intimately involved in the meaning of /white/ for it represents a major class of events *excluded* when one uses the term /white/. The meaning of a word, as we have attempted to show, is a function not only of when the word is used but when it is not used. Antonyms, then, reflect the uses and define the meaning of a term as much as synonyms do, and Osgood's criticism is clearly invalid.

But it is equally clear that *verbal* associations do not represent the *totality* of what we would call the meaning of a word. These associations indeed reflect and are uses of the word, but they are uses made in the restricted environment of the psychology laboratory. Moreover, they are verbal uses only, and words are used in ways other than the purely "intraverbal" one—to use Skinner's term. Thus, the association method does not directly involve the use of the word as a response to non-verbal stimuli, nor does it record the non-verbal responses possible to a word used as a stimulus. However, if we look at associations we can see that they do often appear to reflect verbal *descriptions* of such non-verbal activities. It would appear safe to say that, in general, the associations obtained from the subject in the association method represent a set of verbal descriptions of how the subject uses the words in question. These verbal descriptions do not constitute the meaning of the words, nor do they exhaust the meaning of the words—for words often have uses which cannot be verbalized: consider /of/ as an example. However, the associations are clearly *related* to the meaning of the word. For the purposes of psychological measurement this suffices quite well. We can make accurate inferences about meaning from the results of association studies, in general.*

Now we must ask: what inferences about meaning can we legitimately make from associational data? This will depend on certain critical assumptions about the data. Thus, for example, quantitative inferences are those most frequently made. It is assumed by Noble, among others, that the number of associations represents the meaningfulness or amount of meaning which a word has. Such an inference clearly requires the assumption that a word which has more meanings and, thus, more meaning, will call out more different associations—in our terms; that a word which is used in different ways will call out different verbal descriptions of those uses and that the number of different verbal descriptions will be proportional to the number of different uses. This assumption need not be true. But it is clearly not a far-fetched one either. But there are two different situations within

---

* We must say *in general* since there are, of course, always subjects who clearly ignore the instructions and give associations which represent non-uses of the word, in order to "confuse" the experimenter. What they fail to realize is that by doing this they are giving data potentially as useful as that given by more co-operative subjects. For they are not responding randomly to the stimulus words; and random responses are the only ones which constitute bad measurement to the scientist. By consciously giving words which are not associates of the stimulus they are, of course, defining the meaning of the word as accurately as if they consciously gave associates. To reiterate, meaning is also defined by where a word is not used. No verbal subject can remain independent of verbal stimuli; he may obey or ignore instructions, but he is responding to the stimulus nevertheless.

which we must evaluate the assumption. First, consider the case in which the subject gives many responses to a single stimulus. Here it seems quite safe to assume that the more meanings a word has for the subject, the more verbal descriptions he will give of it. Presumably we might correctly infer something about the number of meanings from the number of responses given.

But what about the case where each subject gives one response per stimulus? Here the number of different descriptions is determined across subjects, rather than within one subject. Are we then willing to assume that the number of different descriptions given here represents the meaningfulness of that stimulus for some particular individual subject? To carry the argument one step further, are we willing to assume that the probability with which a particular response is given by the sample of subjects, represents the probability of giving that response by any particular subject? This is an assumption which has been made by many psychological investigators, covertly or overtly.

We clearly cannot give a definitive answer to such a question. To give a negative answer to it means to reject a vast quantity of psychological research as being meaningless, for it is based on just such an assumption. Such a rejection might prove to be necessary—but it could hardly be done lightly. Certain facts argue in favor of the assumption: if we postulate an individual who has several possible uses for a word, and who must pick one of them to use in an otherwise ambiguous situation, there are certain things we might expect to find. Presuming that some uses are more common than others, we might assume that he would pick accordingly from among the possibilities. In a large sample of subjects, then, the communal probability distribution would be identical to the individual, internal one. Some subjects do in fact report such a random (to them) choice. They do not know what to do, so they "flip a coin" so to speak. But others do not report this. And it is true that a particular distribution of associations could be generated if each subject had only one association but different proportions of the population had different single associations. The latter is, of course, absurd, but some variety of it might be true. A further suggestion in favor of the generality assumption is this: if the language is to function as a language, it must have commonality; it must be shared by members of the linguistic society. Since social agreement is by definition a characteristic of language, we might expect to find agreement among associations as well. Thus the distribution from a sample of subjects would at least resemble the possibilities available to any individual subject. I would suggest that such an assumption is worth making until evidence to the contrary becomes overwhelming. However, the justification for this assumption can come ultimately only from a theory of meaning which allows one to explain why individual language habits would generate the communal distribution of associations.

Thus to return to the original point: we may offer the assumption that the number of different associations given by either association method is proportional to the amount of meaning of the stimulus word. Likewise, the obtained probability of any given association is proportional to the probability of the particular word use that that association describes. We can, of course, go one step further and use the association probabilities to calculate the information in the distribution of associations. This would then be an index of the uncertainty of use of the word—perhaps a better measure of the amount of meaning than the number of associations alone. But in what sense can we *equate* meaning and associations, and not just draw inferences from one to the other?

We can answer this question in two ways: following Osgood, it is clear that verbal associations do not directly constitute meaning; they are interpretable at best as descriptions of meaning or use. But on a different level, Osgood himself defines meaning in terms of a particular kind of association. In this case it is a *theoretical* association between a stimulus and a response. Indeed, this represents an apparent verbal paradox in psychology—for Osgood both is and is not an associational theorist. And we will also attempt to account for meaning by an association theory, while not equating verbal associations per se, and meaning.

Associations as Theoretical Concepts

The history of psychology is filled with theories which have attempted to account for "the mind" by appealing to doctrines of association: Locke spoke of associations between ideas, Titchener of associations between sensations, Thorndike and Hull of associations between stimuli and responses, Tolman of associations between stimuli to give but a few examples (see Boring, 1950). In all cases, the associations referred to are theoretical. That is, they are not observable or directly measurable in any way. They are inferences made from certain behavioral or mental phenomena. They are events of the mind or of the central nervous system, depending on which theory is being considered. In more modern psychological terminology, they are hypothetical constructs or intervening variables. But whatever they are, they are the cornerstone of much psychological thinking.

While associationistic thinking has not remained aloof from the problems of meaning, it has tended to occupy itself with other issues. Thus, E. B. Titchener formulated a theory of meaning in which the meaning was determined by the association between a core of sensations and the context of other sensations, memories, images, and the like—a position not unrelated to the one we are taking here. However, meaning was not Titchener's primary concern; rather, he devoted his efforts to an introspective analysis of the contents of the mind into the basic sensations from which these associations were presumably formed. This approach led to madness—theoretically speaking. Moreover, we often find that associationists have been concerned with the relative innateness of psychological processes and the contents of the mind. They typically side with those who feel that most such processes and contents are learned. At the opposite side are those who speak more of innate mental organizers, ideas, and the like, and who also tend to be non-associationistic in their thinking.

We propose to offer an associationistic account of meaning. To do this we shall have to speak in associationistic language about a great number of things. It seems clear that meaning, particularly the meaning of words, is learned. The assumption of learning is less certain in other areas, for example, the perception of objects, forms, and colors. We propose to be neutral about how much of the mind is learned and only to postulate this: *whether it is learned or innate, it is properly describable in associationistic language.* The implications of this will rapidly become apparent.

Let us first add a few more points about meaning before attempting to explain it. We have partially defined it as the readiness to use words in a particular fashion. We have also assumed verbal associations describe, and can be used to make, inferences about these uses. But it would appear that if meaning is a readiness to use, to respond, or to react to a thing (word), then words are not the only things which have meaning. If we look at a chair, we "see" that it has the properties of shape, color, sit-on-able-ness, and the like; balls are seen to have the property of "able-to-be-thrown-ness"; and people have countless properties —they are seen to be angry, warm, repressed, sick, etc. When we see an object, in addition to its "optical" properties, we customarily also see how to function with respect to that object. This does not mean that we are always aware of the functions of an object whenever we see it; it simply means that the only way to describe the awareness of how to use an object would be to say that we see it that way: "It *looks* as though it is good for. . . ." The readiness to respond or use is then common to both perception and to meaning.

But let us go one step further. Consider some "optical" property of visual perception: size, for example. The perception of size is often explained in a strictly "optical" manner emphasizing only stimulus and receptor organ properties. That is, an object casts an image of a given size on the retina of the eye. A retinal image of a given size could be produced by an infinite array of objects each of a different size. A large object far from the observer could cast an image the same size as that cast by a very small object very close to the observer. Thus, to get an accurate perception of the size of an object, the observer must know its distance from himself. Distance perception is usually explained by appealing to the use of "cues" to distance, of which convergence (or the crossing of the eyes to focus on an object), stereopsis (or binocular disparity), and linear perspective are typical examples. Some theorists go so far as to include familiar or known size in this list.* One major difference among theorists concerns whether or not these cues have to be learned or whether they are "built into" the perceiver. But disregarding the issue of innateness, something appears to be missing here, nevertheless. Does the specification of distance cues really fully account for the awareness of size, or do we need other processes as well?

Consider an example: we are looking at two automobiles of the same make and model, one twenty yards in front of us and the other a block and a half away. If we were asked if they are the same size, we would, of course, answer "yes" and, if asked how we knew, we would simply point or *invite our questioner to look at them himself*. They are obviously and apparently the same size. But nevertheless for many adults, they do not look the same size either; indeed, at sufficient distance they would look "no bigger than ants." Paradoxically, the autos are both seen and not seen as the same size almost simultaneously. Now what is the significance of seeing one thing as "the same size" as another thing? Does it not mean this: the two autos are the same size because we could get into each of them and have the same amount of space remaining in each, could drive each through the same degree of traffic congestion, get each into the same size parking space, arrive at the same measurement of them with a ruler, completely superimpose them part for part if they were brought together, and so on? To say that they look different in our example is to say this; one would be drawn smaller than the other (in Western style art), or photograph smaller, one could be blocked from our view by a smaller object than could the other, one requires a larger sweep of the eyes to go from one

---

* A very readable and comprehensive account of this type of thinking can be found in Gibson, *The Perception of the Visual World*, 1950. He, in fact, rejects known size as a distance cue.

edge to the other, etc. For the same pair of objects, then, we have certain things which tell us that the objects are the same size and other things which tell us that they are different. Small wonder that they are seen as both the same and as a different size. But notice: we have accounted for the perception of size by appealing to things which one can do with or to the object. These actions range from simple organic responses like eye movements, to complex socially conventional acts like drawing. But nevertheless, how big something *looks* becomes a function of what one can *do* with or to it.

We find that on close consideration the so-called optical properties of perception become as "behavioral" as do the functional properties. *What we perceive is a function of what we are prepared to do with respect to the stimulus situation.** Perceiving size, then, involves a readiness to react or use the object in certain ways as much as the perception of "sit-on-able-ness" does. This is not to derogate the importance of the distance cues in perception. We are simply saying that they do not *define* the perception of size. Indeed, if we pursue the matter we must ask how they come to function as distance cues, or why they indicate distance. The answer must be that they instigate certain readinesses to react in a "distance" manner, i.e. to locomote for a greater or smaller length of time or some such.

The conclusion is obvious: there is a basic, unavoidable conceptual similarity between perception and meaning. Both involve a readiness to respond to the stimulus in a particular fashion or fashions. Beyond that we must ask this: is there any basic difference between the awareness of the meaning of a word and the awareness of some property of a seen object? Other than the fact that the latter can be obliterated by closing the eyes, it is difficult to see what difference there is. Piaget (1955) tells us, in fact,

---

* Color may appear to be an obstacle to this approach. Since the issue is too complex to discuss here, I refer the curious to J.G. Taylor's *The Behavioral Basis of Perception* (1962) and to M. Merleau-Ponty's *The Phenomenology of Perception* (1962) in which this and other matters are discussed at more leisure.

that for the child there are few phenomenal differences between the name and the object. This is clearly the extreme of the position we are trying to present.

Now if this psychological similarity between perception and meaning is accurate, we could argue that a theory of meaning must be *based* on a theory of perception. Since perception is developmentally prior to language, it cannot be the other way around. And, moreover, we must use a theory of perception that treats perception as a readiness to react in a particular stimulus situation. Given this perceptual theory, we can then proceed to develop a theory of meaning within it. But first we need the theory of perception.

A theory which has the major properties which we require has been formulated by J. G. Taylor in his *The Behavioral Basis of Perception* (1962). It is impossible to go into all of the perceptual ramifications of this theory here. However, we must outline the basic assumptions of the theory. Essentially three concepts are required by it: stimulus, movement, and readiness to respond.

Stimulus: To Taylor, the effective stimulus in any particular situation consists of the set of all impulses produced by *all* sensory organs at that particular moment in time. Such neural impulses depend not only on what is happening in the environment, but on the present state of the organism as well. To take a simple illustration, but one ignored by many perceptual theories, a particular object stimulating the eye of a human does not produce *a* stimulus, but an entire set of stimuli which vary according to the position of the eye.* The stimulus thus becomes a terribly complex item in this theory. In fact, Taylor shows that if we consider an infant who is able to move only his head and eyes, it would require information from eight stimulus aspects to specify the location of any single object in his visual environment. Specifically, consider yourself visually locating an object—seeing

---

* Taylor uses the term *set* in its technical, logical sense. That is, a set is any collection of objects, properties, things, or the like. The only thing which need be common among the members of a set is that they are members of the set; they need not be alike in any other way.

where it is. If you lack any of the following information, there will be some uncertainty as to where, in fact, it is: (1) the angle at which the light enters the right eye and (2) the left eye, (3) the horizontal position of the left eye and (4) the right eye (both are needed since the eyes can move independently in the infant), (5) the vertical position of the eyes, and the (6) vertical, (7) forward, and (8) sideways tilt of the head. The latter are needed, of course, since they effect the physical position of the eyes. The "stimulus" which effects his eyes is a function of these eight variables.

The stimulus is a concept which is defined totally in terms of "objective" properties; that is, it is not defined in terms of perceived properties or characteristics of perception. We do not see an eight-dimensional world, much less the even more complex one required to specify the stimulus for the mobile adult human. We see a stable three-dimensional world. However, as Taylor correctly points out, it is this fact about perception that we must explain. We cannot just accept it as a foregone conclusion, but must derive it from the manner in which the organism functions. Thus, the stimulus need have no phenomenological resemblance to our ordinary perceptual experience. If we are trying to account for the *behavior* of an adult, it is perfectly proper to take for granted these ordinary facts of perceived experience. If we are interested in trying to explain why the adult is the way he is and perceives the way he does, or how he becomes the way he is, however, we cannot take these facts for granted. Stimuli are in fact complex sets of neural events which could be described only by a large number of dimensions.

Movements: Within Taylor's theory a movement is a set of muscular changes—that is, changes in position of the body or a part of the body. Suppose we set up some arbitrary co-ordinates to describe the physical three-dimensional space in which the organism moves. For convenience we can center these co-ordinates in the body of the particular organism we are studying. Now any movement becomes a change of position of some part or parts of the body—from some point *a* to some point *b* within that co-

ordinate system. Any particular movement from *a* to *b* requires a
set of muscular activities in which some muscles do not move at
all. So the movement can be described as the set of such muscular movements which produce the required movement. Needless
to say, since any set can be empty, not moving at all is a movement within this system.

Moreover, if we are looking at movements from *a* to *b*, we can
see that there is ordinarily a large number of ways in which one
can get from *a* to *b*. If we extend the problem somewhat further
and simply talk about getting to *b* from whatever position we
happen to be in at the time, then an even larger set of movements are involved. We would be inclined to call the set of
movements that gets us to *b*, an *act* or a *behavior*, since psychologists have typically used these terms to refer to goal-directed
movements. That is, an act or a behavior is characterized by the
fact that the organism gets to a particular position from wher-
ever he happens to start out. Taylor does not use this terminology but does recognize the issue. To him, movements become
functionally equivalent if they end the organisms up in the same
spot, i.e. in the same muscular environmental position. The organism, of course, gets stimulation from moving by means of the
kinesthetic receptors in his muscles. Hence he can respond to
changes in his position and can "recognize" when he has arrived
at "the same" position. For the moment, we simply point out
this concept of functional equivalence. We will describe its significance later.

Readiness To Respond: Let us suppose we have an organism who
receives a stimulus and in the presence of this stimulus makes
some movement. Let us further suppose that this movement results in some form of reinforcement. We can now postulate that
on future occasions the occurrence of the stimulus will call out
some tendency or *readiness* to make the same movement. In
symbolizing the neural nature of this readiness, Taylor refers to
it as an *engram*. An engram, then, is the neural representation
of a readiness to make a certain movement in the presence of a
particular stimulus.

There are a few problems here, of course. What makes the animal move in the presence of the stimulus? And what constitutes a reinforcement? Both of these questions must be answered by any association theory of learning. It is apparent that movements by the organism, no matter how young, are not completely random. To the extent that some movements are more likely than others, we have evidence for some selective tendency or predetermination in the organism. The theory must specify the nature of this. Equally clearly, not all movements become associated to concurrent stimuli. Only those which are "rewarded" in some sense, are conditioned. If an associational learning theory is to be successful, it must specify the necessary conditions under which learning will take place. It must, in other words, define reinforcement—although such reinforcement need not necessarily be a reward, in the sense in which it is usually used.

Taylor grapples with these issues, but not with complete success in either case. One of his basic difficulties appears to be a tendency to try to answer the two questions separately, even though they seem to interact mutually. That is, if the organism is getting reinforced, there would appear to be little reason to move to a different locus—unless, of course, movement itself were reinforcing. In either case, the generation of movement and the definition of reinforcement become mutually intermingled issues. We will not go into the details of Taylor's solution. Let us simply accept for the moment the assumption that some satisfactory solution to the reinforcement issue can be obtained in order to see where this theory leads us. The suggestions concerning reinforcement made earlier in the chapter on the development of language have obvious relevance here. But let us assume, for the time being, that it is possible for the organism to form readinesses to respond of the sort defined above.

Taylor takes great pains to demonstrate that all readiness to respond are learned. That is, Taylor claims that at birth the human infant has none at all and, hence, that the infant does not perceive. He makes an amazingly successful defense of the concept that all perception or consciousness *could be* learned. While such a demonstration is something of a logical coup, and, for certain reasons, is a very desirable demonstration, it does not prove that *in fact* all readinesses to respond are learned. The engram is a "neurological" concept which makes a certain movement likely in the presence of a given sensory neural configuration. It is possible that engrams could be built by hereditary or developmental mechanisms. The point is that such built in mechanisms would be no different in form or function from acquired ones. Thus, we need not differentiate between learned engrams and hereditary ones because they may function identically! If we are going to speak of the effects of perception on language or the effects of language upon perception—where language is, of course, learned while all of perception may not be —we must have a scheme whereby the effects of learning and heredity are functionally equivalent. The engram provides such a scheme.

Now we come to the basic issue: perception. Let us consider a relatively mature organism. He is exposed to a stimulus which is a large set of neural events. To at least some of these events he has made responses in the past. Hence, they arouse in him their respective engrams or readinesses to respond. What is important to see here is that there will be *many* engrams activated by any given stimulus. The various parts (subsets) of the stimulus will have occurred in different situations and hence will have different response tendencies attached to them. Thus, this particular set of neural events will arouse a set of engrams where that set will contain many members. It is this set of simultaneously aroused engrams which constitutes perception for Taylor.

Let us be quite specific about this: the set of simultaneously aroused engrams is everything that is meant by the terms "perception," "consciousness," "awareness," and the like in ordinary language. When you are aware of something, you are aware not because you simply have *a* tendency to respond to it, but because you have *many* possibilities of responding to it. One can say that for Taylor consciousness presupposes conflict or choice. If the same response always follows the same stimulus, that stimulus will have one and only one engram attached to it. And the person will not be aware of that stimulus. Only if there are multiple possibilities of response or movement will he be aware. It would appear to be correct to say, then, that the more possibilities there are for movement (the more engrams attached to the particular stimulus), the more aware a person is of that stimulus situation.* If he says he is aware that two things are the same, this means that functionally equivalent engrams are aroused by both relevant stimulus sets. Sameness, then, is defined by the fact that movements resulting from different stimuli "end up" in the same locus. Two things may appear to be the same and not the same simultaneously, since they may simultaneously arouse both functionally equivalent and non-equivalent engram sets.

We cannot begin to outline the perceptual significance of this theory. It appears to provide answers to many vexing psychological problems, although it itself has certain gaps which need much more exacting thought. The question which we must consider is how the problem of language would be treated within this theory. We have defined meaning as a tendency to respond, and Taylor's theory has defined perception as a tendency to respond. But it does not automatically follow that Taylor's position can account for language.†

We must start with the infant and consider first the production of sounds. Let us assume that the infant has, or has acquired, the ability to perceive auditory stimuli; he hears, in other words. In terms of the theory this means that sets of auditory nerve impulses have conditioned to them sets of engrams which represent tendencies to respond to the auditory stimuli. The responses or movements which the engrams arouse would most likely be *orienting* in character. That is, they would involve turning the body toward the sound, adjusting the ear drum as a function of the intensity of the sound, and the like. Now sup-

* A person is not aware of the stimulus itself, nor is he aware of the engrams. He is simply aware. The attributes of that awareness will be the attributes of the movements for which the engrams are the readinesses. *Having* active engrams is being aware.

† In his exposition of the theory, Taylor concerns himself entirely with visual perceptual problems. What follows will be an attempt to extend his theory to cover language and meaning, without, it is hoped, doing violence to Taylor's position.

pose that for one reason or another, the infant makes some sound—crying being the most likely possibility. We would have the situation diagrammed in Figure 4 below. Here we see that the movement which is necessary to produce crying produces

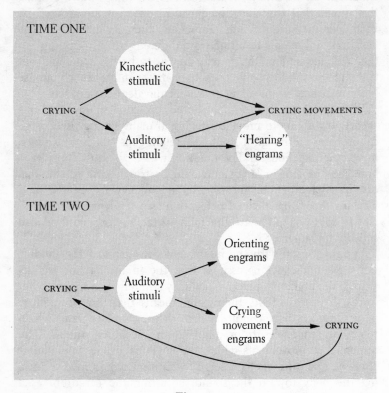

Figure 4

two sets of stimuli: kinesthetic ones from the muscular activity involved in crying, and auditory ones from the air pressure waves produced by the crying noise. We assume that the latter have engrams associated with them, and let us further assume that the infant continues to cry for more than a very short period of time —for longer than two or three seconds, let's say. This means that the infant will be making a crying response *in the presence of the stimuli produced by the kinesthetic and auditory events*, and if the conditions necessary for reinforcement are in force, engrams tending to produce that response will become associated to the stimuli.

Now consider what will happen the next time the infant is exposed to crying, whether or not he cries himself. The auditory stimuli will arouse engrams—i.e. the crying will be perceived. These engrams will involve tendencies to orient toward the sound, and the like, and engrams which are tendencies to produce crying—that is, to make the movements which produce auditory stimuli. This means that the perception of these sounds will include tendencies to make or to reproduce the sounds. Thus, perceiving a sound will acquire a built in imitative tendency. Indeed, it is possible that perceiving a sound at all implies some tendency to reproduce that sound by one's own vocal movements.*

As more self-produced sounds are made by the infant, he will rapidly acquire engrams which lead to the production of any sound which he can possibly make. All sounds will acquire the tendency to imitate themselves, whether or not they originate from the infant himself. Furthermore, we see that the ability to produce a sound allows the infant to control his stimulus environment and perceptions in a way that is impossible for a nonvocal organism. He can extend the duration of a perception by imitating or by producing the movements to which the perceptual engrams are conditioned. To summarize, the infant acquires the ability to hear and produce sounds—abilities which are inseparable from one another.

Now eventually he is able to perceive relatively extended sequences of sounds of which the words used by his parents are typical examples. The auditory perception of a word takes place, of course, in some perceptual context which involves all of the other senses as well. For our purposes we can consider the visual

* Such an idea leads to some interesting speculations. For example, it would imply that a person who is tone deaf is not unable to sing because of his tone deafness, but rather is tone deaf because he cannot sing.

sense primarily. The child sees things at the same time he hears them; in theoretical terms, he has visual and auditory engrams aroused simultaneously. Suppose that he hears a particular sequence of sounds, /ball/, accompanied by visual stimuli which include those produced by the object ball. We will have a situation such as that shown in Figure 5.

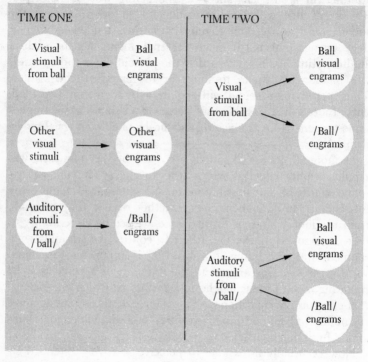

Figure 5

Here we see that three sets of engrams are aroused, those by the visual stimulus of the ball, those by the other visual stimuli present, and those by the auditory stimulus produced by saying /ball/. Assuming that the conditions requisite for reinforcement are present on the next occurrence of /ball/, these stimuli will elicit engrams appropriate to hearing /ball/ *and* engrams appropriate to seeing a ball. They will also elicit engrams appropriate to the other visual stimuli as well, which would suggest that non-ball stimuli would elicit the perception of /ball/ and /ball/ would elicit the perception of non-ball objects. We shall return to this problem.

What has taken place can be summed up in this way: the word /ball/ makes the child think of a ball, be aware of it, have an image of it, etc. Specifically, it arouses tendencies in him to behave toward /ball/ as he would toward an actual ball. Likewise, seeing the object calls out the tendency to produce the name of the object or to be aware of the name of the object. In the awareness of the child, the name and the object become phenomenally inseparable, as Piaget suggested; that is, they both produce identical reactions.

But part of the perception of /ball/ involves a tendency to imitate the sound. The child will, in fact, eventually produce it himself. Once he does this the situation is changed somewhat, for there are now a set of kinesthetic stimuli produced by the vocal movements to which the aroused engrams can be associated, and which in turn arouse engrams which can become associated to the auditory and visual stimuli. But this is a matter of additional complexity only. The major issue is this: the word has acquired meaning in that it has tendencies associated with it. These tendencies include both those associated with the referential object and those involved in the hearing and production of the word itself. Yet, this is still a childish and non-abstract meaning.

To begin with, we have not really accounted for one of the attributes of words—that they are class names. We have conditioned /ball/ to a particular ball in a particular context. In fact the context is as much a determiner of /ball/ as the ball itself is in our illustration. But getting rid of the context is a relatively easy matter. In the first place, the context in which the ball is seen will very likely change from time to time. Thus, merely by frequency alone the ball itself will become more strongly conditioned to the relevant engrams than will its visual context. But frequency alone is not sufficient since most words appear to be *entirely* independent of their visual backgrounds, while the frequency theory would make them only *relatively* independent.

In fact, the problem has somewhat even more scope than this. We have assumed that the meaning of a word is essentially conscious. In general, what gets conditioned is what the child is aware of. Moreover, this theory essentially assumes that objects —visual events—call out the same name or word to the extent that they have common elements. The elements in question are themselves engrams or tendencies to respond, of course. To the extent that each and every ball is called /ball/, the engrams associated with each must be the same. Bear in mind that engrams are tendencies to respond. Thus, one of the engrams associated with the object chair is a tendency to sit in it. This permits us to say that the common characteristics of a class of things may be its function—or even how it is used in a sentence or the like. Common properties as perceived do not necessarily mean common physical or stimulus attributes but rather refer to common engrams, to common response tendencies.

Now to be aware of a ball means that certain engrams are aroused by the object ball. But the object ball can arouse a very large number of engrams. Suppose, for the sake of argument, that only some of those engrams are aroused at the time that /ball/ is heard, and furthermore, suppose they are the "wrong" engrams. For instance, suppose primarily the red engrams from a red ball are aroused rather than those which define the category ball. The child will obviously misuse or mislearn the meaning of /ball/. If he misuses it, he can be corrected by his parents or others and then can learn it correctly. This, in fact, happens all the time. It suggests one thing—engram arousal can be selective. Not all engrams need be aroused at once. In fact, *correct* learning requires that only the *relevant* engrams be associated with the word, not just all that happen to be possible. Now how are we to account for this selective arousal of engrams?

Taylor provides us with a mechanism which will probably serve the purpose—a set of internally produced stimuli which he calls drive stimuli and which essentially represent and are produced by the motives and other internal processes of the individual. All movements, and the engrams resulting therefrom, are in fact conditioned to a set of stimuli which is composed of those stimuli produced by events external to the person and those produced by events internal to him. Seeing something in a particular way, then, is not just a function of optical visual events, but also a function of the motivational state of the organism. Things look differently under different motivational states because the effective stimulus set—and the engrams produced thereby—are different. For the same reason, words will have different meaning—call out different sets of engrams—under different emotional and motivational states. It would appear, then, that when these drive stimuli are in some states, it will be possible to condition a correct (socially acceptable) meaning to a word while in other states such conditioning will be impossible. The drive stimuli can provide the necessary factor for engram selection.

It is assumed that such stimuli are produced by movements of the organism. The movements in this case would be of visceral muscles and glands, primarily.* In some cases, the stimuli produced by these movements will continue for long after the movement itself has ceased—as in the case of an hormonal secretion which produces activation of sensory nerves by its continued presence in the blood long after the gland has stopped secreting it. But in all cases some movement on the part of the individual will initiate the stimuli. It follows that these drive stimuli or specifically the movements which produce them can be conditioned to external events or to other stimuli produced by the person himself. These stimuli are, therefore, potentially controllable by the individual himself. Exactly what variables control them is probably in large part a function of the particular life history of the person under observation. But it becomes quite plausible to assume that once the child has learned some words, perhaps by the more cumbersome method of the reinforcement of common elements by frequency alone, he may also associate the drive-stimulus-producing movements to verbal stimuli. Thus,

* There are other factors as well which will be discussed in the next chapter.

the drive states, which are necessary for the appropriate learning of words, may actually become conditioned to words and in part controlled by words. The child can then be *instructed* to learn correctly (in effect) or even instruct himself. Some words may become the conditioned stimuli for a drive state appropriate to the learning of meaning and for the arousal of the selection process necessary for the choice of the correct engrams to attach to the verbal stimulus. Such a notion would lead to the prediction that the initial learning of words would be slow since it would take place largely by a trial and error process. But following this, a sudden burst of rapid language learning should be observed. This is, of course, exactly what appears to happen in the child.

The major remaining problem to be accounted for is this: how does the word become separated from the object? Up to this point we have the two inseparably intertwined in the experience of the child, and yet it is rapidly obvious that the word and the object are different to the child. How does this take place? We would presume that it occurs primarily because the environment does not present a one-to-one correlation between any object and any word; it cannot offer such a correlation, in fact, if the word is to be meaningful and useful in a language. The child is exposed to the word in the absence of the referential object; he is exposed to it in various verbal contexts. In both cases the result is the same; the word acquires engrams aroused by stimuli other than the referential object. Consider, for example, hearing the word /ball/ in a simple sentence, assuming for simplicity's sake that there are no relevant engrams active other than the auditory ones. We would have the situation diagrammed in Figure 6. Here, following Taylor, we have assumed that any given engram persists for some period of time following the presentation of its eliciting stimulus—for a few seconds, let us say. We will also accept as given, one of the most universal phenomena of classical conditioning—that conditioning will take place when the conditioned and unconditioned stimulus are presented concurrently, *or* when the conditioned precedes the unconditioned stimulus by as much as a few seconds. What we find, then, is that the engrams

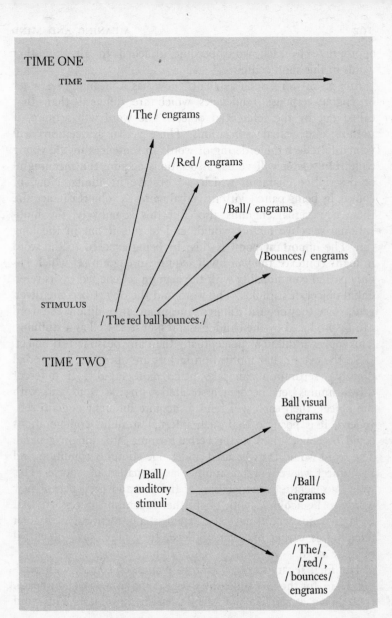

Figure 6

appropriate to each word become attached to all the other words in this short sentence.*

Any given word, such as /ball/, now has a meaning, i.e. a set of engram-response tendencies which are different than that called out by the referential object. The word will acquire, if nothing else, verbal associations. These verbal associations will primarily reflect the ordering of words in sentences in the young child. Only later will verbal associations acquire the meaningful or descriptive character which we observe in adults. Now, of course, by being paired with its verbal name the object can acquire these new verbal engrams also. But this is unlikely; the motivational selective factors would tend to rule it out in the long run. The important point is this: by being exposed to the word in many contexts, the word will acquire an engram set which has only partial commonality with the engram set elicited by its referential object or stimulus. The word and the object become divergent, since they acquire different meanings. In addition, the word can be produced by the child; it is a response as well as a stimulus. This makes it different perceptually than any possible real object.

To the extent that motivation factors are operative, this verbal objective separation can take place more rapidly. If different drive-stimulus sets become associated with the word and with the object, then each will tend to acquire different engram sets. Indeed, it is possible that such internal stimulus configurations could be conditioned to the verbal-learning situation in general. The word would thus be used under one stimulus condition and the object viewed under another as a matter of course. This would accelerate the separation of the two and even permit new words to be acquired with no further separation necessary; that is, later words would never be experientially identical with their referents as earlier ones are. Indeed, they need have no visual referent at all.

The final separation of the word comes, of course, with reading. Here, for the first time, the word can be *seen* as well as heard. It is shown as visually not identical with the object. The word

* The acquisition of grammatical rules will modify this activity somewhat, but we are still dealing with a "pre-grammatical" child.

will now acquire a new set of visual engrams—those produced by the written stimulus. The image aroused by the hearing of the word will call out two objects, the reference object and the "word"—i.e. its written representative.

For the moment we may conclude with the contention that this theory presents the basis for an apparently satisfactory account of meaning. It is based upon the idea that the meaning of a word is in some way a set of tendencies to respond to or to use the word. It appears to satisfactorily account for the phenomenal separation and identity of the word and the perception of its referent. It allows us to predict the growth of vocabulary. And, most important, it treats meaning as something which is appropriate to or relevant to stimulus conditions or states of affairs, and as something which at the same time is independent of them. It treats meaning as uncertain, for all meaning involves sets of response tendencies; these are sets of alternative responses, or choices. They are a necessary condition for meaning, as information theory would suggest. Finally, this theory assumes that meaning can be defined only in terms of a transaction between stimuli and behaviors—as a tendency to behave to a stimulus—and not by stimuli or behaviors alone.

What we have not done yet is to account for the system of language—the rules of grammar by which utterances are generated. This will be the task of the next chapter, which will attempt first to describe the rules of grammar and then to account for them in psychologically meaningful terms.

Bibliography

Bloomfield, L. *Language*. New York, Holt, Rinehart and Winston, 1933.

Boring, E. G. A *history of experimental psychology*. New York, Appleton-Century-Crofts, 1950.

Ebbinghaus, H. *Memory: a contribution to experimental psychology*, New York, Teachers College, Columbia University, 1913.

Gibson, J. J. *The perception of the visual world*. Cambridge, The Riverside Press, 1950.

Glaze, J. A. The association value of non-sense syllables. *J. genet.*
     Psychol., 1928, 35, 255-69.

Kent, G. H. & Rosanoff, A. J. A study of association in insanity. *Amer.*
     J. Insan., 1910, 67, 37-96, 317-90.

Merleau-Ponty, M. *The phenomenology of perception*. New York,
     Humanities Press, 1962.

Noble, C. An analysis of meaning. *Psychol. Rev.*, 1952, 59, 421-30.

Osgood, C. E. Comments on Prof. Bousfield's paper. In Cofer, C. N.
     (Ed.) *Verbal learning and verbal behavior*. New York, Mc-
     Graw-Hill, 1961, pp. 91-105.

Piaget, J. *The language and thought of the child*. New York, Meridian
     Books, 1955.

Taylor, J. G. *The behavioral basis of perception*. New Haven, Yale
     University Press, 1962.

Underwood, B. J., and Schulz, R. *Meaningfulness and verbal learning*.
     Chicago, J. B. Lippincott, 1960.

VII
Grammar

A grammar has been defined as an attempt to describe and account for any speaker's ability to generate correct sequences of words in his language. That is to say, speech follows the rules which the grammarians are trying to discover. From our point of view, it is these rules which constitute an integral part of the *system* which is language. Such a grammar must have two characteristics. (1) It must contain a set of rules which will permit one to create *all* possible sentences by following these rules; and (2) the rules, if followed, must create only correct sentences. The problem of correctness may seem at first to be a very subjective issue and one which should not fall under the purview of objective scientific study. Sentences do have perfectly objective characteristics which can be specified by the scientific linguist or psychologist and which define the grammatical correctness of the sentence, however.

Correctness is, of course, ultimately the judgment of the speakers of the language. If we wish to find out whether or not a sentence is grammatically correct, we must ask someone who is an accomplished speaker of the language—preferably someone for whom the language is the native tongue. One of the things which

Much of what is presented in the opening portion of this chapter can be found in much more detailed and sophisticated form in Noam Chomsky, *Syntactic Structures*, 1957.

must be accepted is this: such a query directed to a speaker of a language will almost invariably get an answer. Speakers of a given language are quite capable of saying, and will say, that such and such an utterance is or is not correct. They will even go one step further and phrase it correctly for you. The speaker of the language is a perfectly accurate measuring instrument of the language. He will accurately describe what is a correct sentence. He can follow the rules of the grammar. But typically he has little conscious awareness of these rules of grammar. This is important for the psychologist; to correctly account for grammar we must not only postulate a mechanism which explains the fact that utterances follow rules, but also make this mechanism unconscious.*

The objectivity of a grammar comes from the fact that its rules, once known, can be used by anyone to generate a correct sentence. If there is any question about the correctness of the sentence, a speaker of the language can inform us regarding this issue. There is, of course, a grey area in which sentences are ambiguously correct. That is, to some speakers the sentence may be a correct one, while to others, it is not. This may be a result of differences in dialect; each dialect is governed by a slightly different grammar. That dialect differences seem to reflect socio-economic differences is quite irrelevant to linguists per se. The "lower classes" do not speak "bad" grammar while the "upper classes" speak "correct" grammar. They use *different* grammars and neither can be said to be more correct or better than another so long as they both permit language to function to its maximum potentials—as in fact they do. The standardization of a language, such as that observed in France where Parisian French is the standard tongue taught in the schools, etc., is linguistically arbi-

---

* Many psychological theorists, e.g. Dollard and Miller (1950), including to some extent Freud (1960) himself, have defined consciousness as that which can be verbalized or spoken of. It is of interest, then, to see that conscious verbal processes are regulated in the normal individual by rules which are themselves unconscious. There is some amusement to be derived from speculating about whether or not linguistic studies therefore provide a confirmation of Freudian mental theories, which assume that conscious processes are primarily under the control of unconscious ones.

trary. It may be a political necessity to the extent that perhaps members of an economic or political community could not communicate with one another because of dialect differences. But such a standardization cannot be accepted as a *linguistic* critique. All dialects are in some sense equally good. The dialect of the socially powerful may be accepted as the "correct" one—the King's English, as we say—but it is grammatically no better than any other dialect.

To reiterate, a grammar is a set of rules which if followed will produce only correct and all correct utterances within a language as spoken by a particular community of people. Since there are an infinite number of possible sentences within any language, the grammar must permit the generation of an infinite number of sentences. In case there is any question about this infinite characteristic of language, we need only point out that the phrase /the old man/ can be extended to /the old, old man/, /the old, old, old man/, ad infinitum. Such an extension may be senseless or incomprehensible when too many /old's/ are involved but no matter how many there are, the sentence is still grammatically correct.

Some grammatically oriented linguists believe that the study of grammar can take place without reference to the issue of meaning. Such a statement does not deny the fact that language is intimately involved with meaning, for it is obvious that no one would study grammar unless it were part of the meaningful system called language. It does not even deny the fact that meaning is affected by grammar: thus the meaning or sense of a string of words is profoundly altered by their ordering, as in /Boy bites dog./ and /Dog bites boy/. What the statement does imply, however, is that there are sentences which are grammatically correct but are at the same time senseless or meaningless to the ordinary speaker of the language. To take one of Chomsky's examples /Colorless green ideas sleep furiously./ is a perfectly correct sentence, grammatically. But it is also somewhat less than meaningful in any ordinary sense of that term. It is, therefore, possible to speak of the grammatical correctness of an utterance without questioning what meaning is involved.

STATISTICAL GRAMMAR

For the purposes of the psychologist, there appear to be only two
interesting theories of grammar among those currently available.
The first is essentially a statistical or probabilistic one. Let us
begin by briefly outlining the facts: there are determinant probabilities of words following one another in the language. Moreover these probabilities can easily be shown to be psychologically
meaningful. That is, if we take a large sample of English text, we
can, by counting, determine the relative frequency (probability)
with which one word follows another. We will find, for example,
that out of all occurrences of /the/ in the text, /man/ has a far
higher probability of occurrences immediately following /the/
than does /is/. We will also notice that both probabilities are
very small, since there are a very large number of words which
will follow /the/. Hence the probability of any *particular* one
will be small. However, some probabilities are still much larger
than others. If we wish to extend this procedure, we can calculate
the probability of any particular word following any two particular preceding ones: thus we could count the frequency with which
different words followed /the man/. We can clearly extend this
process up to as many preceding words as we wish, with the general result that as the number of preceding items increases, the
number of possibilities (the number of words actually used in that
position in the utterance) decreases and hence each particular
possibility will have a higher and higher probability of being correct.

If we want to make the situation less cumbersome, and also
get higher probability values, we can ask people to generate
sequences of words for us. That is, we can take a sample of subjects, give them the word /the/ and ask them to guess what word
will follow it in a sentence. We can give them /the man/ and ask
them to guess what word will follow that, etc. We will find that
the number of different words guessed is relatively small—probably since the experimental context restricts the range of words
about which the subjects think. They may not guess the "correct"

next word at all, but they will produce a distribution of guesses, some of which are more common than others. We can then calculate the probability of guessing that any particular word will follow any other particular sequence of words. Typically, we find that the more preceding words we give subjects, the fewer different guesses they produce, and the more agreement there is among subjects on the guesses given. The probability of guessing the correct third word in a sentence is typically higher than the probability of guessing the correct second word, the fourth higher than the third, etc. These probabilities are "real facts." But their existence is, of course, not sufficient reason for saying that they are grammar.

These probabilities have an additional psychological import related to the recall of verbal material. Using a method analogous to the guessing method described above, Miller and Selfridge (1953) showed that recall of strings of words increased as the words were more highly determined by the strings of other preceding words in the text. Thus, a string of words compiled from guesses made to only one preceding word was recalled much less accurately than a string generated from guesses based on two preceding words. They carried this procedure up through words which were dependent on seven preceding guesses. Using the immediate recall of the material as a measure, they showed that steady improvement in recall was observed up through lists dependent on five preceding words. Beyond this point recall was as good for all conditions as it was for grammatically correct sentences. This study could be interpreted as suggesting that there is a connection between word probability and grammar. High probability strings of words, of course, resemble grammatical strings more than low probability strings do. And as far as recall is concerned, words that have a high statistical dependency on one another produce the same effects as strings of words which are grammatically correct. That this variable affects recall does not mean that it is an accurate description or theory of grammar, however.

What would a grammar based on probabilistic connections between words be like? Presumably, we would have a model which was essentially linear; that is, we would start with the first word and produce each successive word in order. We can ignore the problem of where we get the first word from for the moment, since, as you will see, this model does not work anyway. Given the first word, there would be a set of second words which were possible, each of which had a finite probability of occurrence. We can add, if we wish, that in different stimulus situations, different sets of words would be available. One of these second words would be chosen, and this choice would determine a set of possible third words—and then fourth words, etc., until the sentence was finished. Of course the possible words from which one chooses at any given point would have differing probabilities of being chosen, but any word which *could* follow another would have to have *some* probability of being chosen, no matter how small that probability was.

Two difficulties exist here. First of all, we must account for where these probabilistic tendencies in the individual come from. Since it is possible—and even common—for any speaker of the language to generate a sentence which is totally novel and unfamiliar to him, this clearly implies that these particular word combinations have, in the words of this model, a tendency of calling out each other. But how did they get this tendency if they have never occurred in the life of the individual? Clearly we cannot postulate some innate factor here. We might assume, instead, that a given word has a probability of being followed by certain specific words and all other words of the same form class. Perhaps it is not too farfetched to think that an entire part of speech could be probabilistically conditioned. But where does this lead us? It means that we would necessarily have a certain probability of making mistakes in grammar and that this probability would be quite large. If, for example, verbs in general were conditioned to /he/, even though specific ones have higher probabilities than others, we should find a large number of statements such as /He do, He are, He go/. All the second words are, after all, legitimate verbs.

We have a difficulty here. If we construct a model so that it is possible to utter novel sentences, then non-grammatical sentences become statistically probable. If, on the other hand, it is not possible to say anything other than those grammatical forms which have been previously experienced, then no novel sentences can be uttered. Consider in addition the following examples:

/They said./
/They said, "the."/
/They said, "the man."/
/"They," said the man./
/They said the man was hot./
/"They," said the man, "were hot."/

It would seem to be impossible to account for the construction of these sentences by any linear probabilistic model—that is, by a model which starts with the first word and cranks out the succeeding ones by probabilistic rules. At least two additional things would be required to account for these sentences. The first would be some straightforward notion of *intention* on the part of the speaker. It should be clear that we could have any sentence go on for ever, simply by adding /and/ or /or/ at the "end" and continuing. By simple probabilistic laws, we should find such sentences. They might be rare but they would occur. Moreover, it is clear that nearly any word can be the final word in a sentence. Hence, there is probability of *not going on after any particular word*. By this reasoning we should find a high proportion of senseless incomplete sentences. In fact, while we do often observe incomplete sentences, they are almost never senseless. In other words, sentences have a beginning and an end. One utters words until the sentence is finished. There is no way of accounting for this form of a sentence except to appeal to some desire or intention in the speaker. He knows what he wants to say and he knows when he has said it. In other words, the beginning and ending of an utterance are controlled in part by extra-grammatical factors. To be quite metaphorical, a sentence is the expression of an idea. Probabilities do not respect the boundaries of ideas. One could never guarantee complete or finished sentences considering only the probabilities of words following one another.

Second, if we consider the last two sentences in our example, we find that they differ in only one word. Assuming for the moment that there is some probabilistic representation of the quotation marks in the last sentence (which seems a debatable assumption), we must still come to this conclusion: the individual cannot make the correct choice between /was/ and /were/ in these two sentences unless he is able to "refer back" to the subject of the sentence. Here we have a common case of agreement of number between the subject and the predicate of a sentence or clause. In order to be able to do this, the individual must "know" what the subject of the sentence is. In making the choice among the possible words which can probabilistically follow /man/, he must take into account both /they/ and the fact that /they/ is part of a quotation. To give a probabilistic basis for the fact that something is a quotation would appear to be very difficult. If another example is required, the reader is invited to account for the following utterance probabilistically, in light of the preceding sentences: /"They," said the man, "was not the correct word."/

In summary, then, the theory that postulates words as being generated from probabilistic distributions conditioned to the preceding stimulus or stimuli is untenable. No sentence can be understood without an appeal to non-verbal characteristics of the speaker. And no sentence can be generated without referring backward, or forward, to other words in the sentence. Consider a question: /What were the men doing?/ To account for the agreement between the verb and the subject here one must have the verb chosen in light of a word which has not yet been chosen. The model assumes that early words in the sentence are chosen prior to later ones; one starts at the beginning and goes step by step. Yet, later words obviously influence the choices of earlier ones. This is clearly contrary to the theory. Now there is no question about the fact that the probabilistic model is almost infinitely flexible. It can be adjusted to account for nearly any specific fact. Yet such adjustments must involve either the addition or removal of constraints from the model. Thus, if we assign a probability of /were/ following /man/, as we must do to account for one of the above sentences, then we allow for the possibility of /the man were hot/ as a grammatical sentence. If we refuse the right of /were/ to follow man, then we say that the above grammatically correct sentence is impossible. This is a simple, but typical, example. It is put quite succinctly by Chomsky (1957):

If a grammar of this type produces all English sentences, it will produce many non-sentences as well. If it produces only English sentences, we can be sure that there will be an infinite number of true sentences, false sentences, reasonable questions, etc., which it simply will not produce (*Syntactic Structures*, p. 24).

TRANSFORMATION THEORY

Chomsky has offered an alternative to the probabilistic model. He first assumes that all sentences have a structure which he calls *phrase structure*. Thus, for example, any sentence will consist of two parts, a noun phrase and a verb phrase. A noun phrase may consist solely of a noun, or it may consist of a noun and modifiers such as /the/. A verb phrase may contain only a verb, or it may, in addition, contain a noun phrase as well. Thus we can conceive of a hierarchy such as that described below:

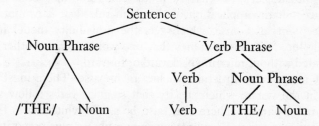

Having arrived at the bottom of the "pyramid," we can proceed to substitute specific nouns and verbs in the sentence. The result will be a grammatically correct sentence—within limits. We will see the limits in a moment.

The idea of phrase-structure grammar is quite straightforward and elegant in intent. The notion is to start at some beginning point, labeled sentence above, and to terminate with a correct sentence by following a specific set of rules. Each rule involves the change or rewriting of one part of the sentence into another form. Thus the diagram specifies that the sentence be rewritten as noun phrase plus verb phrase. This in turn is rewritten as /the/ plus noun plus verb phrase, and so on. By following each single specific rule, one after the other, one is going to end up with a correct sentence.

But this is clearly a simple example, as Chomsky indicates. We would need many additional rules, for example a rule which would specify that the verb phrase was to be written as singular if the noun phrase was singular, etc. To specify each of these grammatical conventions would clearly require a long list of rules, but length is not a criticism of a theory if that theory is correct. The difficulty with this theory is, surprisingly, analogous to the difficulty which exists with the probabilistic model. That is, the theory specifies a set of rules for rewriting which must be followed, one at a time and one after the other in a fixed order. There is no going back permitted; that is, a particular rule cannot "take into account" what some preceding rule has done. Each rule is applied independently of all others. But one could not make the subject and verb agree in number unless one knew what the subject was—that is, unless the verb rule could take into account the application of the noun rule. But it cannot. It is this point, of course, which gets the probability model into trouble too, for it also requires that one word after the other be generated without referring backward or forward.

But now phrase structure reaches an impasse. There must be rules in the system which specify that singular verbs follow singular noun phrases. There must also be a rule which states that any noun phrase can be rewritten as noun phrase plus preposition plus noun phrase. Without the latter we could not generate sentences such as /The men at the bar were drinking/. But now we can ask which rule comes first. If we permit the noun phrase to be written in the prepositional form and then apply the rule that singular verbs follow singular noun phrases, we may get /The men at the bar was drinking/. But we cannot apply the singular rule first, since there are two noun phrases. The speaker would have to know which phrase was the subject of the sentence in order to know whether to make the verb singular or plural. In other words, the prepositional form must be written first. But if it is, then ungrammatical sentences result. In order to resolve this problem, Chomsky introduces a new grammatical device which he calls a *transformation*.

What exactly are these transformations? While it is impossible to do full justice to the elegance of Chomsky's theory in such a short space, we can say simply that they are rules for rewriting complete sentences. Essentially, his grammar would work like this: we would start with the sentence as above. Then we would apply all of the phrase-structure rules. Each of these rules involves, as we have seen, rewriting one specific part of a sentence at a time without refering to any preceding or succeeding parts of the sentence. Having finished this phrase-structure procedure we change the sentence according to transformational rules which allow us to rewrite the sentence as a whole, with all of its parts taken into consideration. What we are in fact rewriting at any given time is, of course, the result of the preceding application of the phrase structure rules and the application of any preceding transformational rules. What we are rewriting may not look much like a real sentence at any given time, but when all the rules have been applied, it will—if the grammar is correct, that is.

For the sake of elegance, Chomsky would add that we must then apply a third set of rules—those which translate the abstract words of the sentence into phonemes or, presumably, written letters. For up to this time we have been dealing only with abstractions, the ideal word, sentence, and the like. We therefore need some rule to translate the abstract into the concrete, into behavior. We will not go into these rules here. Suffice it to say that they are necessary for a complete linguistic grammar.

Now what exactly is a transformation? Let us take a specific example. One transformation might read something like this, in informal language: A sentence of the form, noun phrase (one) plus verb auxiliary plus verb plus noun phrase (two), may be rewritten as noun phrase (two) plus verb auxiliary plus a form of the verb /to be/ plus verb plus /by/ plus noun phrase (one). If you substitute words into this abstraction, you will see that this transformational rule has changed the sentence from the active to the passive state. Thus by the transformation we could change /The dog is biting the boy./ into /The boy is being bitten by the dog/.

The passive transformation does not directly produce this grammatically correct sentence, however. Notice, for example, that /biting/ in the first active sentence is changed into /bitten/ in the passive one. There is a verb ending change from the active to the passive voice. This change can be written into the transformation directly by having it read, ". . . /to be/ plus participle ending plus verb. . . ." However even here the participle endings for different verbs are different. The /-en/ for /bite/ would become /-ed/ if we had said /The dog is chasing the boy/. This is no criticism against the transformational theory. It simply shows that applying one transformation is not sufficient. Other rules, in this case those specifying participle endings, must be applied as well.

But most of these other rules will also be transformations since they must refer to the sentence as a whole—as the passive transformation does. As we tried to show above, agreement between subject and verb in number, agreement between the auxiliary and the verb in ending, etc. all require a reference to a large part of the sentence. They cannot be accounted for simply by fixed rewritings of specific items in the sentence, for such specific rules can never take into account all possibilities.

This argument suggests, however, that there are two types of transformations. Transformations involving the agreement of subject and verb, for example, *must* be used if we are to arrive at a grammatical sentence. Chomsky refers to these as *obligatory transformations* and states that when all obligatory transformations have been applied to the result of the phrase-structure rules, we have what has been called a *kernel sentence*. On the other hand, there is nothing compelling about a transformation from the active to the passive voice. This would ordinarily be conceived as being a matter of choice for the individual speaker. Hence this type of transformation falls into the class of *optional transformations*. Among these optional transformations we would find those which permit rewriting the kernel sentence as a question, in the negative, or rewriting two sentences as one joined by a conjunction. The term "optional" should not mislead one, however. These transformations are optional in the sense that one may elect to use them or not. Once their use has been elected, however, they contain specific and rigid rules for rewriting the sentence. There is no optionality within a transformation.

We will make no attempt to present a complete picture of all the transformations necessary to account for a complete grammar of English. What should be clear is this: once the grammar has permitted rules which allow complete sentences to change, it should, logically, be possible to create a set of rules which allow one to generate all grammatical sentences and only grammatical sentences. In other words, one would have a logically perfect grammar.

In addition, we see that the transformational approach can shed some understanding on verbal ambiguities of a certain kind. Chomsky points out that certain sentences are ambiguous with regard to their referent. As Fries (1952) points out, when considered only as a string of words, /have the men paid/ is ambiguous. It could be either a question or a command, although of course if one heard the sentence spoken, the intonation of the two would be distinctly different. Chomsky's example is /John was frightened by the new methods/. Here we have an ambiguity: are there new methods *which* frighten or new methods *to* frighten John? The point which Chomsky wishes to demonstrate is that in any example of this sort, we will find that each of the two different senses of the sentence is derived by means of a different set of transformations. Thus one sense of the sentence is the direct passive transformation of /The new methods frightened John/. The second sense is a double transformation of a sentence like /Someone frightened John by the new methods/.

Here we might first have the passive transformation into /John was frightened by someone by the new methods/, and then what Chomsky calls the elliptical transformation which permits the dropping of /by someone/. Two different transformational histories, then, can produce the same string of words. To the extent that a string of words has more than one possible transformational history, its sense will be ambiguous, and most likely all such ambiguity which is not purely due to individual words can be reduced to differences in the transformation history of the string of words.

At this stage of the development of transformational theory it seems quite fair to say that it shows exceptional promise. While the particular transformation rules proposed by Chomsky may be changed, and while the present list may prove to be incomplete, the approach in general seems eminently fruitful. It would seem quite likely that a *model* of correct grammar could be generated by these means. As a logical analysis of language, then, this transformation grammar is excellent. The question we must face is this: what is its psychological status? That is, should one assign a psychological reality to what originated as a logical analysis of language. There is little doubt but that Chomsky does assign such a psychological reality to his theory.

Before attempting to criticize this approach, let us point out that there is some empirical evidence which is at least consonant with the theory. Miller (1962) has shown, for example, that the time it takes for a subject to translate one form of a sentence into another is a function of how many optional transformations this translation would require. Thus it takes less time to shift from active to passive than it does to shift from active to negative passive. The former would require only one optional transformation while the latter would require two. One could easily offer alternative explanations to these results, of course; for example, more word changes are required to go from active to negative passive than to passive alone. More changes will doubtless require more time. Transformations need not be considered at all. Yet this alternative explanation does not deny the fact that these data also follow quite clearly from a psychological transformation theory.* In addition, Johnson (1965) has shown that the recall of sentences by experimental subjects tends to follow phrase-structure rules. That is, if only a part of a sentence is recalled, it will tend to be a complete unit of the phrase structure of the sentence—an entire noun phrase or an entire verb phrase, for example. It will be rare that one will recall an incomplete structure, and even rarer that one recalls *parts* of two adjacent structures, e.g. part of the noun phrase and part of the verb phrase. Again, a probabilistic theory could account for these results since inter-word probabilities are higher within particular phrase structures than they are between them. A probabilistic theory might say that what you call a part of the phrase structure is merely a group of words which have a relatively high probability of following one another. But again, the results must be taken primarily as confirmation of the theory from which they were derived—the transformation approach.

But even to its adherents, we see that the transformation theory poses problems. The theory is quite complex; the list of rules, both for phrase structure and for transformations is long. As they are verbalized in Chomsky's writings, these rules appear terribly complex, in addition to being quite specific and detailed. The apparent complexity of the rules is probably just that—apparent. Grammatical rules are not something which we are normally aware of. Hence we have developed no vocabulary to describe them and any description must take place by means of relatively enormous circumlocutions. The fact, then, that the rules are verbally cumbersome does not mean that they are not basically simple. But simple or not, they are numerous; the generation of any single sentence requires the application of a very large num-

---

* It should be noted that any fact is by itself scientifically ambiguous. It could have stemmed from any number of possible causes, and any of a large, perhaps infinite number of theories that can account for *all* facts accurately. Part of the evaluation of a theory, then, rests on the question of what facts it makes you look for. The fact that transformational theory suggested that an experimenter go out and look for those facts is evidence in favor of the theory, despite the fact that other theories could explain it as well. Those theories did not suggest that we find the fact, hence they acquire less status by its demonstration.

ber of these rules. By what psychological means can this take place?

Let us go even further. The application of the grammatical rules is generally unconscious. Even the optional transformations we are aware of only dimly. We are aware of the difference between the active and passive. But under ordinary circumstances we are not aware of making the choice of the particular option, nor are we usually aware of what the rule is. We are only aware of the *result* of applying the rule. In general, then, the average speaker can correctly identify active and passive sentences, or correctly give examples of them. But he cannot tell you the rule for converting one into the other. The rules themselves are unconscious. At best only the results of the optional transformations enter one's awareness. A complete psychological theory of grammar must account for these phenomenological facts.

Finally, we have certain temporal difficulties. We have the fact that the child quite rapidly acquires the capacity to utter sentences. While these are not always correct by an adult grammar, they are correct enough to be understood. He is following some of the rules of language. Was he not, the child would simply utter random strings of words. Grammar is, after all, the set of rules or constraints which define the non-random aspects of language. The fact that any string of words is not random is de facto evidence for the existence of some sort of grammar.

The child learns rules and he learns them rapidly. Even more striking is the ease with which he, and the adult as well, applies these rules. A vocalized sentence can quite literally be generated in a split second. It can be generated with no thought on the part of the speaker, and with no hesitation. And it is more often than not a grammatically correct sentence also. This is an amazing feat of skill when you stop to think about it. No psychological theory is going to find this an easy skill to explain. The question for the moment is this: can a theory as complex as the transformation theory account for the *ease* of using language?

The Critical Period: Chomsky (1964) has faced, in part, the problem of the acquisition of grammar. He recognizes how difficult it will be to account for the acquisition of grammatical rules, particularly during the time span in which they are in fact acquired. This difficulty becomes exceptionally great if one is bound to a trial and error theory of learning of the sort espoused by most contemporary learning theorists. He removes himself from the difficulty in a most startling way: he says, in effect, that grammar is innate.

It seems not unlikely that the organism brings, as its contribution to acquisition of a particular language, a highly restrictive characterization of a class of generative systems (potential theories) from which the grammar of its language is selected on the basis of the presented linguistic data (Chomsky, 1964, p. 112).

Specifically, what we might apparently envision is a sort of grammatical *critical period*. The concept of a critical period is one derived originally in the study of instincts in the lower animals. It appears that certain instinctual behaviors are acquired in a peculiar manner. During a particular stage of development, the animal suddenly achieves the readiness or capacity to perform some particular behavior. If a specific stimulus occurs during this critical period of readiness, the animal will emit the behavior and will thereafter continue to emit it whenever the stimulus is presented. It should be noted that the stimuli in question are quite specific and that they do not "force" the behavior out of the animal. Rather they provide the necessary conditions for the behavior. They are *releasing stimuli*, to use the quite descriptive term originated by Tinbergen (1951). If the necessary releasing stimuli do not occur in the animal's environment during the critical period—for there is an end to this period of readiness—then the behavior will not occur in the future, at least not as a reaction to these stimuli.

Let us consider a specific example, the so-called *fixation* of the barnyard fowl—chickens, ducks, geese, etc. By fixation we refer to the behavior of the young in following some adult member of the species, usually the mother. The following of the mother by the long string of ducklings, so striking to behold, is an instinctive behavior in the most ordinary sense of that term. All duck-lings do it under normal conditions. In fact this behavior develops as follows (Ramsey and Hess, 1954): from about ten hours fol-lowing birth until about seventeen hours following birth, the Mallard duckling is in a critical period. Any moving object which he is permitted to follow he will fixate on. Moving objects prior to this time will not produce fixation; the first moving object during the critical period will be the one fixated upon. Normally, of course, the first moving object will be another member of the same species. In most cases this will be the mother, who is on the nest. In the laboratory, however, we can produce abnormal fixations. Ducklings have been thus fixated on inanimate objects or on the human experimenter, for example. Once fixated, they follow the specific object of their fixation throughout their youth. At sexual maturity, they attempt to mate with a member of the species on which they have fixated. If the moving stimulus oc-curs prior to the critical period, it will not lead to fixation. If it does not occur until after the critical period no fixation will take place. In the duck, this means that he will not flock with other ducks, nor will he mate with them. Normally, this means that he will die.

The critical period concept hypothesizes a specific time during which learning can take place. Before or after this time, learning is no longer possible. But of even greater importance, during the critical period, the learning is both rapid and permanent. It is in some cases what some psychologists might call one-trial learn-ing; one presentation of the stimulus is all that is required to attach it to the correct response. If we could presume a "gram-matical" critical period in this sense, we would clearly be in a most fortunate position.

It is not immediately clear how such a critical period would operate. Since the grammatical transformations involved in dif-ferent languages would appear to be at least partially different, there can be no possibility of *specific* innate grammatical trans-formation, or even of readinesses for specific transformations. Grammar, in this sense, must be learned; it is the exposure to a particular language which makes one acquire the transformations for that particular language.* But it is here that the conceptual difficulty arises, for it is not easy to fit the notion of a generalized readiness for grammatical transformations into the notion of a critical period. The critical periods with which we are familiar in psychology tend to be about highly specific things. If there is a generalized readiness or critical period, it is of a different sort than that with which we are familiar. But we must be sure to realize that the uniqueness of the concept does not make it wrong.

One of the implications of this critical period notion is that language must be learned within a specific period of time; we would guess that this period would have to be between approximately the second and fourth years of life. This period is that during which the normal child in any society masters the language of that society. Presumably if he does not learn it by then, he never will. We therefore can make the prediction that one cannot (really) learn a second language, becoming bi- or multi-lingual, unless one learns those other languages during this time also. This prediction follows from the notion of the critical period which assumes that the "learning" must take place during a specified time and *cannot* take place after that time. But this prediction would appear to be contrary to the facts.

There appear to be many people who are bilingual and who have not acquired their second language until relatively late in life. In some cases the second language may even have been learned in school. Now one might argue, of course, that having acquired the transformations of one's native language would

---

* The grammar that is learned in school is, of course, simply a routine for describing the grammar that is already acquired by the speaker of the language. It is an unsatisfactory description at that, for it only deals with the most superficial aspects of grammar. School grammar, for example, never teaches that the verb auxiliary must precede the verb. It needs no teaching for everyone automatically does it; yet, this is clearly an aspect of grammar, as is all word ordering. School grammar teaches those aspects of grammar about which people make "mistakes." It teaches them "correct" English. Therefore, it follows from what we said earlier, that school grammar teaches the child the class structure of the society in which he lives and nothing of any real significance about language.

facilitate this more conscious acquisition of the transformations of the second language. But an even more serious and more ambiguous question can be raised. One is tempted to pose it this way: have they "really" learned the second language? To be more specific, we have assumed in this book that the acquisition of a language alters the basic mental structure of the individual. The mechanisms and devices of the language become part of the mechanisms and devices of his "mind," his awareness, his personality, or what have you. Moreover, they become basic in the sense that they cannot be taken away or distinguished from non-linguistic mechanisms in the operation of the individual's psychic structure. Now we can ask, does the second language have this sort of basic "mental" influence that the first language does, or is it somehow more superficial?

Asked in this manner the question is both meaningful and significant. But it is also nearly impossible to answer. It is clear that the critical-period theory of grammar acquisition would have to predict that at some level one could not become "really" bilingual unless this were done at a very early age. The apparent bilingualism of many adults would appear to contradict this hypothesis unless one makes some interpretation of "true" bilingualism like that proposed above. But if one makes this interpretation, we will have some uncomfortable facts. Short of the difficulty of acquiring a perfect accent, most bilinguals can perform quite nicely in the second language. The necessary grammatical mechanisms are at their disposal. How are they acquired? They must be learned by rote, consciously or in some manner unlike the critical-period learning of grammar. The postulation of the critical period will also require the postulation of processes for the more traditional learned acquisition of grammar. But if standard learning will account for the learning of the second language, why do we need to postulate the critical period? Why assume two processes if one can be shown to account for the facts? Or does pronunciation argue for a critical-period hypothesis, while the rest of grammar can be said to be more traditionally learned?

But what are the facts? Chomsky is faced with an enormously

complex logical system which he feels the speaker must absorb, somehow, in order to be able to speak grammatically. The only way he can understand how such a staggering amount of material could be accounted for would be to build it into the individual in some way—the critical period is one such possibility. But if we pay less attention to logical elegance and more to psychological data, perhaps this issue does not arise.

We see that, in fact, the transformational theory leaves many psychological issues of grammar aside. It does not, for example, attempt to account for the unawareness of grammatical principles which most speakers have. Of even greater importance, it does not seem to *really* account for the way people *speak* or *use* language. In fact, people *do* make grammatical errors. Their use of the language violates, at times, the rules of the language. We can accept this statement as true since they themselves will tell us that they have made mistakes. I may, for example, utter a sentence in which the subject and the verb do not agree in number. I will often become aware of this error and, verbally, go back and correct it. Such grammatical mistakes may have a low probability, but they have a high frequency of occurrence, nevertheless.

Granted that such grammatical errors often seem to occur in relatively complex sentences, we still are faced with a difficulty: the transformational system of grammar does not account for this possibility of errors. By definition, it is a system for deriving all grammatical sentences and *only* grammatical sentences. But by the usual operational definitions of grammatical correctness (whether or not a speaker of the language says that the sentence is acceptable in the language) people do not always talk correctly. The logical conclusion of this is inevitable: they do not follow transformational grammar. More likely, they do not use transformations (psychologically) in the way in which Chomsky has proposed. But if we are to reject the transformation system, despite its logical elegance and its ability to account for many linguistic facts, what are we to put in its place?

Perhaps the best place to start is by questioning the entire assumption underlying all of the theory presented in this chapter. We have assumed that there is *a* grammatical system underlying the use of language. The fact that all of language may be described by the rules of one system (after the fact, as it were), does not constitute evidence for the hypothesis that the behavior in question is *produced* by one system alone. Perhaps there are several grammatical systems. Each grammar would be relatively simple and restricted in its use, but each grammar would have to have certain commonalities with the others so that one could call the results of each the same language. Psychologically, however, they could be quite different mechanisms. In such a case the apparent complexity of grammar could be the result of simply lumping together the results of many simple, but different, grammars.

This may seem farfetched: but I do not think it actually is. Let us look at the use of language again. Fries has indicated that a vocabulary of only a few hundred words would allow one to understand most of the telephone conversations which take place in normal circumstances. A further analysis would unquestionably show that the sentences of these conversations were quite short, and that they were grammatically simple. The use of subjunctive clauses, parenthetical remarks, and the like is quite rare in such conversations. If someone introduces a complex sentence into a situation such as that, one thing will almost invariably result— the listener will say, "What did you say?" The unexpected—in this case, the grammatically unusual—is not understood and a repetition is required for the listener to comprehend it.

In other situations, the style of the language may be totally different. In professional speaking and writing, for instance, sentence complexity is not only usual, it is even "required." The scholarliness of speaking and writing is identified by the grammatical complexity of its presentation. Certain classes of simple sentences are not only not used, they are "incorrect." In psychology journals, for example, we will find the frequent use of constructions such as, "One might feel that. . . ." and the like, rather than the everyday equivalent, "I feel. . . ." The purported objectivity of science* frowns on first-person statements as being less valid than the consensually validated third-person statement.

* An objectivity which appears quite dubious to some. The interested reader is referred to M. Polanyi, *Personal Knowledge*, 1958.

In another case, the poet uses language in a way which defies grammatical description at times and yet in a way which is universally regarded as a legitimate and comprehensible use of the language.

It is customary to refer to these different sorts of uses of the language as *styles*—and to assume that they are unrelated to the problems of grammar—since the latter is a system which may account for all styles.

As an alternative, let us assume that a difference in style quite clearly signifies a difference in the grammatical rules with which the speaker is operating. That any individual speaker of any language may operate and process language which is presented to him in several different styles indicates that he has several different grammatical systems at his disposal. This in itself is important for psychology. But even more important is that each of these systems will be logically simpler than some single system which attempts to describe all of them at once. Not only that, the simple systems will be considerably more real, psychologically, than will the complex. As an example, we could assume that in a "telephone situation" the person will be equipped with a system which will produce simple declarative sentences and simple questions and little else. At the typewriter, the same individual may be under the control of a system which produces only complex, multi-claused sentences and which is incapable of producing simple ones. This latter system probably produces complex sentences directly, not by derivation from the simpler ones which can be logically analyzed from them.* Phrase-structure grammar assumes, of course, that the complex is built from the simple. Our argument says that the complex can be produced by itself. But we still have not offered a mechanism by which any sentence can be constructed, much less a complex one.

We must start with certain "stimulus" factors. Essentially

---

* Many things can be analyzed into parts. This analysis is real and valid, but does not necessarily support any genetic arguments. Thus, the fact that perceptions can be analyzed into sensations does not mean that perception is ontogenetically constituted by sensations. And the fact that complex sentences can be analyzed into simple ones does not mean that the complex were constructed out of the union of simple ones.

there are two sets of stimuli acting at any given moment of time
on the individual; those which arise from outside him, and those
which arise from within. The latter we have come to see as produced by motivational or intentional determinants. In order that
the individual utter a sentence, both of these factors—the internal
and the external—will be operative and will determine the nature
of the sentence uttered. Thus, for example, in order for the individual to speak at all, the internal stimuli must be such that
they give rise to readinesses to respond (engrams) involving the
organs of speech; commonsensically this means that the individual wants (though not necessarily on a conscious level) to
speak. The external stimuli will partially determine what he
speaks about, in a number of ways. The content of the sentence
will, of course, be relevant to the current environmental conditions, including what others are saying to him. The environment
of the individual includes his own internal environment, his intentions and the like, and they too may be reflected in the content of an utterance. Certain grosser features as well determine
the features of the utterance, particularly its grammatical form.
Thus, the individual will often respond to a question with a
declarative sentence, and we can assume that at some level this
sentence form is conditioned to the stimuli arising from a question.* Likewise, at some level the grammar of the telephone is
associated to "telephone situations," the grammar of the professional journal to "journal" situations and so on. To have any
merit, our theory must account for the details of this association
since all we have done so far is to restate obvious facts; nothing
has been explained.

Let us assume that the individual in his normal environment
is in a state of readiness to speak. That is, the stimulus conditions
are such that they have normally been followed by talking. In

---

* One might ask how a question is perceived as a question so that one is required to answer it. Within the scope of the theory presented, perception is
a function of action. Thus, utterances can be perceived as questions and will
be so perceived only if the person is capable of using that grammatical
form. Hence, the major issue remains how the individual *utters* the various
grammatical forms.

addition, the stimulus conditions provide him with certain possible contents for speech. That is, the readiness to say certain specific words has been aroused by the environment.* To understand this process, then, we must understand the readiness to speak, and to do this we must go back to simpler forms of behavior.

It is customary in psychology to talk of *acts*, which are generally conceived of as goal directed behaviors; that is, these are behaviors which are defined in terms of the ends they achieve. Taylor (1962), in the presentation of his theory, is faced with the problem of getting from the muscular movements, which are the basis of his theory, to acts which seem to characterize adult life so completely. For the adult, behavior is oriented toward a goal. When one learns to go to a goal, one learns to get there, if not by one way then by another. But movements themselves have no goal. Hence, Taylor assumes that movements which terminate in the same position and, hence, produce the same kinesthetic stimuli in their terminal state becomes a functional unit, which we can call a simple act. The animal can learn eventually to go to *a* from other points, rather than just to move from *b* to *a*, for example. Given "act" learning, if we put him at *c*, he may stand a good chance of getting to *a* also. Presumably after a considerable history (months) of moving, the child will increasingly organize his movements into acts. One of the remarkable powers of Taylor's position is that he can demonstrate that the organization of behavior will facilitate further organization along the same lines. Learning one act will facilitate the learning of a second. The result is that the organization becomes simpler and simpler—more natural—over time.

* It is not necessarily correct to say that the individual is aware of what he wants to say, or to associate these readinesses with ideas or the like. In general, most people do not think about what they are going to say. In general, it is most often correct to say that they do not know what they want to say until they have said it. Awareness depends not on the presence of an engram but on the presence of a multiplicity of engrams. Thus, a readiness for a particular speech act may be aroused but not be a content of awareness if it is essentially a solitary engram, which may often be the case, particularly if the intentional stimuli require it.

Now then, once we have permitted acts, we can speak of speech acts; the readiness to speak will consist in the readiness to make a speech act, where each speech act must have some common terminus. Let us be more specific and concrete and assume that the speech acts in question are noun phrases and verbs. We are assuming that the individual is in a situation where the stimuli are eliciting a "declarative sentence" readiness to speak. More precisely, we are assuming that the stimuli elicit a readiness to utter a noun phrase. We can call a noun phrase a speech act as long as we can defend the notion that all noun phrases have a common terminus; that the stimuli resulting from the conclusion of a noun phrase have some common property. This means, of course, that all nouns must have some common property since the noun is the terminal utterance in the noun phrase. If we can defend the theory that nouns have common properties, then, it would appear, we might defend this entire notion of a grammar based on association.

It is a fact that the parts of speech have no common physical properties by which they may be identified. Following Fries, parts of speech can be given functional definitions. But these will certainly not suit us. We cannot explain *why* something functions as a noun by appealing to the fact that it *does* function as a noun. Moreover, we are faced with the at first appalling fact that any word in the English language can function as a noun. As an example take /"of" is a preposition/. But to get bogged down in this sort of morass would be quite unnecessary. We are first of all concerned with getting the *child* to learn to talk; his talk, by definition, is childish. It is that out of which adult talk grows, but it certainly does not require us to explain adult talk as though it sprang full grown from the head of the child. Children do not use all words as nouns. They largely use those which fulfill the grade-school definition—a noun is the name of a person, place, or thing. More precisely, the original nouns are those words associated with objects, and somewhat later, to all functional units in the child's world. An object is something which the child can manipulate, and later, anything which functions as a unit. It must be perceived as a functional unit to be an object and for its "name" to function as a noun. Hence, we occasionally see difficulties with certain proper names in children, particularly, "obvious" names such as those for cities, states, and countries, which have no obvious functional significance for the child— if they do for anyone. The terminal point, the common characteristic of the noun for the child is that of manipulation and use. The utterance of a noun calls up engrams appropriate to the objective referent itself; these engrams all have readiness to respond to the object as a totality, to have it move as a totality, etc. Hence all nouns have a common property of "seen" movement or function.

We could continue ad infinitum. Childish verbs probably have the property of readiness for the child himself to move, etc. Given the fact that for the child nouns, verbs, and the like *do* have common properties, we can account for the conditioning of sentence forms. A consideration of the grammatical errors made by children will help us in this. Thus, for example, a grammar must account for sentences of the form, noun phrase plus verb plus noun phrase. But which particular noun phrase comes first will determine whether the verb is written in the active or passive voice. We see by observation that the child utters active sentences long before passive. Indeed, I have heard children use a passive noun-phrase arrangement with an active verb—making a grammatical error in the process. Such an error involves saying something like /The boy bites the dog./ when in fact the dog was biting the boy. To use the passive properly, indeed to understand the words properly, he must acquire the notion that there is a *directionality* attached to the verb. Given this, he can then use the appropriate verb form no matter which noun phrase happens to come first. But directionality is also an action tendency and, hence, is expressible in our engram form.

Language becomes more and more complex, but it does not originate that way. While any word may function as a noun for an adult, they may not do so for the child. He must learn nouns by a simple definition. Thus, when he has learned that *words* are objects too, he can use any word as a noun. But even here the childish basis of the grammar remains.* The point is that grammar develops. It starts simply and becomes complex. But each successive complexity becomes less complex because the preceding simplicities have been mastered.

We see that grammar, because the use of its rules is a function of stimuli and stimuli are ambiguous, will never be infallible. The individual will make mistakes, and a close consideration of the stimuli, both environmental and verbal, will probably reveal the reasons for these mistakes. We should point out that the consideration of grammar in developmental, associational terms does not completely invalidate the Chomsky approach. Indeed, we have made use of this phrase-structure analysis. A fair reason for the choice of phrase structure is that the normal patterns and cadences of speech support such an analysis. The pauses in speech seem to fall in the places where the structural members join, as if the speaker were filling in one structure at a time, as we have suggested that he is.

Finally, we see that most of grammar will not be conscious. That is, the readiness to utter a noun phrase will involve a single, particular, ordered act of speech controlled by a single engram. No other engrams—which would be readinesses to produce other orderings—will be present. Since there are no multiple engrams present, there will be no awareness of the ordering principle. There will, of course, be awareness of the utterance and *its* order as objects of perception. But the determinants of the form of the utterance of the sentence itself generally exist on a level not open to the awareness of the speaker.

We cannot develop this theory more fully. We have given only an outline which must be filled in in considerable detail before one can feel with any certainty that the position is completely valid. But it does appear to show more promise for the psychol-

---

* Since, we have argued, the real perception of the word as an object comes with writing, grammatical theories would develop only in literate societies. It does seem that many literate—but independent—cultures have developed and studied formal grammars, while (to my knowledge) no preliterate cultures have.

ogist than do any of the other contemporary approaches to grammar.

Up to this point we have considered language in the normal individual. For a fuller understanding, we must now consider some of the abnormalities of language. This we shall do in the next chapter.

Bibliography

Chomsky, N. *Syntactic structures*. The Hague, Mouton, 1957.

Chomsky, N. *Current issues in linguistic theory*. The Hague, Mouton, 1964.

Dollard, J., and Miller, N. *Personality and psychotherapy*. New York, McGraw-Hill, 1950.

Freud, S. *The ego and the id*. New York, W. W. Norton, 1960.

Fries, C. C. *The structure of English*. New York, Harcourt, Brace & World, 1952.

Johnson, N. F. The psychological reality of phrase structure rules. *J. verb Learn. ver. Beh.*, 1965, 4, 469-75.

Miller, G. Some psychological studies of grammar. *Amer. Psychologist*, 1962, 17, 748-62.

Miller, G., and Selfridge, J. Verbal context and the recall of meaningful material. *Amer. J. Psychol.*, 1953, 63, 176-85.

Polanyi, M. *Personal knowledge: towards a post-critical philosophy*. Chicago, University of Chicago Press, 1958.

Ramsey, A. O., and Hess, E. H. A laboratory approach to the study of imprinting. *Wilson Bull.*, 1954, 66, 196-206.

Taylor, J. G. *The behavioral basis of perception*. New Haven, Yale University Press, 1962.

Tinbergen, N. *The study of instinct*. London, Oxford University Press, 1951.

VIII
Language Disturbances

Language disturbances may be grouped into two categories: those which stem from organic causes and those which are functional in origin. These two categories correspond to the traditional psychological division of mental disturbances in general. The organic disturbances are presumably due to some wound or injury to the central nervous system itself, while the functional disorders are "psychological" in nature. That is, they are learned or in some sense a product of the individual's life experience. The Freudian hypothesis that neurosis often stems from some emotionally traumatic experience is an example of the latter sort of thinking.

This division is somewhat oversimplified at best. To the extent that we assume a physiological process underlying all psychological events, then all the functional disorders have an organic base. But these disturbances are not due to an injury to the central nervous system, at least in the normal sense of that term— although we may choose to call a malfunctioning nervous system an injured one. Likewise, the presence of an organic wound in the nervous system does not mean that the wound per se produces the symptoms observed. The wound affects the functioning of the nervous system, making the disturbances observed in that sense functional. But in addition, the individual *reacts* to the knowledge that he has the wound, which produces other "functional" disturbances that are "due" to the wound but not directly caused by it. As you can see, an organic-functional distinction is arbitrary. We shall be arbitrary, for ease of presentation if nothing else.

Functional Disturbances

We shall start with the functional disturbances, since we propose to treat them much more lightly than the organic. We do find many severe disorders of language which are due to functional disturbances. Some forms of stuttering are perhaps the most common examples of such disturbances. But, in fact, we know very little about these disturbances other than that they are not organic. Even the nature of functional symptoms, the *particular* disorders of actual language behavior, have not been well recorded in many cases. All we can offer is some generalities, which are of some interest, but by no means completely conclusive. In addition, we have the problem that the diagnostic categories for functional disturbances are often vague, ambiguous, and fluctuating. Schizophrenia, for example, is a mental disturbance which commonly produces extreme functional language disturbances. Yet there is no hard and fast rule about what makes someone a schizophrenic, not only in terms of how he got that way, but in terms of how he behaves when he is that way. The various subtypes of schizophrenia are even more vaguely defined. There is no assurance that any particular typology is the most fruitful or correct one. Hence, to say that schizophrenics show such-and-such behavior may be totally misleading if one is trying to understand either the nature of mental disturbance or the nature of language. But we must start somewhere, so let it be with schizophrenia.[*]

Schizophrenia is that disturbance which is commonly referred

[*] There is a division of opinion in psychiatric circles about whether schizophrenia is an organic or functional disturbance. We cannot settle this issue, but since schizophrenia involves no *obvious* organic injuries, we will retain the classification of it as functional.

to as "split personality." By this, we do not mean that the individual thinks he is more than one person, or that he has two or more individual lives (that would be called multiple personality), but that his personality is split from reality in some manner or other. The schizophrenic lives in "his own little world" which has little or no contact with the everyday social world of the "normal" people around him. His world is often characterized by extreme delusions and hallucinations. He takes his fantasy life as being as real as the real world; he sees and hears things which are not there because his thinking of them is perhaps more real than if they were there. He is the inhabitant of the violent wards; he is the human vegetable seen squatting in his own urine in the corridors of the mental hospitals; he is the man who thinks he is Napoleon; he is at present virtually incurable.

It is not surprising that a person as withdrawn from social contact as is the schizophrenic would show disturbances in his use of language; for language is, after all, a social behavior by definition. It is difficult to provide an accurate description of the sorts of language disturbances we find, perhaps because they have not been described accurately, and perhaps because there is no single symptom to point to. At the most obvious and global level, we find that it is almost impossible to talk to schizophrenics. They do not use words in the same way that the more socially oriented person does. The meanings which they give to words are idiosyncratically rather than consensually defined. Thus the therapist, approaching schizophrenia with his stock instruments—all of which are verbal—finds it impossible to do anything. One cannot psychoanalyze schizophrenics, because one cannot talk to them; and talk is the basis of most contemporary therapies.*

* In part this may be the therapist's problem. Laing (1965) suggests that much of the observed pathology in schizophrenic speech may be due to the hostility of the patient toward the therapist for not understanding him, for treating him as a "case" rather than as a person. In other words, the symptoms may be a function of the clinical situation as much as the pathology itself.

A study of the meaning system of a particular schizophrenic can throw considerable light on his personality structure. But its particulars will be of little use in understanding the next schizophrenic. Moreover, it may be exceptionally difficult for the "normal" individual to use language in the way that the schizophrenic does. So even understanding what he means by a word does not guarantee that one will be able to communicate with him.

Beyond this global linguistic problem, we often see more specific difficulties. Cameron (1964) has reported extensively on the fact that in schizophrenic language, words often seem to come out all mixed up together. The usual normal grammatical rules of ordering are lacking or disturbed, as are any divisions of words into separate utterances expressing separate ideas. The schizophrenic seems merely to spout words. Typically, it would seem that the words are mainly those of the major form classes. The function words which serve the purpose of ordering and relating words to each other are missing. It is, of course, the use of the function words which makes language an instrument of communication, for the function words are verbalizations of the consensually valid rules of ordering and relating substantive words. The "word salad" and the loss of function words logically follows, then, from the schizophrenic's not using language in a socially valid manner generally.

Another way of describing the schizophrenic "language" is to borrow a term from the psychiatrist Harry Stack Sullivan (1964) and call it *parataxic*. Sullivan hypothesizes that all human experience can fall into one of three modes. The most primitive mode is called *prototaxic*, in which

[e]xternal events and their internal consequences are perceived dimly, are organized in a primitive manner, and may be reacted to through primitive signals before their actual development is at all sharply comprehended. . . . These states are much more generalized ("cosmic") than will be the case later on. They are not organized serially in time or related to the yet unformed distinction between the self and the outside world (Munroe, 1955, p. 399).

The prototaxic mode is developmentally prior to the other two and is necessary in that the other two develop out of this type of experience. It is essentially prelinguistic.

The next mode of experience is the parataxic mode.

It is characteristic of the parataxic mode . . . that the various percepts and symbols and more or less differentiated kinds of experience are not yet connected with one another in an orderly way. They exist side by side. . . . Each symbol has its own referent, which may be entirely disconnected from other symbols that are logically very close for the objectively minded outsider but that remain separate for the child, or for the adult in so far as he is operating in the parataxic mode. . . . The parataxic mode in childhood—and often later life—is further characterized by its *autistic* quality. The child naturally develops rather arbitrary, highly personalized symbols, which are not checked and tested against "reality" (Munroe, 1955, p. 401).

This mode is characteristic of the young child who is just developing language. Finally, out of this parataxic mode grows the mode of "normal" adult experience—with which we are presumably all familiar—and which Sullivan calls the *syntaxic* mode. As the name suggests, experience here is ordered and consensually validated. It follows the logic and rules of a grammar.

According to Sullivan, one matures through these various types of experience. But under abnormal conditions, particularly those of heightened anxiety, one may return or regress to a more immature level of experience. Thus, under threat, or during mental disturbance, the adult may leave the syntaxic mode of experience and return to the parataxic. This is apparently what the schizophrenic does, according to Sullivan. It is no coincidence that the description of the parataxic mode resembles that of the linguistic behavior of the schizophrenic, for Sullivan was one of the most astute students of schizophrenia. His developmental theory, in fact, stemmed from an attempt to account for this disease which he apparently viewed as a social pathology. Disturbed language was one of the defining characteristics of schizophrenia for Sullivan.

We have now entered the realm of theories of schizophrenia. In Sullivan we see an attempt to account for the disease by postulating that it involves, among other things, the immature use of language. How far one can extend this notion is somewhat debatable. Those patients—and there are some—who formulate their own languages, which may often be undecipherable by the doctors, do not appear to be too immature in their use of language. They are only disturbed. But theorizing about mental illness in terms of language is not confined to Sullivan, for the apparently essential connection between language and schizophrenia has occurred to most observers.

A somewhat different approach is presented by Bateson and others (1956), who attribute at least some mental disturbances to conflicts which are generated by or within the patient's language system. They refer to these conflicts as *double binds*, the characteristics of which are that words (or their referents in the physical world) acquire multiple and contradictory meanings which are of a highly emotional nature. To take a simplified example, imagine an environment in which the child learns to react to his mother in an emotionally ambiguous way. His mother is associated, to him, with love and protection; she feeds and cares for him. But she is also aggressive and hostile toward him, which produces in him reactions of hate. The word /mother/, then, will acquire at least these two response tendencies also— one which leads to reactions of love and one which leads to reactions of hate or aggression. The emotional significance of /mother/ is not only ambiguous, because of the ambivalence felt toward his mother, but it is contradictory, since we must assume that for the individual love and hate suggest incompatible modes of behavior. Until this point there is no real problem: probably everyone has words which have this contradictory emotional quality in his vocabulary. /Mother/ is very likely one of them. But now suppose that this individual's environment is one step further and forces *both* emotional reactions simultaneously. His mother may, for example, attack or threaten him and then immediately try to elicit protestations of love from him. Or she may react to his loving gestures as ag-

gressive and vice versa since both meanings are attached to the
same vehicles in this social world. It is clear that his perception
of his mother will tend to elicit simultaneously both emotional
reactions. And that his behaviors will be stunted since it is
literally impossible for him to do anything right. The word
/mother/ will likewise have this character for him; in fact, the
process might be acquired through the use of the word alone.
Anyway, as far as this person is concerned, he is attempting to
do two things at once or avoid both at once, which he cannot
possibly do. And these incompatible things are, by definition,
highly emotional for him. The resulting conflict, frustration or
what have you, will clearly be severe. To the extent that the
word is involved in this conflict situation, the emotional reaction
can be produced even in situations in which the physical environment does not warrant it. The word /mother/ alone will then
set off the conflict, and for the child, there is little distinction
between meaning (verbal) and perception, as we have indicated.
The result could easily become an almost unending conflict situation for the child, which could distort his personality for life.
Whether it will produce schizophrenia is another matter, but for
our purposes it is interesting to see how psychological disturbances might arise out of the sorts of meanings acquired by words,
if those words are used in peculiar ways.

The possibility of verbal or semantic determinants of mental
disturbance has received a different but interesting treatment
at the hands of the general semanticists, particularly Hayakawa
(1949) and Korzybski (1958). According to Hayakawa, any ambiguity in word meaning is a possible source of conflict. At the
very least, it can render the act of communication suspect. One
can too easily become misled by what others are saying. The
ambiguity of meaning leads to ambiguity in communication.
This in turn suggests that the entire basis of social interaction is
ambiguous and that there is no real contact or communication
between people. The society as a whole can become "sick" as a
result of this lack of interpersonal contact, and as a result of
the conflicts generated by the ambiguous meanings of words.

To rectify this sort of situation, Hayakawa suggests that we perform therapy on language itself. For example, language is often enough ambiguous about two things, *time* and the *object of reference*. That is, the use of the past tense—and sometimes even the present—does not specify the time period referred to except as being "before" now. Obviously /before/ itself is ambiguous since it might be two hours or two centuries before. Of course what is true of an individual at one period of his life, may not be true at some other period. But to say that a person "was so and so" is, in effect, to label him with this attribute for his entire past life. For clarity, then, one must specify the particular time period to which one refers. You must not just refer to Robert Terwilliger in general but must refer to Robert Terwilliger (1966) who is in all likelihood not completely identical to Robert Terwilliger of 1965.

In the case of reference we have a similar problem. If I mention /the cow/, it is not obvious what particular cow I am referring to unless the context itself provides the necessary definition. But if we have been talking about several specific cows, any reference to "the cow" is clearly ambiguous; I could be talking about any one of the particular cows we were discussing. The fact is, of course, that words are in some sense class names; they may be used in reference to all sorts of objects of the specific type. Words are not proper names; they do not single out individual members of the class for our consideration but refer helter-skelter to all members of the class. This can produce ambiguity, confusion, and conflict. The therapy is simple. One labels each individual member who is under discussion. We do not speak of /the cow/ but of /cow (1)/, /cow (2)/, etc.

Now it should be clear that Hayakawa has isolated a significant problem here—that is, that words can be used in numerous different ways. And it is a fact that this ambiguity can lead to misunderstandings—even to outright conflict and hostility under certain situations. The history of philosophy is filled with cases in point: certain philosophers use a word in one way while others use it a totally different way. Since each philosophic school works totally from within its own definition, the word of the other school appears nonsensical. Each accuses the other of misusing the word in question, if not of outright stupidity. Yet there is *no right* way of using a word; there are only different ways of using them. Clearly these conflicts are arbitrary and semantic in nature and involve a lack of comprehension that the same word may have a different use for another person and that this use is legitimate. Such conflicts can become emotional, to say the least, but insofar as they deal with academic problems this emotionality need cause no practical fears.

But unfortunately such conflicts are not confined to academic matters. Consider, for example, the term /peaceful coexistence/ which has been bandied about the international scene for some time. To the average citizen, this term clearly suggests something along the following lines: "You leave me alone and I'll leave you alone and we will not engage in any overt conflict whatsoever. We each have our spheres of influence and you stay out of mine and I'll stay out of yours—more or less." For the USSR, on the other hand, the meaning of this phrase seems to go something like this: "We will not have a war with you. We do not want a war under any circumstances. We will, however, attempt to get the better of you (bury you) in matters economic, both within and without our spheres of influence, and we will, of course, give our support to any revolutionary activities against you in any part of the world."*

Now what is the result of this? Let us assume for the sake of argument that both countries sincerely desire peaceful coexistence—as they see it, of course. It soon becomes obvious that from the point of view of our country the USSR is doing things which are not in line with "peaceful coexistence" as we see it. Since we apparently do not see or do not care to see the possibility that there might in fact be more than one way to interpret "peaceful coexistence," we immediately brand the USSR as treaty breakers, hypocrites, war agitators, and so on. For the moment, we can even ignore the fact that they are already labeled with "scurrilous" terms such as /communist/ and the like. To us, they are saying one thing and doing another. At this point,

* This is an *interpretation* from a hypothetical, average Western point of view. The real meaning of this term is much more complex.

the Russian clearly has the right to be puzzled when we get so upset about his doing something that we agreed to. He sees no more than one meaning to a word or phrase either, and so our actions appear to him to be hypocritical, war mongering, imperialistic, and so on. Carried to its extreme, it is not farfetched to think that a conflict situation of this order could lead to war and the eventual destruction of mankind.

Bearing in mind, then, the potential gravity of the symptom to which Hayakawa addresses himself—one which could also happen on an individual psychological level—we must still disagree with his solution. It does not appear that his treatment does sufficient justice to the nature of language. In fact, words *do* have multiple meanings and in fact they *must* have multiple meanings if they are to function as words. At some level ambiguity is a necessary condition for language. Without it no transmission of information could possibly take place. The fact that language can be used, the fact that it is general and infinite in its scope, necessitates that the words in that language *not* be restricted in their use to specific referents, temporal or objective. One can get the impression reading Hayakawa (perhaps erroneously) that he wishes to solve these linguistically generated problems by reducing language to a set of proper names. Yet, as we have indicated earlier, proper names have no real meaning. They cannot be the basis for a viable language. Hence this can be no solution to our problems, for the result would be worse than the problem; we would not communicate at all. A somewhat more realistic approach might be to say that people should have a fuller understanding of the nature of language. People would then be less likely to commit such semantic blunders. This may perhaps be the case but we cannot pursue the issue at present. We will return to it later.

What we have attempted to do here is to indicate some possible relationships between language and psychological disturbances. We have seen language treated both as a symptom of disturbance and as the potential cause of such disturbances. It is clear that such a consideration of language can shed light both on the nature of the disturbance and on the nature of language.

The words the "patient" uses reveal to us something about the disturbance from which he is suffering. The non-linguistic nature of the disturbance reveals to us something about the language he is using. It suggests what a language must be like in order to be used in this manner by the disturbed individual. But the most systematic and historically important study of language through disturbances concerns not the psychological disturbances but the physiological or organic ones.

Organic Disturbances

The type of language disturbance with which we will concern ourselves here is that commonly called *aphasia*. By "aphasia" we refer to several things. First, that the disturbance is initiated by some injury to the central nervous system. While the observed symptoms may be due to things other than this injury, we must assume that the injury plays some causal role in it. Second, we are talking about a disturbance in language; that is, we are not talking about disturbances in the sensory receptors necessary to hear or talk, nor about disturbances in the motor ability to talk. The aphasic can often enough hear and see perfectly. Moreover, he may make all sorts of noises and in many cases can use language to some degree. The disturbance lies in the fact that he cannot use language, either because he cannot comprehend speech (or writing) or because he cannot produce the sequences of sounds (or letters) necessary to utter language. Finally, we refer to a great cluster of specific symptoms ranging from almost total inability to speak to very slight disturbances in relatively specific aspects of language. It has been clear to most investigators that there are many types of asphasia; but unfortunately there is often little agreement about what those types are.

We will see that the study of aphasia is also a means to the study of the physiology of thinking, for underlying the problem of aphasia is the problem of how the central nervous system works. In particular we are faced with the issue of whether or not *specific functions*, such as speaking, are located in *specific* *areas* of the brain or the cortex.* Thus, to do anything like an adequate job of discussing aphasia, we must also delve into some physiological issues. We will see that physiologists have become more and more linguistically oriented as they have studied this problem, as indeed linguists have become increasingly concerned with this physiologically derived issue.

We may begin with the two cases reported by the nineteenth-century French physician, Broca. He presented evidence obtained from two patients, both men, suffering from wounds in the head. Their behavioral symptoms, as reported by Broca, involved severe disturbances in the use and comprehension of language with no apparent injury to either the sensory or motor organs or nerves. In at least one case the actual speech of the patient was limited to a very few words with which he could express something about agreement, size, or numerosity, and emotional arousal. But he could in no case apparently utter a complete, well-organized sentence. His understanding of spoken language was, apparently, better than his production of it. From this brief picture it is not at all clear what sorts of general intellectual deficits the patient might have been suffering from, or whether, in fact, his only disturbance was in language. Following the death of the two patients their brains were studied, and from this examination Broca concluded that the injury in both patients was localized in the third frontal convolution of the cerebral cortex.†

Broca concluded from this evidence that the speech mechanism was localized in a particular place in the brain—specifically in the third frontal convolution, which was henceforward known as Broca's area, or as the motor speech center. These findings ap-

* The cerebral cortex, or "grey matter" of the brain is actually six layers of unmyelinated cells which covers the cerebrum.

† The cerebrum is customarily divided into four lobes. These are (1) the occipital lobe located in the back of the brain (skull), (2) the parietal lobe located in front of the occipital and on the top part of the brain, (3) the temporal lobes, each of which lie on the side of the cerebrum approximately over each ear, and (4) the frontal lobe which lies in the front (forehead) area of the brain. The frontal and parietal lobes are separated by a major fissure in the cortex known as the central sulcus.

peared at the time to be decisive evidence for the concept of specific localization of brain function, a theory which many upheld but for which there had been little conclusive evidence. Prior to this time the only evidence for the specific localization of functions in the brain came from Gall and his school of phrenologists. While Gall's theory was both elegant and sophisticated, his methods of diagnosing brain functions from bumps on the skull (a large brain area indicated high skill in that function and meant that a large bump would be needed to contain that larger part of the brain) were justifiably suspect. At one stroke Broca appeared to be able to consign a specific function—speech—to a specific area of the brain.

With this impetus, a multitude of theories of aphasia and its kindred disorders were advanced, all based on the notion that for specific functions there are specific cortical loci, and that an injury in a specific area of the cortex will produce a specific set of symptoms. Both symptoms and cortical areas proliferated. Thus while Broca started with about three categories, we end with a multitude. To be specific, Broca spoke of *motor aphasia* which was the inability to produce spoken language. The patient of this disorder cannot say words. *Verbal amnesia*, on the other hand, signifies a disorder in which the patient can produce words, he can speak, but he cannot recognize or cannot respond to the connection between the word and its referent. In some sense he does not know what the word means. Thirdly, we have *agraphia* in which the patient is unable to write; that is, he cannot integrate words into sentences or letters into words, although there is no apparent paralysis or disorder to the motor nerves themselves. These are all central disturbances.

To Broca's list we find that Bastian added *word deafness* and *word blindness* which, as the names suggest, indicate an inability to comprehend spoken or written words as the case may be. But here as in the prior case, there is no apparent sensory malfunction. The individual can, supposedly, hear and see as well as he could normally. His acuity is fine, but spoken or written symbols have lost their meanings for him. Henschen goes even further and adds a host of things including *visual* and *auditory agnosia* (the inability to recognize spoken or written words or symbols), *alexia* (the inability to read), *acalculia* (the inability to perform arithmetic operations), *amusia* (the inability to comprehend music), and so on. Underlying all of this classification of symptoms lies the assumption that for each class we will find a corresponding cortical area which controls the function. In most cases, however, no direct evidence for the existence of these cortical areas is offered.

The cortical theorists of a similar persuasion tended to propose alternate theories. Wernicke, for example, postulated essentially four areas in the cortex—that is, four with which he concerns himself. There is the auditory area, the visual area, the motor speech center, and the motor writing center. These various centers interconnected so that the person can write what he hears, say what he reads, and the like. From such a structural hypothesis we can derive a set of possible disturbances. Injuries to the sensory areas will produce the sensory aphasias, agnosias, or amnesias. Injuries to the motor areas will produce the agraphia, Broca's aphasia, and the like. Injuries to the connections between areas will produce certain disturbances in the manipulation of words; one will not be able to switch from one mode to another, or organize words properly. Finally, of course, injuries can be so extensive that total aphasia results in which the patient, apparently cannot do anything linguistic at all.

Wernicke's school provides us with a particularly interesting example of the results of pure theorizing, without sufficient regard for data at any level. These men had a firm conception of how the brain *should* function, namely as a set of specific areas, each of which performed a certain highly specific role. They naturally enough interpreted their available physiological data in this light, although such an interpretation was not logically required by the data. But this is no crime nor is it any different from what any scientist does when he theorizes about data. But it is important to realize that Wernicke's school treated as discrete symptoms things which had only been observed as parts of more global symptoms.

What we find, in looking at aphasia, is that the individual is disturbed in several areas simultaneously. While there may be, in fact, one symptom which is so obvious that one is tempted to classify the patient in that particular category, closer inspection reveals that he will always have other disturbances as well. Thus, it would be rare indeed for the motor aphasic not to be affected in his writing as well. In addition, his comprehension of language will doubtless also be affected. To reverse the situation, the agraphic will also show speech deficits. The person who cannot comprehend arithmetic will likely not be able to comprehend music either, or for that matter, many sorts of abstract activity. The point is this: any one of the symptoms these investigators reported are in fact observed in patients. These disturbances do exist. But they do not exist as isolated symptoms. Aphasia appears as a more global disorder.

To a localist, however, any specific symptom must be the sign of a particular injury in a particular spot. If two symptoms are observed, then two spots are injured. Clearly by looking at patients, then, one can never disprove the localist's position. But one has the right to ask him why is it that symptoms *always* appear in clusters and never isolated as the theory would predict? In fact, it would appear to be correct to say that these diseases do not exist; they are the products of a theory and not observable facts. And, unfortunately, the theory is wrong. It gives a totally distorted and erroneous picture of the nature of aphasia, and it stems from a totally erroneous conception of the brain and how it works.

Let us look at the physiological evidence. To begin with, we find by re-examining the brains of the patients observed by Broca which were fortunately preserved, that the injuries are by no means as highly localized as Broca reports. There is a chunk of cortex missing in the third frontal convolution just as Broca reports. But the damage is not restricted to this area. It is now known that the nerve fibres in the brain tend to run up and down; that is, they run from the center of the brain (subcortex) up to the cortex and back down to the subcortex. It is not surprising to find, then, that an injury to the cortex will produce considerable damage to subcortical areas, first to the fibres connected to the particular cortical area, then, by atrophy, to fibres connected with the latter, and so on. An injury can in such a manner spread out to cover a considerable area of the brain, much of which is, of course, subcortical. That is exactly the state of Broca's patients. Their actual neurological damage is extensive and by no means can be said to be localized in a specific spot.

We have, by now, considerable evidence against the notion of specific localization of highly specialized functions. Part of this evidence is behavioral and stems from the fact that indeed one can retrain aphasics in the use of language. Since there is apparently little regrowth of injured brain tissue, the only way in which we can account for this is to assume that some other area of the brain is taking over a function performed previously by the injured area. This implies, of course, that in fact there is little necessity that a particular area perform a particular function.

Aside from this rather inferential data, we have a body of direct physiological experiments which refute the notion of highly specific localization of function. Much of this research has been conducted in an attempt to demonstrate that the brain functions as a totality and that all of the brain is involved in all higher mental functions. The general results of this research indicate that within the specific lobes of the brain are located definite but highly general functions. Thus, for the occipital lobe we find the following: this lobe controls vision and visual discriminations.* If the occipital lobe is removed, we have a blind organism, and an organism incapable of performing any visual discriminations except those based on brightness. All previously acquired visual discriminations are lost to him, and no amount of retraining following the ablation will permit the reacquisition of these discriminations. If, however, only a part of the lobe is missing, we find that the loss to visually acquired habits is roughly pro-

---

* Specifically it controls all visual discriminations except those of brightness. The latter are under the control of the superior colliculi, which are subcortical centers.

portional to the amount of cortical loss. And, in such cases, if any reasonable amount of the occipital cortex remains, it is possible to reacquire the lost discriminations.

The results for other lobes are quite similar to this. The parietal lobe appears to regulate motor functions, tactile and kinesthetic sensitivity, the temporal-lobe hearing, and the frontal-lobe temporal factors, including the ability to delay responses and the like. In all cases, the loss in function is roughly proportional to the amount of cortical loss. Retraining is possible so long as some cortex remains in the relevant lobe and is apparently impossible so long as the cortex is completely gone. We have, then, a certain kind of specificity of function here; the lobes have different and specific functions. But within any given lobe it is impossible to locate specific functions related to the more general function of the lobe. Any given habit or engram cannot be precisely located in any given lobe. Between lobes there is localization of function, but within there is mass action; the lobe functions as a unit or whole.

We have, of course, no direct evidence on the problem of aphasia from these studies. Since the studies involve surgical tampering with the brain, they naturally involve subhuman subjects. There is, however, no reason to assume that the human brain is constructed in a manner which is basically different from that of a monkey or an ape. And we do have data on both of these species. The evidence of comparative anatomy suggests strongly that the human brain is simply a more complex primate brain. There is no data which would suggest the existence of highly specified localization in the human brain while the opposite is true in the subhuman brain. In this situation it appears safe to generalize to humans from lower species. There is, then, no evidence to suggest that the various functions involved in language are specifically localized in the brain, although there is little direct evidence from linguistic animals. Clearly the very complexity of language as a system of behavior would suggest this same conclusion even if the physiological data were more ambiguous. Language requires a large number of "simpler" functions, both sensory and motor, if it is to function properly. Hence its cortical determinants are quite *unlikely* to be located in some few particular small areas of the cortex.

Moreover, the studies of experimental ablation of parts of the brain, as well as more modern clinical studies of human patients, have suggested that a brain injury is not a simple thing to interpret. That is, suppose we know that a particular individual has a cortical injury in a specific location on the brain. We could determine this locus quite precisely if we wanted by surgically opening his skull and looking for the injury. We cannot, of course, look under the cortex. In addition to knowledge of the cortical wound, we also know the behavioral symptoms which the patient is exhibiting. The question is this: what sort of relationship can we infer between the injury and the symptoms? The answer is by no means clear. There are, in fact, several effects of brain damage which *could* produce any observed symptoms. We can, then, classify symptoms according to their possible physiological causes.

(1) *Negative Symptoms:* By "negative symptoms" we refer to the fact that the removal of the cortical material in the injury deprives the individual of performing those functions controlled by that area of the cortex. This is, of course, the traditional way of looking at the effects of the injury. We need not necessarily assume specific localization to treat the injury-symptom relationship in this way. We can simply say that any function in which this area of the cortex is *involved* will be prohibited or hindered by its removal. The brain cannot do what it should since it is not all there, and behavior will suffer accordingly.

(2) *Symptoms Due to Subcortical Damage:* It is clear, of course, that an injury need not be restricted to the cortex itself but can extend rather deeply into the brain. This injury will produce negative symptoms as will cortical injury itself. The fact that subcortical injury is difficult to determine on a living patient throws a certain uncertainty into the relation between the symptoms and the injury. But beyond this, assuming that the original wound was restricted to the cortex, it is still likely that subcortical

damage will develop. The fact that the cortical cells to which certain subcortical cells transmit are no longer there may result in the atrophy and eventual death of those subcortical cells. It is possible for this process to continue through a large chain of cells until an originally highly localized injury has spread to cover a large area of the subcortical brain. It is possible, then, that the symptomatology can *develop* over time due to this subcortical deterioration. Again, the difficulty of observing subcortical loss, particularly when it is due to atrophy, renders the symptom-injury relation obscure, at least until the patient dies and an autopsy can be performed. Even then the diagnosis would be difficult. Suffice it to say that symptoms can develop as a result of the deterioration following a cortical injury.

(3) *Positive Symptoms:* Here we refer to the fact that the cortex has been shown to perform certain *inhibitory* functions. To take an extreme example, we find that the domestic cat with a complete brain is capable of normal feline emotions, of which rage is a rather rare and fleeting one. Minus the cortex, however, the subcortical cat is subject to fits of what has been called *sham rage.* Any unusual stimulus will provoke a seizure of hissing and spitting, with hair raised and fangs bared, which lasts for a considerable period of time but which apparently has no meaning for the cat. The general interpretation of this is that the emotional mechanisms known to exist in subcortical areas have been *released* from their normal control, i.e. inhibition, by the cortex. They run rampant. Now the subcortex in general is a large and complex nervous mechanism. It controls many functions of extreme psychological importance; it is known to have a bearing on most appetitive needs, sexuality, emotionality, sleep, and the like, as well as certain sensory processes such as smell and brightness vision. In the normal brain these mechanisms are integrated with the cortex; they function jointly. When the requisite cortex is gone, however, the normal control is also gone. The lower centers can now behave differently than under normal situations, thus creating a set of symptoms which are produced by the release from control of certain mechanisms. In this sense we

speak of positive symptoms; they are new behaviors produced by a new sort of nerve functioning rather than the loss of behavior resulting from the loss of nerve tissue.

(4) *Symptoms of Malfunction:* In the ordinary case of injury we are not dealing with the "clean" removal of a part of the brain. Typically the brain is pushed, mashed, and otherwise insulted as well. The possibilities of unseen injuries other than direct loss are thus considerable. But beyond this, in nearly any injury to the body, the natural healing functions of the body produce a layer of scar tissue to partially replace the tissue missing as a result of the wound. The brain is no exception to this, and cortical injury results in the growth of scar tissue on the surface of the brain. The brain, unlike other organs, cannot regrow missing parts. Thus, this scar tissue is essentially a foreign body in the brain and as such induces neural malfunction. Its very presence causes otherwise healthy tissue to function in a manner other than it would without the scar. It has been shown, for example, that the removal of scar tissue from the brain can alleviate or even cure completely certain epileptic seizures. These seizures are not due to the loss of cortex, but to the *malfunction* of the remainder of the brain. If the cause of malfunction, the scar tissue, is removed, the symptoms will also go. Clearly, then, the presence of scar tissue can itself create symptoms which are not due to the nerve damage directly, but which are due to the malfunction of the brain as a whole.

(5) *Psychogenic Symptoms:* In dealing with an injured human being we cannot overlook the fact that he knows he is injured as do other people in his social environment. It is not uncommon to find aphasics, particularly among the less severe ones, humiliated by their inability to speak normally. Their awareness of their own behavioral inadequacy can produce anxiety, conflict, feelings of inferiority, and any number of other states which can lead to severe emotional disturbance. The psychological reaction to the injury, and particularly to the behavioral symptoms resulting from the injury, can lead to emotional states which are

themselves generative of symptoms. It is clearly not easy to distinguish the psychogenic symptoms from the organic ones. In fact, the diagnosis of brain damage in general is often impossible on a purely behavioral level.

(6) *Any Combination of the Above:* Here, of course, we get to the crux of the matter. Any particular set of symptoms is the result of some combination of the above five causes, perhaps of all five acting at once. There is no known way of determining the particular causes of a particular set of symptoms. Indeed, it is likely that any particular behavior symptom could have itself been produced by any one of the five causes. A constellation of symptoms, such as we typically observe in the aphasic patient, could have come from nearly anywhere. This suggests, then, that a somewhat different approach to aphasia is warranted. Rather than worry about the precise relations between symptoms and damage, perhaps it would be more profitable to construct a global picture of what appears to be global disorder. This is, in effect, the direction in which thinking about aphasia has been moving since the time of the localists. Moreover, it is a direction of thinking which is common both to linguists and to physiologists who are concerned with the problem.

This approach to the study of aphasia started in the nineteenth century with the work of the English physiologist, Hughlings Jackson. He was the first person who clearly recognized the global character of the symptoms of aphasia. He saw, for example, that alexia did not mean that the ability to write was completely absent, nor did it have symptoms only in the area of writing. The alexic patient could easily have speech problems as well. In fact, he suggested, the best way of describing the effects of brain damage would be to say that it effects *abstract* behavior. The more abstract the behavior, the smaller the injury required to effect it; and the larger the injury, the less abstract the behavior which will be effected. But abstract behavior goes first. The implication seems to be that highly abstract behavior, e.g. logical reasoning and linguistic behaviors in general, requires more of the cortex and, hence, will be disturbed by almost any injury, no matter where in the brain it is located and how small in extent. Simpler behaviors require less brain functioning, hence a larger and more specific lesion to abolish them.

Jackson suggested that an intensive look at the actual behaviors of patients would support his contention. Let us see what they do, rather than worrying about what our theory says they should do, as the localists were doing.What he suggested, in effect, was a theory of the nature of language. The meaning of a word, he claimed, lay only in its relationship to other words. The unit of speech is the sentence or proposition, not the single isolated word.* Now the forming of propositions is a relatively abstract behavior, and hence, by his reasoning, is very likely to be effected by almost any sort of cortical brain injury. To Jackson, then, the symptoms of aphasia may be a result of the loss of the ability to form propositions. Since the propositions whereby words gain their meaning are no longer available, the words themselves lose all significance. It is not that speech is gone; it is rather that words are no longer used since they serve no purpose; they have no meaning. In fact this hypothesis seems to have considerable validity, as we shall see when we discuss Goldstein.

The twentieth-century British physiologist, Sir Henry Head, followed the Jacksonian tradition and defined aphasia as a disorder of a symbolic functioning and expression. There were, he felt, essentially four types of aphasia: (1) Verbal aphasia in which the patient appears to be unable to form words but shows adequate understanding of them. This appears to be roughly comparable to Broca's motor aphasia. This patient may, for example, be quite capable of following instructions but unable to speak about what he is doing. This is probably somewhat of an oversimplified picture, since, if nothing else, understanding will

---

* In the terminology of this book, we would say that words must belong to a system in order to constitute parts of a language. Without being part of a language, they have no meaning in the ordinary sense. Since the essence of a language is that it is used or uttered, the utterance is the basic unit of language. An utterance need not be a proposition in any formal, logical sense, of course.

doubtless be affected also. But we shall return to this. (2) Syntactical aphasia in which the patient is unable to form recognizable sentences, although he appears capable of uttering recognizable words. Essentially this patient often seems unable to handle the function words and other devices used to relate words to one another. (3) Nominal aphasia, in which the patient seems unable to name objects. That is, he may describe the object by means of some circumlocution, e.g. a pen becomes "something to write with," but he will not be able to dredge up the appropriate name for the object. The patient often seems to be quite cognizant of the use or function of the object, and can describe it in these terms, but seems unable to recognize the object as a member of a class of similar objects. It appears to be mainly class names which are affected in this disorder. (4) Semantic aphasia, in which the patient does not appear able to write complete sentences, although the phrases which he utters are formulated in a grammatically acceptable manner. His understanding is similarly affected. This patient at some level appears to be able to follow rote or routine verbal formulas, but is not able to use language productively or to generate a complete proposition, where he might be required to do something other than the familiar. Thus, he can count, providing he starts from one and advances one digit at a time, but he cannot do arithmetic.

We need not consider Head in any greater detail since his work is similar to and supplemented by that of Kurt Goldstein and his associates. To Goldstein (1948), aphasia was also a disorder of symbolic, abstract abilities or what he referred to as the "categorial attitude." That is, the patient's behavior is hopelessly concrete. He cannot assume any sort of abstract set or carry out any sort of complex instructions. He is incapable of using words as class names. Corresponding to this is the inability to see the similarities among object characteristics which the normal person can see. If, for example, he is given a sample of yarns of various colors, he will identify colors as the same only if they are in fact almost identical in hue and brightness. He cannot group all shades of one color together, for, to him, they are not the same color any longer.

The patient will typically suffer an extreme vocabulary loss when tested in any normal manner; that is, if he is asked to name something he will not be able to do so. Yet the next minute he may use the word he could not think of in a sentence. Sentences are particularly interesting, for they indicate that the patient's ability to use grammar in a creative manner has apparently disappeared. He is at a loss to talk about a new circumstance, and the more abstract the topic of conversation, the more at a loss he is. Nevertheless, he is able to generate grammatical sentences at times. Typically, these will be rote sentences. If he is asked to describe some past event, he may be able to do so, but a second description of the same event will be an almost verbatim repetition of the first, even after a relatively long period of time.

The patient appears absorbed with the *functioning* of objects. He can say what they do, but not what properties they have or what class they belong to, for that is too abstract. To him, each object and each word has its proper function. The object or word will not be recognized if it is performing some other function, nor will the patient be able to conceive of its performing some other function. Thus, the patient cannot have fantasies, nor can he lie, since both require the use of words about states of affairs that are merely imaginary. As an extreme example, one patient was unable to recognize Goldstein's house on a day when he was not supposed to go there for treatment. The patient's response in this sort of situation was something like this: "It can't be Dr. Goldstein's house because today isn't Wednesday."

Goldstein's work is noted for its particularly brilliant descriptions of the patient's symptomatology, a description which does suggest strongly that aphasia is something quite different than the localists' conception of it. To him, aphasia is not merely a language disturbance; it is a disturbance of the mind—of thought and of behavior. It is a disturbance which results from the loss of an ability which cuts across all these things and which is determined, apparently, by the functioning of the brain in its entirety. It is difficult, indeed impossible, to account for the wealth of symptoms observed by pointing to the particular cortical area injured. Even though lost behaviors do not stem from the area, the area had played a role in their determination. Any injury removes certain capacities which are necessary as part of a system, or sets of capacities which must function jointly in order to produce the sorts of behaviors typical of the normal, non-injured human.

To *explain* all his findings in terms of the abstract attitude—or in terms of Head's symbolic functioning or Jackson's proposition formation, for that matter—appears unsatisfactory, however. While, on some level, saying that the patient's behavior is concrete or not abstract does *describe* that behavior quite well, it does not constitute an acceptable *explanation* for it. Clearly, we do not want to postulate the existence of some "abstract attitude" floating around the brain someplace. We must explain the effects of aphasia in terms of more basic psychological and physiological mechanisms. We need, in other words, a psychological theory of language constructed in such a way that we can account for the observed symptoms when disturbances occur in the human system. Goldstein's contribution lies not in his explanations of aphasia, but in his establishment of what it was that we had to explain. He has, in fact, set the requirements for a theory of language; if it cannot explain his data, it is not adequate. And if nothing else, we see that language disturbances cannot be separated from disturbances in other modes of behavior. The patients have difficulty in relating to objects just as they do to words. Hence our theory of language must be something other than just a theory of language. It must be a complete theory of behavior, of perception or of the mind (depending on your terminological preferences) as well.

Before attempting to pull together the threads of our discussion on aphasia, some recent trends in the study of aphasia must be noted. We have seen that nearly all theorists of aphasia have attempted to develop some typology or set of pigeonholes into which each patient may be stuck. Such diagnostic categories not only have an aesthetic value, but they can in fact be of considerable use (1) if the categories relate to the *causes* of the disturbance, or (2) if the categories relate to the *types of treatment* required by the disturbance. Typologies have, then, a pragmatic significance and must be evaluated accordingly. Therapists, in general, have found none of the typologies we have discussed to be completely useful.

The most frequently used typology is that proposed by Weisenberg and McBride (1935) which divides aphasia into four types: (1) expressive, (2) receptive, (3) expressive and receptive, and (4) amnesic. These labels are quite self-explanatory. In fact, in practice they are generally referred to as "primarily expressive," etc., to reflect the obvious fact that no aphasic ever shows only disorders in speaking a language with no disorder in understanding it, and the like. It should be obvious that these categories also suggest a type of training or therapeutic procedure. The expressive aphasic needs training in uttering language, while the receptive needs it in hearing language. The amnesic needs to be given a vocabulary. The appeal of this system is obvious, and despite the ambiguity of symptoms in general, this system is, in fact, relatively effective in use.

More recently, Schuell and Jenkins (1959) have criticized the typological notion and have proposed instead that there is simply *aphasia*. That is, we are dealing with a unitary disease wherein the patients differ from one another in terms of *how* disturbed they are, but not in terms of *what* sort of disturbance they have. There are different amounts of aphasia, but not different kinds of it. Considering the facts about aphasic symptomatology which we have outlined above, there is a great deal to be said for this argument. All typologies appear somewhat arbitrary, and none appears to do justice to the symptoms in the way that a global assumption such as "the loss of an abstract attitude" does. Their idea, then, has the seeds of validity to it.

What is of interest is that they then attempt to demonstrate the validity of this assumption by means of an extremely sophisticated piece of research. They essentially attempt to construct a diagnostic test that will contain a series of items such that the score obtained on the totality of items will indicate the severity of the disturbance the patient is suffering. A scale analysis of the items which had proved to differentiate among patients known to be severe and those known to be mild aphasics would indicate this: whether there is one or several underlying traits or dimensions which are being measured. If there is one trait, we can talk about aphasia in a generic sense. If there are two or more traits, we may have to conceive of expressive versus receptive aphasia, or some other category system.

But now let us look at the test itself. We will consider only items which Scheull and Jenkins themselves report to be discriminating and which have been validated by them on repeated uses of the test. Let us look at these items from this point of view: if there were two kinds of aphasia, for example, expressive and receptive, how would a patient of each type perform on the item? The expressive, we will assume, is a person who understands language but who is unable to translate his understanding into action, while the receptive is capable of action but cannot understand written or spoken language. Consider now the two best items of their test:

A series of cards, each containing five or six letters or numbers are presented individually, and the patient is required to point to the symbol named by the examiner.

Card with single printed word is displayed, and patient is required to point to appropriate picture. The pictures are the same as those used for auditory recognition.

In both of these items, in fact on all the items in the test, we find that the patient is required to do two things: (1) to understand the directions and the particular stimulus presented to him and (2) to translate that understanding into action, in this case the action of making a gesture which is itself a kind of symbolic or linguistic act. Clearly, from our definition, either a receptive or an expressive aphasic would have equal difficulty with these problems. They would perform indistinguishably since all the problems require both receptive and expressive powers.

The fallacy both undermines the research and validates the assumption of the research. We cannot measure a receptive versus expressive distinction, since all measurement requires the use of *both* capacities. But then the use of language itself requires both capacities, and a disabling of one power will have effects on the other proportional to the severity of the injury. Spoken language is a system of acts or behaviors, and the understanding of language requires the ability to act. One does not understand a word unless one knows how to use it or how to react to it. Hence, the receptive and expressive aspects of language are logically mutual. They cannot be separated and, on this level, it is correct to say that there is but one type of aphasia. But this is clearly not the point that Schuell and Jenkins wished to make; rather than saying that one cannot tell the difference between expressive and receptive aphasics, they wished, it seems, to show that there was in fact no difference.

Nevertheless, the assumption underlying the experiment may still be correct; there may be only one kind of aphasia. But no experiment can possibly prove this when the very measurement confounds the two. And, in addition, an instrument which can measure the severity of the disturbances cannot be underrated, for it is at least a step in the direction of a successful diagnostic instrument. The true nature of aphasia cannot be determined from a measuring instrument alone, however.

Among other recent empirical studies in aphasia, we must cite the work of Lambert and Fillenbaum (1959) on aphasia in bilingual individuals. They start with the assumption that there are two kinds of bilinguals. (1) *Compound bilinguals* for whom the two languages share a common meaning system. That is, in our terminology, there would be a common set of engrams elicited by the equivalent words in each of the two languages. (2) *Co-ordinate bilinguals*, for whom the two languages have, at least to some extent, different meaning systems. Thus for words in the two languages that are roughly synonymous, one would call out one set of engrams and the second another, independent set. There is no need to assume that the co-ordinated state holds for all words in either language, but it should hold for a fair number of them.

From this simple theoretical notion, it is clear that the compound and co-ordinate bilinguals would have to learn their two languages in different contexts. That is, the compound bilingual would tend to use the two languages in the same environment, thus permitting the perceptual and other engrams to be commonly associated to words in both languages. The co-ordinate bilingual, on the other hand, would have acquired the two languages in different contexts, so that the perceptual and other engrams associated with the two would be different. Lambert, Havelka, and Crosby (1958) have, in fact, demonstrated that the more different the learning contexts, the more separate the meanings of two translated equivalents will tend to be.

Lambert and Fillenbaum reason that European-born bilinguals will tend to be co-ordinate in their bilingualism. For the European, any second language will typically be acquired in a different context from the native language; it may be in school, in business, or in a new country to which the individual has emigrated. Whatever the circumstance, it will tend to be co-ordinate, since the two languages are not, for instance, used at home, at play, or in any similar surroundings. In the French districts of Canada, as in Montreal, however, English-French bilingualism will tend to be compound. It will not be uncommon for both languages to be spoken at home, at social activities in school, at play, and the like. By sharing the same environment in which they are used, the meaning systems of the two languages will overlap. This will produce compound bilingualism.

From the definitions of the two sorts of bilingualism, it is easy to progress to an hypothesis about aphasia. That is, a given injury is more likely to hinder only one language in the case of the co-ordinate bilingual, but will effect both languages in the case of the compound bilingual. The reason is, of course, that the meanings of words are separate for the two languages in the former case, and thus it is possible to affect one language without the other's being harmed. In the compound case, however, there is only one meaning system, and any damage to it will simultaneously and equally effect both languages. The data indicate that:

If we assume that the European and Montreal scenes encourage co-ordinate and compound bilingualism respectively, then the data offer some support for our hypothesis since the Montreal cases typically show a generalized disorder affecting both languages, while the European cases typically show a more specific-language disorder following aphasia (Lambert and Fillenbaum, 1959, p. 32).

Moreover:

The generalization therefore seems appropriate that the language (or languages) which bilinguals use continuously from early life will probably be least vulnerable to aphasia. The Montreal cases are also consistent with this generalization in that two languages are more likely to be learned early in life and used concurrently in Quebec (Lambert and Fillenbaum, 1959, p. 32).

We would be more inclined to look at these data in a somewhat different light. It is an implication of the theory, which we attempted to develop previously, that words can differ in the amount of meaning which they have. Now it would appear likely that on the average, a word which is used frequently will have more meaning than a word which is used infrequently. The word used frequently is, of course, more likely to be used in several different contexts, rather than only one or a few. And by being used in many contexts, it will acquire a large set of associated engrams, taken from the perceptions, emotions, and behaviors performed in those contexts. Specifically, we can say that in the case of the bilinguals, the language used most frequently will be the one with the most meaning. It will consequently suffer the least loss if a constant amount of "meaning" is "subtracted" by the aphasic injury.

But if we are to develop this idea, we must propose some general account of aphasia in the language of our theory. This is, of course, no easy thing to do. However, we can tentatively approach the issue anyway. We have seen that making an utterance, or a speech act, is a behavior which is under the control of an exceedingly complex set of stimuli. We have first, the external environmental events which determine in part what we will speak about. In addition, there are internal events which will determine both what will be spoken of and the grammatical form of the utterance. Moreover, these internal events deter-

mine that there will be an utterance, for they reflect the existence of an intention to speak. Then we have seen that the individual must be capable of dealing with or classifying words as
members of the same part of speech, for without this classification he could not utter a correct sentence. And finally we see
that the large set of engrams aroused by the words as perceived
stimuli constitute conscious events. These conscious events in
turn constitute the significance or meaning of what is said. Without this meaning, the behavior would not constitute a linguistic
act.

We have, of course, ignored the fact that the sensory receptors
and speech organs must be able to perform their necessary functions. But then a deficit in either of these would not typically be
termed aphasic. We must have available the necessary mechanisms whereby incoming stimuli can arouse and select their
appropriate engrams, however; the person must be able to perceive and be aware in order for the whole processes to take
place. We have, in other words, an extraordinary process and a
process of exceeding complexity. It is hardly surprising that a
small injury in the nervous system at a place from which stems
any of these nearly simultaneous activities would produce damage to the language system as a whole.

But what is equally apparent is that the processes involved
in the utterance of a speech act are not processes which are
unique to language. They are processes which are common to all
sorts of mental activities, from "simple" perception on up. What
we would expect to find is that an aphasia would be a disturbance which was not, in fact, restricted to language, but which
would extend to all sorts of mental functions. It is a disorder of
thinking, if you will; a disorder of the mind. It is, in other words,
the sort of disorder which Goldstein reported; one which has
symptoms not only in speech but in the perception of colors, the
recognition of objects, and so on.

We must offer a somewhat different picture of the apparently
concrete behavior of the aphasic, however. This concreteness is
not abnormal in any sense. In fact it is the *basis* of perception
and of meaning. The abstractness of language and thought is

just that—an abstraction. It is a characteristic imposed by the adult mind, which is capable after a period of growth of conceiving of "ideas" which lie behind things and of abstract and transcendental "properties," of "sensations," and the like. The important thing to realize is that these are *creations* of the mind. As such they are valuable and important. But they do not represent any necessary truths, nor are they a picture of the way the mind develops and functions.

The mind *functions*. That is its nature. It is the mind of an organism which moves, behaves, and functions in a world. All perception and awareness, as we have suggested, is the arousal of possible ways of moving, behaving, and functioning. All meaning is likewise a set of possible *uses* of and responses to words. All meaning is in this sense functional. To define a pen as "something to write with" is not primitive or concrete—it is *basic*. There is no definition which approaches the essence of a pen more closely than that it is something with which one writes. No definition of a pen in terms of properties such as shape, size, and structure does as much justice to the pen as the simple statement that one writes with it. That the aphasic is not capable of going beyond this basic functional definition says something about aphasia; aphasia involves a lack of certain kinds of behavior. But it does not imply that he is behaving abnormally; what he does is also quite characteristic of normals. He is expressing the definition out of which the more abstract ones arise.

The concreteness in the use of words which we see in the aphasic is likewise basic to the use of language. Words are parts of things to the child. They become objects in themselves with age and as literacy is acquired. Moreover, the meanings of these words are concrete in that they consist of a set of specific uses in specific contexts. The idea that a word is necessarily abstract stems from a faulty psychology, one which assumes a particular kind of *adult* mind as the basic psychological given. It stems from the notion that consciousness is produced by sense impressions passively recorded by the organism, and then "interpreted" by some entity—generally called "the mind"—which is independent of these sense impressions (or of the body). It follows from such a conception that the assignment of a word as the "name" of an object is arbitrary or contingent. It could have been otherwise. The word becomes, then, an abstraction by definition, an abstraction by nature, and any concretization of the word becomes pathological.

But all this is based on a psychology which is totally wrong. Both consciousness and meaning stem from the way the organism behaves. And there is nothing abstract or arbitrary about behavior. If one makes an error in behavior, the environment is very quick to let one know about it and often does so in a violent manner. Neither perception nor meaning are passive, and as such, the concept of meaning imposed by the interpretations of a disembodied mind has no psychological validity, objectively or, most importantly, subjectively. It may be logically true that what I call /red/ could have been called /blue/. But I submit that the honest abstract thinker must struggle manfully to overcome the following rebuttal: "But it is not blue; it is red." This rebuttal is the natural response, and it is natural because that is the way language is. It is a concrete functional tool. The language of the aphasic, on this level, then, is no more concrete than the language of the normal.

But his language is *limited* in a way that the language of the normal is not. He cannot, if you will, think. He cannot use the language in all the ways that the normal can. It is as if his meaning system has become limited, as if the set of engrams which could be aroused at any given moment of time were much smaller and more restricted than in the normal. His awareness is not as large, and the possibilities for action open to him are restricted. The damaged brain cannot handle sets of engrams as large as can the normal brain. Hence, the behavior of the aphasic appears rigid and restricted. He appears to respond rotely since he no longer has the choice of a large set of possible actions. His actions for words are limited to a very few. These meanings will typically be those most basic, those used most often and learned earliest. He lives, then, in a world which is but a shadow, a fraction of that occupied by you or by me.

But we cannot go further with this analysis here. We have

already stepped into the realm of thinking and of other "higher mental processes." We are obliged, then, to discuss the relationships which hold between language, thought, reason, and the mind in general. This we shall do in the next chapter.

Bibliography

Bateson, G., Jackson, D., Haley, J., and Weckland, J. Toward a theory of schizophrenia. *Behavioral Sci.*, 1956, 1, 251-64.

Cameron, N. Experimental analysis of schizophrenic thinking. In Kasanin, J. S. (Ed.) *Language and thought in schizophrenia.* New York, W. W. Norton, 1964.

Goldstein, K. *Language and language disturbances.* New York, Grune & Stratton, 1948.

Hayakawa, S. I. *Language in thought and action.* New York, Harcourt, Brace, 1949.

Korzybski, A. *Science and sanity; an introduction to non-Aristotelian systems and general semantics.* Lakeville, Conn., International Non-Aristotelian Literary Publishing Company, 1958.

Laing, R. D. *The divided self.* Middlesex, Penguin Books, 1965.

Lambert, J. W., and Fillenbaum, S. A pilot study of aphasia among bilinguals. *Canad. J. Psychol.*, 1959, 13, 28-34.

Lambert, W. E., Havelka, J., and Crosby, C. The influence of language acquisition contexts on bilingualism. *J. abnorm. soc. Psychol.*, 1958, 56, 239-44.

Munroe, R. *Schools of psychoanalytic thought.* New York, Dryden Press, 1955.

Schuell, H. and Jenkins, J. J. The nature of language deficit in aphasia. *Psychol. Rev.*, 1959, 66, 45-67.

Sullivan, H. S. *The fusion of psychiatry and social science.* New York, W. W. Norton, 1964.

Weisenberg, T., and McBride, K. *Aphasia, a clinical and psychological study.* New York, The Commonwealth Fund, 1935.

IX
Language and the Mind

The development of human experience seems to require that a theory of meaning emanate from a theory of perception or consciousness. But how is language related to the various functions or attributes of the mind, e.g. perception, thinking, imagining, feeling, etc.? Is it one feature among many, having roughly equal status with but no necessary connection to the others? Or is it in some way casually related to the other features of the mind? It is to this question that we must address ourselves. We must determine to what extent the mind is dependent on language, and to what extent language is simply a "tool of thought" to be used or rejected as we see fit.

Psychologists seem to be rather uncertain about this issue. Within limits it is possible to avoid it altogether. The behavioristic tradition has generally managed to do this by treating language solely as a response. Thus, for example, in a well-known attempt to formulate Freudian principles in stimulus-response terms, Dollard and Miller (1950) identify "consciousness" as that which can be verbalized. Any stimulus is conscious if we can make a verbal, naming response to it. There is apparently no causality intended by this definition; words are not what makes something conscious. Rather, Dollard and Miller intend that this is *what we mean* when we say something is conscious. To them, the meaning of the term conscious is that one can describe something—make a verbal response to something—while the meaning of unconscious is that one cannot make such a verbal response to it. The attachment of a verbal response to some stimulus shifts it from the unconscious to the conscious *by definition*. Here is the crux of the issue. There is no change in some internal mental state by virtue of the ability to verbalize something, for there are no such things as internal mental states. At least, any such states are beyond the pale of science, as conceived of by the behaviorist. All that exists is what people do and what stimuli they receive. We find that we can dichotomize stimuli into those to which verbal responses may be made and those to which they may not. Hence, this becomes the meaning of conscious and unconscious to the behaviorist. But as you can see, this is not a statement about the relationship between language and the mind; it is a denial of the mind and an attempt to substitute verbal behavior for it.

A further illustration of the same mode of thought can be found in the experimental work on discrimination learning and the *transposition problem*. By "transposition" we refer to the fact that animals appear to respond to the relationships between stimuli or objects rather than to the absolute qualities of the objects themselves. Thus, given a choice between two objects, say circles of different sizes, the animal is quite capable of learning which one of these has food behind it. If we suppose that the two circles are 2 inches and 3 inches in diameter, respectively, and that the food is behind the 3-inch circle, we can now ask the following question: Is the animal responding to the size of this particular circle, i.e. is he learning that 3 inches is the correct size, or is he responding to the relationship? That is, is he learning to go to the larger circle?

We can attempt to find out the answer to this by testing him on another pair of circles. If we now face him with a 3-inch circle and a 4½-inch circle, we may be able to get some sort of answer to our question. If the animal chooses the 3-inch circle, we can say that he is learning to respond to the absolute size of the stimulus object. That is, he is still choosing the stimulus which was previously correct and, hence, is making a choice based on absolute stimulus properties. If, on the other hand, he chooses the 4½-inch circle, he must be responding to the relationship between stimulus objects. He is choosing the larger stimulus even though he has never seen it before and even though the previously correct one is there for him to choose. In this sort of test the animal subjects will typically choose the larger circle; they will respond to the relationship between stimuli.

This evidence produces something of a difficulty for behaviorist psychologists who wish to treat stimuli as objective physical entities or energies. It is clear that if one wishes to conceive of a stimulus as defined by light energy striking the retina of the eye, for example, that one cannot talk about relationships between stimuli in this language. There will be no stimulus which corresponds to the relationship itself, and hence relationships cannot properly be called stimuli in this sort of theory. To be somewhat less behavioristic about it, a relationship is a characteristic of perception, not of objects or of stimulus energies. Since no behaviorist wishes to talk of perception—it is, they maintain, an unobservable, mentalistic concept—it follows that they will not accept speaking of relationships as stimuli. As we shall see, this concept is one which cannot be avoided.

Now, in fact, the transposition data does not give the behaviorist too much difficulty, at least as long as we use subhuman animal subjects. In a particularly brilliant piece of theoretical model building, Kenneth Spence (1937) was able to account for the transposition data in terms quite acceptable to the behaviorist. We will not go into the details except to say that the theory made use of the concept of generalization, a term used to describe the fact that responses seem to be conditioned not only to particular stimulus energies, but to energies similar to the original stimulus as well. The strength of conditioning will be proportional to the similarity to the original conditioned stimulus. Using such an approach, Spence was not only able to account for the fact of transposition, but able to predict that it would *not* occur under certain conditions—namely when the test stimuli were quite different from the original training stimuli. In such a case, the animal will choose the one most similar to the original training stimulus and not respond to the "relationship" at all.

Spence was very careful to add that this model would in all likelihood not apply to verbal subjects, however. They would be able to attach verbal labels (i.e. responses) to the stimuli and respond to these labels rather than to the objective stimulus characteristics themselves. Thus, by virtue of words, people will respond to relationships. Only in making relational verbal responses can we give the appearance of making relational discriminations. However, it is clear that there is no change in the basic sensory processes implied by this. The stimuli are the same, and the reactions of the receptors to those stimuli are the same. All that happens is that verbal responses become conditioned to these stimuli, and our discrimination behavior is conditioned to the verbal responses rather than to the stimuli themselves.

To support this view, Spence cites the work of his student Margaret Kuenne (1946) who demonstrated that pre-verbal children showed the same sort of transposition behavior as sub-human animals—i.e. transposition which broke down with extremely different test stimuli—while verbal children showed complete transposition over all test stimuli. Leaving aside the difficulties posed by the fact that the verbal children tend to be older or more intelligent or both than the non-verbal children, we can still see that this study in fact poses more difficulty for the behaviorist than it resolves. We can ask the question: how does the verbal label get conditioned to the stimuli? To be specific, how is "larger than" conditioned to the 3-inch circle and "smaller than" to the 2-inch circle in our original example?

We can, of course, assume that one has learned these specific connections, except that this will not then account for the transposition effect. Our 3-inch circle has to call out "larger than" in this situation, and "smaller than" when it is paired with a 4-inch circle. But how is this possible? If we assume that "larger than" and "smaller than" are both conditioned to the 3-inch circle, we must assume that they are both conditioned to many other sizes of circles as well, since transposition works over a relatively large range of stimuli even at its least efficient state. But if both the

3-inch and the 2-inch circles call out both "larger than" and "smaller than" then there is no verbal difference between the stimuli, and we would have to assume that one could not use verbal labels as the basis of a discrimination. Since the discrimination is made, this explanation must be wrong.

As an alternative, we could assume that the pair of stimulus objects themselves was the stimulus. Thus "larger than" is only called out when there is more than one stimulus object, and, moreover let us assume that it is called out only when the objects are different and only when they are different in size. For the moment, let us assume that we can find some satisfactory stimulus definition of both "difference" and "size"—a task which is not as easy as it may at first seem. We are still faced with the problem that "larger than" is not indiscriminately "conditioned" to the pair, but is specifically "conditioned" to the 3-inch and not the 2-inch circle. How are we to account for this? Could we not say that the response "larger than" is conditioned to that member of the pair which has the greater magnitude? That sounds objective enough, but is it? Is it not simply saying that the individual calls something larger than something else, if it is in fact larger or if he sees it as larger. But this would mean that either the stimulus must be defined relationally, or that the subject must see or perceive a relationship in order to use the verbal label properly. After all, "greater magnitude" is a relational definition. But this is exactly what Spence and his colleagues said could not happen, and it is what they were trying to escape by reporting to the verbal-response concept. Yet we see that in order to account for the verbal response, we must appeal to the very concept that the verbal response was trying to explain. Spence is led to this impasse by two basic mistakes. First, by trying to explain everything in terms of stimuli as physically defined, rather than phenomenally treated, and second by assuming that language is only a response and ignoring the fact that language refers to things. Once you realize that language has meaning, in the sense of referring to classes or concepts, then you are faced with the problem of how one can learn to use the language *properly*.

How can one refer to a relationship unless something is there for him to refer to?

In the case of the notion of relationship, there are only three possibilities for such an "object of reference." Either the relationship is in the stimulus itself, is in one's awareness of the stimulus, or is in some other ordering principle provided by the subject himself. The concept of a relationship implies a dependence between certain parts of the world or between experiences. Such a dependence cannot exist between stimulus energies which are, in fact, independent of one another. If one changes or interrupts the light energies proceeding to one part of the retina, this has no effect on energies proceeding to another part. The energies are independent, but a relationship implies a dependency. It implies a reference of one part to another; but independent stimulus energies cannot refer to one another; hence, they cannot provide the information required to respond to a relationship or to use relational terms.*

Thus, in order to account for the correct use of "larger than" we are left with two possibilities. The organism organizes the relationship either by perception or by some other ordering principle which the organism has. Such a principle might be the past history of responses made by the individual, in which case it is, of course, possible for a response to define a relationship. But we have already assumed that this sort of organizing principle underlies the organization of *perception itself*, which has been defined as a readiness to respond in some particular fashion. If there is, in fact, such a non-perceptual ordering principle, then either language and perception precede and develop from the same ordering principle on parallel but separate paths, or there is some precedence and dependence of one on the other. That

---

* This is not to say that certain stimulus conditions are not necessary for the perception of a relationship. Indeed, there must be a pair of stimuli which are different in magnitude for the term "larger than" to be employed appropriately. But these conditions alone will not account for the correct use of the term since they do not provide the necessary *comparison* between magnitudes. The stimulus conditions, then, are necessary but not sufficient.

is, the organization of language depends on the organization of perception, or vice versa. Clearly the latter cannot be completely true since one perceives before one has language; yet, it might be partly true. If the ordering principles for language and perception are the same, then any ordering given to language might be expected to have its effects on perception and vice versa. It is this problem which we must discuss. No amount of behavioristic philosophy can remove us from it. Indeed, a careful consideration of behaviorism raises the issue as strongly as anything could.

We have reached the position that there must be an interdependence of language and perception and, for that matter, between language and other mental activities—most of which are also dependent on perception for their material. We can hardly think or feel without something to think or feel about. But we must face the uncomfortable fact that the empirical evidence suggesting a relationship between language and the other mental processes is quite minute, and much of it quite unconvincing. Let us summarize some of it.

Consider first the problem of perception. We have a relatively enormous literature dealing with the perception of words—which is not quite the same as an influence of language on perception. Much of this research is designed to show that meaning does in fact influence perception. But it is almost entirely clouded by certain extreme methodological flaws. Consider, for example, one general issue: that the emotional tone of a word should determine either whether it is seen, or the ease or rapidity with which it is seen. Notice that we are dealing here with the perception of the word itself, and not with the effects of words on other non-linguistic perceptions. Hence, at best the studies would be of limited scope in making conclusions about the effects of language on perception in general. But beyond this we find that the effects observed can be attributed to a set of trivial variables, most of which deal with the familiarity of the material. The more familiar the material is, the more likely the subject is to report it, or even to *guess* it. And the more socially unacceptable the material, the more likely he is not to report it. The whole thing seems contingent on the subject's willingness to *say* the word, which is clearly not what we mean by perception. At this level, the relationship between language and perception appears quite hypothetical.

A somewhat more interesting set of data is reported by Brown and Lenneberg (1954) as a test of a theory proposed by Whorf (1956) to be discussed more fully later. This study concerns the functions performed by the words which describe sensory qualities and attributes, in this case color. The languages of different cultures do not all have the same vocabulary for describing sensory qualities. Thus, what we call /blue/ and /green/ may be called by one single name in some other language. Even within our own language, we find that different groups of people have different sensory vocabularies as a function of their occupations and interests. Thus clothing designers and painters, as well as people interested in clothes and painting, will have a richer usable color vocabulary than will others. They will speak knowingly of /magenta/, /beige/, and /prussian blue/ whereas the ordinary man in the street may have difficulty in denoting these colors and will rarely if ever use these color names.

One interpretation of the theory offered by Whorf is that the existence of color names, for example, determines the ability to perceive the colors in question. Thus, the Iakuti who calls blue and green by the same name (let's call it x) would presumably be unable to see the difference between what we call blue and green, while in parallel fashion our man in the street would fail to see any difference between Prussian blue and navy blue. Initially, this theory seems farfetched, and in general this has been the reaction of many critics of the Whorf theory. In part the validity of this hypothesis depends on the sense one gives to the word "see." Let us look at the Brown and Lenneberg data before continuing this discussion.

These authors had English-speaking subjects name a series of colored patches of known physical character. From this naming task they were able to ascertain what they called the "codability" of the colors in question. That is, they obtained a measure of the agreement among subjects about the correct name of the color. As one would expect, the agreement among subjects increased when the color could be called by a single-word name, e.g. /red/ and decreased when a multi-word "name" was required, e.g. /red-orange/. Thus, codability reflects the degree of agreement among people as to how to use the language in the description of sensory qualities of color.

A second group of subjects were shown samples of color and asked to identify the ones they had just seen from a chart containing a large number of color samples. The accuracy of this identification was related to the codability of the color sample in question. That is, if the color had a single-word which was used unequivocally by speakers of the language, then that color was easy to identify from memory. But we can see that the relationship between this study and the Whorf hypothesis is ambiguous at best. That naming helps recall is one thing; that the existence of a name makes something *look* different is another thing entirely. Or is it? The difficulty with this study is that it follows from both of two contradictory hypotheses. First, the data would be consonant with a hypothesis that states that language influences perception. Obviously such a theory would have to predict that identification would improve with the existence of names for the things to be identified. Things which had the same name should look the same, as should things with no names. Hence, codability and identification would go hand in hand. On the other hand, if we assume that codability reflects the speaker's general familiarity with the sensory quality in question, then we have the second possible interpretation. That is, we will not have names for things which we rarely if ever encounter, or which are functionally ambiguous. In addition, the more that we have to deal with a particular sensory event, the more likely it is that we will develop single-word names for those events. This is the sort of idea that we find expressed in Zipf's law (1949). In other words, the existence of a name is testimony to the fact that the named event is familiar, and the absence of a name, testimony to the fact that it is unfamiliar. Color codability, then, becomes an index of color familiarity, and, of course, it comes as no great surprise that the familiar is recognized and identified more easily than the unfamiliar. By this hypothesis the data can be accounted for with no mention of perception at all.

We are forced to conclude that this study gives us no evidence that any linguistic unit has some effect on perception. The existence of a name does not make something look different—or at least we cannot prove it from this study. But could this be owing to the fact that we are looking at the wrong sort of perception? What exactly is it that we expect language to influence? The child is exposed from birth to an extraordinarily rich and varied array of visual stimuli, which, in all known human ecologies, will cover the whole range of light wavelengths to which the human eye is sensitive. Moreover, the existence of these wavelengths is not random in the environment. Different sorts of objects tend to be of different colors. Animals are differently colored than are plants. Houses are differently colored than automobiles or rocks or sand or snow (although not in all cultures) and so on. There is not only a color *similarity* between members of classes of objects, but there is a color *difference* between almost any pair of objects one encounters. All this indicates that the pre-verbal infant has ample opportunity to learn to discriminate among the varieties of color which are physically and humanly possible. There is no reason to assume that he will not so discriminate. And language is not a crucial factor here, even if it does play some role. Colors may be reacted to differently simply because things are reacted to differently, and color differentiates things as well as do other sensory qualities.

Given this state of affairs, what can we expect language to do? In general we will find that perceptual studies emphasize accuracy. That is, they instruct the subject to treat any sort of difference between two stimuli as a real difference. Things are identical only if they are identical in all detail. Brown and Lenneberg did not want their subjects to identify colors on the basis of /well, it was some kind of x/ and then pick any instance of x. They wanted subjects to pick the identical color, not a member of the same class of colors. The subjects, of course, understood this and performed accordingly as they do in all psychological experiments involving sensory discriminations.*

Now let's suppose we take the subject out of the laboratory and put him in the real world. Is he not likely to tell us that two things look the same, or look similar, because they are both colored shades of x? And yet in a psychological experiment he would also tell us that the two hues were distinctly different, which, in fact they are perceptually. Let us take an extreme example. Suppose some hypothetical Iakuti was telling us about his culture and that he mentioned that typically people painted all of the rooms in their houses the same color. In his case, he had painted his entire interior x. Now we happen to be in his house at the time and are quite surprised to see that his living room is blue and his bedroom is green. Here is the crux of the issue: both the Iakuti and I would agree that the hues of the living room and the bedroom were different. But at the same time to him they are similar colors, while to me they are not. To him they resemble one another while to me they do not. To him they "look the same" while to me they do not. Here is a clear linguistic influence on something. The only thing which the psychologists would argue about is what is being influenced. Is this a perceptual phenomenon or is it not? Certainly we might agree that it is some sort of cognitive phenomenon, and thus we have at least some hypothetical evidence for an effect of language on cognition. I would be inclined to say that it is specifically an effect of language on perception, but then I define perception in a way which would not be agreed upon by most other perceptual psychologists. We must, unfortunately, leave this issue, since obtaining a proper definition of perception would require a book in itself.†

* One cannot resist speculating about the similarity between the experimental subject's behavior and that of the aphasic. Both seem incapable of responding to the class membership of a stimulus and both insist on responding only to strict identity. How general, then, are the findings of experimentation? This is, of course, a function of the experimenter's instructions, including most importantly those which he implies and does not overtly say.

† Essentially the problem is this: Most psychologists maintain a dualistic view of perception, in which there are pure experiences of sensations, which

But it would seem that we still have not produced the kind of hard experimental evidence that indicates that language influences conscious processes in any really basic way. The author has recently conducted a study which may offer some advance, however. Subjects were asked to view words, one at a time, in a darkened chamber.* The words in question were four-letter monosyllables about which normative data have been previously gathered on separate samples of subjects. The word-letters were transparent and illuminated from behind, so that one saw relatively bright letters against an otherwise totally dark background. The light source was in actuality a flickering light, flickering so rapidly that the light appeared stable—not flickering—to all subjects. Its rate of flicker was above that known as the critical flicker fusion threshold for the subjects. Then the experimenter adjusted the rate of flicker by slowly increasing the on-time of the light. The rate of flicker eventually became slow enough for the subjects to perceive it. The subjects were instructed simply to look at the word and to report when they saw the first signs of flicker; they had been shown flicker previously so they knew what to look for.

The experimenter found the perception of the flicker to be a function of certain totally semantic characteristics of the words themselves. Specifically, flicker was seen sooner in words which

---

are a function of physical stimuli alone, and then there are interpretations, judgments, inferences, associations, or whatever that are made using this pure sensory material. To these theorists, language might conceivably effect the latter cognitive processes, but it could not conceivably effect the pure sensation. Another group of theorists, notably the Gestalt school, has rejected this so-called constancy hypothesis and assumes that incoming sensory events are never sufficient to account for consciousness or perception. Other internal organizers are required. Once one accepts this position, as I do, it becomes difficult if not impossible to differentiate between perceptual and other conscious processes. To say that language influences perception is simply to say that language influences conscious processes in a situation where it is impossible to tell what is purely perceptual consciousness and what is not.

* Specifically a tachistoscope, which is an apparatus for regulating the duration of exposure of a stimulus.

are less meaningful, and in words which are less redundant in their letters. Redundancy was assessed by asking subjects to guess the sequences of letters, with a high probability of correct guesses indicating a highly predictable or redundant sequence of letters. Meaningfulness was indexed by obtaining single free associations from a sample of subjects and totaling the number of different associations obtained. In addition, a measure of the familiarity of the word was obtained which did not appear related to the appearance of the flicker.

For our purposes, we need consider only the data related to associations. These, we would assume, measure or reflect the amount of meaning possessed by the word. And we see, then, that words with more meaning are seen to flicker later, at slower rates, than words with less meaning. To reverse the statement, meaningful words are more perceptually stable than less meaningful words. This appears to be a rather striking correspondence between a perceptual process and our ordinary conceptions of meaning. If something has meaning, it is knowable. Meaning gives stability in the sense that it removes uncertainty and ambiguity on some level. We know what to do with a meaningful unit. And here we find that the clarity of use implied by having a large quantity of meaning is paralleled by the perception of stability of the word; the meaningful word does not appear to change as easily as the less meaningful one. We cannot go into the perceptual implications of this study here; however, we will point out some of its methodological advantages. We are not dealing with the perception of the word itself. The subjects see and recognize the word easily. We are dealing with the perception of an attribute of the written word, namely, its flicker. Hence, there is no possibility of a response bias producing this effect. The likelihood or willingness of saying the word is irrelevant here. Moreover, the perceptual process involved is one which all perceptual psychologists would agree upon as "pure" perception. Hence, we have, in fact, evidence for the influence of meaning, or at least meaningfulness, on "real" perception. However, the effect is academic. How far we can generalize it remains to be seen. With this at least suggestive data, let us leave perception and go to something more "mental"—problem solving and thinking.

There are a number of phenomena which suggest an intimate relationship between linguistic behavior and thinking. For example, we have the *Einstellung* effect which has been studied by Luchins (1942). Here the subject is given a series of simple mathematical problems to solve. For example, he may be asked to say how, given $a = 40$, $b = 21$, and $c = 4$, one could arrive at $d = 27$. The answer is, of course, $a - b + 2c$. He is generally given a series of such problems, all of which can be solved by the same formula—although he is not specifically told that this will be the case. Following this period, he is given a test problem which may be either one like $a = 40$, $b = 20$, and $c = 4$ to find $d = 28$, or one like this except where $d = 24$ or $d = 25$. In these problems we have in the first situation one in which both the original and two alternative formulae ($b + 2c$ or $a - 3c$) will give the correct answer, and in which the latter are in some sense simpler than the original. In the second and third problems, we find that the old formula does not work at all and either that a new solution is required, or that there is no solution at all. Given the original training conditions, subjects tend to find these problems quite difficult. Often they seem unable to solve the problems where a new formula is required, and they practically never see that a new formula would be easier than the old in the problem in which several solutions are possible.

There are numerous ways in which one could interpret such a set of results. One way is clearly in terms of the labeling of the situation. We can assume that once the subjects have arrived at what appears to be a satisfactory verbal label for the situation —in this case for the set of problems—they will generalize this label (the formula) completely. They will, in other words, respond more to the label, to their linguistic description of the situation, than they do to the problem itself. It is as if the presence of an apparently viable verbal label actually blinds the subjects to the realities of the environment. They see only what the words would lead them to expect and do not respond to the objective problem at all.

Such an interpretation is, of course, suggesting that words have great power. It is assuming that they can control or direct a person's behavior, perhaps even his life. We will discuss this implication more thoroughly in the next chapter. But for the moment, we will point out that such an interpretation seems consonant with behavior in a totally different area—namely social stereotyping. By stereotyping we refer to the fact that all people of a certain type, class, race, religion, or what have you, are seen and responded to identically or similarly simply because they are seen as members of this type. One is responding to the type and not to the individual at all. Thus, in the language of the bigot we find that all Negroes are the same; indeed, that they all look the same, they all smell, they all have wonderful senses of rhythm, and so on. And similarly for any other group of people one wishes to find. There are stereotypes for Jews, Catholics, children, cripples, students, professors, doctors, advertising men, commuters, and so on. The point of the stereotype is not that people can be classed into groups or types. The point is that others react to people on the basis of certain impressions about the groups in which they are classed, and not to the idiosyncratic individual at all who just *happens* to be a Jewish, Negro, commuting advertising man.

It is a fact that when one is able to label, to verbally classify a person, one has the option of responding to the attributes of that classification rather than to the attributes of the individual. One's behavior toward others can change as a function of the labels attached to the other. The literature on prejudice bears eloquent testimony to this fact (Allport, 1954). Again we see the word dominating the behavior. But we still cannot say exactly *why* this domination occurs. There are at least two reasons why it might. First of all, it is more economical; the individual is required to do less work, to make fewer discriminations, and the like, if he responds to a label than if he responds to each individual separately. This alone might favor the stereotyping of behavior along convenient verbal classifications. A second alternative is that something about the nature of language forces this sort of reaction. If, for example, meaning is a tendency to respond, once one has labeled something, all the response tendencies to the label become active in the presence of the stimulus object which calls out the label. One cannot help but react to the label since it is, in fact, part of the way in which the person is seen. But more of this later. A third possibility, of course, is that both of the above theories are correct, since they are by no means mutually incompatible.

To continue in the area of thinking and problem solving, the works of Maier (1931) on problem solving are of interest here. His studies involved giving subjects rather elaborate problems in which they were required to use some familiar object in a rather novel way in order to solve the problem. Thus, for example, they might have to hammer some nails, since the problem requires them to build a box of wood. But there is no hammer present, and the only "tool" which will solve this dilemma is the leather heel of a shoe. Or, they may be required to tie two ropes together, both of which are suspended from the ceiling, but which cannot be reached simultaneously by the subject. He must bring the ropes within reach of each other to solve the problem. They cannot be untied from the ceiling. The solution lies in making one of the ropes swing so that it can be caught at its nearest approach to the other rope. This will bring them within reach of one another. To swing the rope, a weight must be tied at its end so that a crude pendulum is made. For our purposes we can ignore the question of how the subjects get to the point of realizing that swinging the rope is required, and that a pendulum weight is necessary, and deal instead with the selection of the pendulum weight itself.

The only appropriate object in their environment which can serve as a weight is an ordinary claw hammer. Whether or not the subject will choose the hammer, and the rapidity with which he will choose it, is a function of the recent past use to which the hammer has been put. Thus, if the subject has, in a previous study, used a hammer for hammering he will tend to not see the hammer as suitable for a weight in this study, whereas, for example, if he has used the hammer to keep something closed— as a weight—he will more rapidly achieve the required solution here. This sort of activity Maier names *functional fixedness*. The prior uses of an object determine how it is seen in a given situation. It is not farfetched to assume that there is a verbal element involved here. If the subject calls the hammer "for pounding" rather than "heavy object" his reactions will be different. He will respond to the verbal classification made of the object, rather than to the objective characteristics of the object itself. We can see that words can put a set of blinders on the individual—but we can also see that they may facilitate his behavior in other situations. Again we have anecdotal evidence for the importance of words in thinking.

Clearly, this is not the strongest evidence in the world. But if we are willing to admit that thinking can be affected by language, we must ascertain exactly how widespread the role of language is. Is language *necessary* for thinking—in which case clearly the nature of the language would completely determine the nature of thought, or is it not—in which case there could be at least partial independence of the two? It probably appears self-evident that language is not necessary for thought, since we can easily see that subhuman, non-linguistic animals are competent problem solvers and the like. On the other hand, it is equally clear that the other animals are not as creative, intelligent, and thoughtful as humans. And it is also true that the great examples of creativity which we have are all *symbolic* in nature. While they may not involve verbal language per se, they all involve working within some system of symbols—whether of numbers, sounds, colors, forms, etc. It is proper to think of music, art, mathematics, and the like as being kinds of languages, since they are behavior systems which are social in nature. Thus "creative" thinking requires a language. But that does not mean that one actually *thinks* in the language, that the mental processes themselves are the manipulation of words or symbols. In other words, we are asking whether language is the tool by which we think, or only the *expression which we give to thought*, or both.

The doctrine that thinking requires language, or to be more blunt, that thinking is talking to oneself, is by no means uncommon in psychological thought. The most well-known proponent of this view is J. B. Watson, the founder of behavioristic psychology. As one might expect from a doctrine that excluded not only the study of consciousness, but its very existence, verbal behavior became the answer to many problems. The process by which problems were solved and by which "thinking" took place was reduced to talking to oneself. And this statement was meant quite literally. It was assumed by Watson that if one had instruments precise enough, it would be possible to record actual—but microscopic—speech movements, whenever the subject reported that he was thinking. Thinking, then, became another form of behavior rather than some mysterious entity which effects behavior but which cannot be directly studied.

Needless to say, this hypothesis is too straightforward (straightforwardness is in general one of the great virtues of behaviorists) not to have been empirically tested. By the 1930's electronic instrumentation was far enough advanced so that one could record such implicit speech movements if they in fact existed. The data are characteristically ambiguous. If we take a simple example and ask a subject to think about performing some physical act, say playing tennis or even merely moving his arm, it is generally possible to record simultaneous activity in the relevant muscle groups. The arms and legs in fact show small twitches during this thinking. We can directly observe extreme examples of this in dreaming, where the sleeping subject will often move violently while he is dreaming of violent movement. But this is clearly but one rather restricted sort of thinking; and it does not involve language at all.

Studies involving the recording of speech movements have been much less convincing. The essence of the problem involves the comparison of any observed movement in the muscles of the speech organs during periods of silent thought, with movements in the same muscles during actual talking. Presumably there should be a close resemblance, and the "thinking" movements should be miniatures—and perhaps abbreviations—of normal speaking movements. It is this comparison which poses the difficulty. There is no question about the presence of movements in the speech organs during thinking. Such movements are quite generally there. But there does not appear to be any obvious—

or even any subtle—resemblance between these movements and those of normal speech. How then, does this affect the behaviorist position? Muscular movements are there, but there is doubt as to whether they are indeed miniature speech movements.* It would seem that we can reject this hypothesis on the grounds that the parallels between observed movements and speech movements have never been conclusively demonstrated. This demonstration, if it could have been made, would have been crucial evidence in favor of the behaviorist theory.

But this sort of investigation does not nullify the more general theory that language is required for thought. In some sense, this hypothesis still exists in the work of Spence, as we saw earlier in this chapter, in Skinner, and in other behaviorist descendants. One may even formulate this hypothesis so that it becomes impossible to refute. The hypothesis states that thought processes involve the use of language. Now our observation of a subject solving a problem is evidence enough for us that he is, in fact, thinking about something. But to study the "thought process" we must find out about this thinking. There appears to be no way to find out thinking except to ask the subject to tell us about his thought. To the extent, then, that he is able to tell us about his thinking, we face a difficulty. Our subject can formulate his thinking in words—after the problem has been solved. This clearly indicates that he could have done so—at least logically— before or during the problem solution. The fact that thinking can be verbally formulated clearly indicates that these verbal formulations *could* have been the basis of thinking itself. Now even if our subject claims that he could not describe his thinking, or even if he claims to have been unaware of thinking in words, this is still not evidence against the theory. It is certainly plausible that one could be unaware of language, or unconscious, even

---

* It is commonly observed that people often move their vocal apparatus while reading. This may be called thinking by means of speech muscle movements, but it is certainly not the strongest evidence for the hypothesis that all thinking is talking to oneself. Thinking about talking, or about words, may indeed involve talking to oneself, but that is not necessarily generalizable to all thought.

if that language is one's own. Moreover, our studies of language have indicated that there are significant aspects of language which are habitually unconscious—specifically the rules of grammar. Hence, some "unconscious" elements in thinking are to be expected. Clearly, at this level it will be difficult if not impossible to even conceive of evidence which would refute the hypothesis that thinking requires or is done by means of language. To the extent that we find ourselves in these sorts of paradoxical conclusions, we must conclude that we are asking the wrong question, or that we have asked it in the wrong way. If this is the case, then let us leave it and approach the relation between language and thinking in another way.

In this case let us ask for negative evidence. Clearly, one implication of the theory that there is a casual relationship between language and the other operations of the mind is this: people who speak different languages will think (and perceive) differently. To the extent, then, that one can find evidence that there are similarities among individuals despite the languages that they speak, one has evidence against this hypothesis. This is particularly true if one finds similarities among languages themselves. If it is true that all languages have certain attributes in common, particularly if it is true that there are common cores of meaning which cut across all languages, then it is clear to some extent that there is an independence of language and other processes of the mind. Since all people are exposed to the same physical world, in the sense that the laws of physics and biology are universal, common cores of meaning which transcend language families may be taken as indicating that one's thinking about the world is reflected in the language and not that language is the sole determiner of one's thinking about the world.

For the moment, let us consider only two pieces of evidence here. The first is data which we have already cited in our discussion of Osgood's theory of meaning. You will recall that Osgood (1962) and his associates administered the semantic differential to members of many different linguistic groups and found that for all languages, the same three factors of meaning were obtained—evaluation, activity, and potency. It appears that Osgood sees this sort of evidence as indicating a common core of mental process which is independent of the nature of the particular language. All meaning is the same in this basic sense, despite the vagaries and differences of language families. Thus, one's thinking about the world is at least partially independent of one's language.

But is this evidence really that strong? Let us remember, first of all, the weaknesses of the semantic-differential methodology. The subjects are rating words taken out of context on scales, defined by "opposite" adjectives, which are selected arbitrarily by the experimenter. Even if these scales do indeed reflect true opposites, it is still clear that it is very difficult to rate some concepts on some of these scales. The ratings obtained, then, have an unavoidable flavor of arbitrariness and artificiality. But consider some other problems pertaining to the cross-culture situation. First of all, we have the problem of selecting the scales in a foreign language. The English scales were selected, at least to some extent, from a relatively large sample of adjectives. Not all details are available concerning the scales selected in foreign languages, but one thing is certain: translated equivalents of the English scales have been included. They would naturally be included in order to test the generality of the English factors. The selection of the scales, however, determines the possibility of finding the factors—and, moreover, the economics of testing require that other factors will not be found, since not enough other scales could be practically included.

Now what do the factors themselves indicate? For scales to appear on the same factor, it must mean that they be responded to similarly. Subjects use all the scales on a given factor in a similar fashion, and all the scales on another factor in a different but similar fashion. Strictly speaking, then, the factors are indices of how the scales are used and Osgood's data shows that the scales which are used similarly to one another in our society are used similarly to one another in other societies as well. But is this the same thing as saying that words mean the same to members of those societies as to us, or that the meaning systems of the cultures are the same? I think not. Osgood, in fact, gives us no evidence that the *factors* mean the same to the different cultures. We are concerned here with, essentially, the problem of translation. The researcher is faced with the problem of translating an English word into its closest single-word equivalent in another language. Clearly the presumption is that such translation is possible with no shifts in meaning at all—and clearly such a presumption is nonsense. There is no evidence at all, either that the translation is the best possible one—a phrase may have been more accurate than a single word—or that the words in the two languages actually have the same meaning. That is, the translated equivalents may, in fact, be used in quite different fashions in two languages, and thus have truly different meanings. To take a simple example, we may translate the French *"amie"* as "friend" which is a perfectly correct translation—in some situations. But the French word clearly has sexual tones to it which our word equally clearly does not. And French is a language which is closely related to ours. What conceivably might happen in switching to Japanese, for example? The point is, then, that even if three dimensions involving the "same" scales are obtained, this does not mean that the meaning of the scales is the same in two different languages, for the words defining the scales may have quite different uses.

The factors obtained by Osgood seem to reflect something about the affective states of the individual. Wundt many years ago indicated that an emotion, by definition, must involve something about (1) approaching (seeking) or avoiding some situation—which is one way of speaking of the pleasantness or unpleasantness of the emotion, (2) about acting or not acting, moving or not moving, and the like, and (3) about the intensity or vigor of the action or feeling itself. Freud (1963) presented a similar three-dimensional scheme for the development of the "instincts," which for him have a clear emotional content. These three necessary characteristics of emotions seem to be what Osgood has found in his three factors of evaluation, activity, and potency. These dimensions are true of all feelings, at least of all feelings in man, simply because man is built the way he is. On this level it is hardly surprising to find them cross-culturally. One would find them in the *man* on the moon too. Thus, all emotional words will have these three characteristics. But that does not mean that one will approach and avoid the same thing, or be active or passive about the same thing in another culture as in ours. Osgood's data could be interpreted as a demonstration of the obvious—that all feelings have the same basic, necessary characteristics. From this he appears to jump to the conclusion that things which have feeling in our society have the same feeling in another. This is clearly not warranted. From a statement that meaning must have such-and-such characteristics in general, one cannot conclude that specific things will have similar meanings. Hence, we must reject Osgood's evidence concerning the commonality of meanings, at least insofar as we use meaning in the relatively precise sense of "how a word is used in the language."

A different and somewhat more interesting approach to the same problem is provided in the work on phonetic symbolism. This hypothesis assumes that certain sounds tend to have the same meanings in all societies, which, if true would again indicate a common mental attitude despite the heterogeneity of language. Thus, for example, small sounds—those produced by small mouth openings, tight vocal chords, lowered palate, and the like —might tend to be associated with words denoting small objects or characteristics, according to the notion of phonetic symbolism. Thus, for example, we find small vowel sounds in certain words denoting smallness, for example /tiny/, /petite/, /klein/, /piccolo/, etc. But we do not find that sound in /small/, notice. Here is part of the problem—there are always exceptions to the "rules" of phonetic symbolism.

But let us consider the evidence. There are a large number of studies all of which essentially demonstrate the following sort of effect. If a subject is presented with an English word and asked to guess which of a pair of words in some foreign language means the same as the English word, he will typically be able to do this better than chance. That is, by chance alone he would be able to make half of the guesses correctly—even if he merely flipped a coin, let us say. But in fact he is able to do significantly better than chance. This suggests, then, that there is some resemblance between words in different languages; translated synonyms can be identified, presumably by their sound patterns alone, since there would appear to be no other factors which could determine the correct choices observed.

We are assuming, of course, that the subjects involved are totally unfamiliar with the foreign language. And this is a correct assumption insofar as a formal training in the language is concerned. But there are, of course resemblances between languages of the sort we described in the second chapter in talking about the history and comparison of languages. Indo-European languages have *formal* similarities by definition. All of the synonyms in these languages, or at least many of them, are presumably derived from some common ancestor word in the hypothetical Indo-European tongue. Clearly, then, to the extent that one finds people identifying synonyms in unfamiliar Indo-European languages, we might be able to account for this by pointing to the formal and historical similarities of the languages. On this level, English speakers are familiar with French, German, and other modern tongues because these languages are "cousins" to the one which they themselves speak. If the phonetic symbolism data were restricted to examples taken only from Indo-European-derived languages, then, one would be justified in rejecting this data as not indicative of anything greater than a family resemblance between languages; and that we already know exists.

This criticism does, in fact, eliminate certain studies of phonetic symbolism as demonstrating nothing more than familial resemblances among languages. However, other studies have been made using non-Indo-European languages, such as Hungarian, Japanese, Hawiian, etc. Even in these cases we do in fact find some evidence for the phonetic symbolism hypothesis. The subjects do perform better than chance on many of the identification tests given to them. Now even here the "family-resemblance" hypothesis cannot be rejected out of hand. Languages do, in fact, borrow from one another, even across family lines. There is perfectly good reason to suppose that Hungarian con-

tains words which are Indo-European derivatives, for despite its
Asiatic origins, Hungarian has been spoken in Europe for a good
many centuries. Similarly, Hawaiian might have been expected
to pick up English derivatives. Japanese is clearly not so easily
written off; nor, on the other hand, is it easy to assume that the
particular words which happen to be in the experiment are those
which are Indo-European derivatives. But this assumption must
be made if one is to rule out the phonetic symbolism hypothesis
on the grounds of this criticism.

There is another point which must be considered, however.
Someone must select the words for the experiment. It is generally
the case that one can find several words in one language which
may be given a reasonably accurate translation by one word in
another language. Thus /klein/ could be translated correctly as
either /little/ or /small/ or /tiny/, etc. The experimenter, then,
is faced with the issue of picking from among several equally
"correct" translations of his key stimulus words. No matter which
way he approaches the problem—from English or from the foreign language—he is still faced with this decision. How does one
solve a problem like this? It is, of course, possible to select words
which stack the experiment in your favor, by selecting only those
translations which do resemble each other in their phonetic constitution. It is doubtful that any experimenter has done this sort
of thing consciously. Some may have done it unwittingly, either
because they were unaware of the translation problem or because
of some other relatively unconscious bias. In a sense, it is difficult
to avoid a bias here; you must select words, and they will, in general, be either phonetically similar or phonetically dissimilar to
their translated synonyms. Thus, either you select words which
will clearly prove or clearly disprove the phonetic symbolism hypothesis. But even if one can completely avoid one's own personal biases—say by selecting words randomly from a dictionary
—the problem in fact remains. But now it is the problem of the
lexicographer, the compiler of the dictionary. He does his work,
of course, with no intent to test any hypothesis of phonetic
symbolism. But let us simply ask this hypothetical question: if
you were compiling a dictionary, say German-English, and you

came to the entry /klein/, how would you translate it; which would you list as its best synonym, /little/ or /small/? I cannot shake the suspicion that most translators would respond to the phonetic similarity. And the conclusion here is that it is impossible to avoid a built-in bias *in favor* of the hypothesis of phonetic symbolism. Methodologically it appears impossible to devise an experiment which will yield results which disprove the hypothesis.

The fact is, of course, that people respond to similarities between things, and phonetic similarities are no different in this regard than others. The joy of phonetic similarity can be seen to its fullest in rhyming poetry. Given no other similarity to respond to than the phonetic one, experimental subjects will obviously respond to it, particularly when the experimenter tells them to. Likewise the experimenter and the lexicographer respond to it as well. But clearly this says nothing about the nature of language per se. Regarding language, there is the fact that there are phonetic resemblances between translations in two unrelated languages. But why is this so? Is it because there is some inherent meaning in the sound, or is it for some other reason? I strongly suspect the latter. Specifically, notice the fact that most phonetic symbolism studies depend on similarities among vowel sounds for their demonstrations. At least it is with vowels that the most striking effects seem to be found. But notice that there are relatively few vowels in any given language proportionately to consonants. Suppose, then, that we are dealing with a relatively familiar word—as all these studies do. Now using the data of Zipf (1949), we can assume that most of these familiar words will tend to be rather short—say monosyllabic or di-syllabic at most—since familiar words which are used a lot tend to be short words. For ease of demonstration, assume that we are dealing with a monosyllable which has one vowel sound and two consonant sounds, and that this is so for both languages. Now further suppose that there are eight vowel sounds in each language and that the languages are roughly similar phonetically. What this means is that, given a particular vowel sound in such a monosyllable in one language, there is one chance out of eight that the word in the other language will have a similar vowel phoneme. In other words, considering only such monosyllables, one out of every eight such "synonymic" words will have similar vowel sounds by *chance alone*. Considering the size of modern language vocabularies this gives the experimenter ample chance to select a large sample of words which show both phonetic and meaning similarity. But this can clearly happen, not because of any meaning effect, but simply because the number of sounds in any language is limited to a relatively small number. A little consideration will convince you that in dealing with a di-syllable, the odds are considerably greater that the two words will have one vowel in common—hence that our illustration above is on the conservative side. Taken from this point of view, there would seem to be no earthly reason to maintain the phonetic symbolism argument unless some a priori reason can be given for its validity.

The only such a priori reason which has been offered is that the means of producing the sound determine its meaning. Thus small sounds are associated with words denoting small things, etc. At one level it would take a complete analysis of the morphemes of a language to fully evaluate this theory. There are two arguments against it, however. The first of these is the obvious fact that there are many words which simply contradict it. This is clearly not sufficient, however, since no one at all would maintain that phonetic symbolism is the only source of meaning. That there is *some* true phonetic symbolism is all that the theory requires. But beyond this, the hypothesis that the means of sound production effects the meaning of the sound appears ridiculous in terms of what it presupposes. For it seems to assume that the speakers of a language, or at least the original creators of languages in general, had some detailed consciousness of how they were making these sounds. If we take the average speaker of any modern language, such an assumption about him is ridiculous. Practically no one knows how to talk on this level. If you were to ask someone how to make a particular phoneme, the best he could do would be to actually make it for you. Knowledge that a sound is small in the sense outlined above is knowledge possessed only by a very small number of technical experts who have been thoroughly and exhaustively trained to learn just this. And even they are not all able to translate their verbal knowledge into action. People who can produce any sound by knowing how it should be produced are very rare indeed. To assume some knowledge of this order in average people is clearly false, and would appear, then, to undermine at least this a priori reason for assuming the phonetic symbolism hypothesis.

In general, then, I would maintain that there is no evidence which strongly supports any notions of common meaning systems underlying different languages, at least in the sense of there being some necessary and inevitable facts about language. There is no logical reason to assume anything other than that languages can be completely independent of one another with no dimensions in common. Yet there is a commonness of another sort, for it is a fact that different languages can be translated into one another. This would clearly not be possible unless there were similar meanings in the two languages. And such similarity there indeed is, but it is of a different sort than that we were just discussing. This sort of similarity in meaning arises because we *Homo sapiens* live in the same world—a world governed by the same physical laws, a world in which animals and plants have uniform characteristics, a world of seasonal regularities, and so on. Language must concern itself with the physical and biological attributes of man's ecology. It is these things which we talk about. Since they are common to us all, we will all have concepts to deal with them. But the similarity and commoness need not be attributed either to a similarity among people—to some essence of man—nor to some necessary similarities among languages or meaning. The similarity exists because things outside the individual, the world, has constant features and dimensions. Since all languages must deal with this world, they must all have some constant or comparable features.

But in many cases it is possible to deal with, categorize, and conceptualize a given state of affairs in the world in different ways. From these natural ambiguities will arise differences between languages. It is now time to decide what effects *these* differences may have on the mind in general, or on any specific mental function in particular. Since the most far-reaching theory concerning this problem was advanced by the anthropologists, B. L. Whorf (1956) and E. Sapir (1956), we will return to a discussion of their hypothesis, which is often referred to as *linguistic relativity*.

In its broadest terms the theory states that the functions of one's mind are determined by the nature of the language which one speaks. But there are several ways of interpreting such a broad statement. Clearly the hypothesis would predict that meaning per se would be a determining variable in mental functioning. That is, evidence which showed that meaning influenced certain perceptual functions would be quite consonant with the Whorfian hypothesis. But it would be very weak evidence for that hypothesis since a great number of other theoretical positions would maintain the importance of meaning also without at the same time being theories of linguistic relativism or determinism. As Joshua Fishman (1960) points out, the Whorfian hypothesis is concerned with the " 'Englishness' of English and how it effects cognition." The *particular* language which an individual speaks will influence him and make him a different person than if he had spoken some other language.

But there are still at least four levels on which one can interpret an hypothesis like this. The Whorfian hypothesis can be interpreted as (1) referring primarily to the lexicon of the language or (2) primarily to its syntax; and it can be interpreted (3) as making statements about basic sensory or behavioral states of affairs or (4) about more cognitive and cultural states of affairs.

(1) The availability of words in a given language determines the sorts of sensory and behavioral classifications which a speaker of the language can make. This, of course, is relevant to the sort of issue we discussed earlier. Do the Iakuti see the difference between blue and green even though they have only one name for the two hues, or do they not? And, as we have seen, an unequivocal answer to this question is difficult to obtain, although if one interprets this on the level of laboratory psychophysics, it

does appear to be false that the language influences the sensory perception of the individual speaker.

(2) The availability of words in a language will determine the sorts of cognitive and cultural classifications which a person may make. One possible example of this sort of thing might be in the area of kinship. Some societies have two different words for our word /aunt/, for example. One word denotes the mother's sister and another word denotes the father's sister. Typically in such cultures there will be quite different behaviors demanded of one in relating to these two aunts. It might be argued that the availability of these words—different words for different people—demands that one treat and relate to these two people differently, while the presence of only one word, /aunt/, in our language demands that we treat them as formally the same. Clearly there are a great number of "ifs" required in this sort of interpretation. What we actually observe, of course, is a difference in formal cultural behavior which is *correlated* with a vocabulary difference. To get from this fact to a statement of causal necessity is a large jump, and no matter how elegantly it is phrased, this jump impresses one as extreme and somewhat unjustified. Nevertheless, it is still not beyond reason to assume that the existence of certain labels per se determines that a person will make certain discriminations which he would not otherwise make. The difficulty in validating this assumption arises from the fact that the existence of the labels may have arisen from some cultural, economic need which in some sense is the real determiner of the discriminations. Thus, the Arabs have a large vocabulary of terms referring to camels, where we, of course, have only two. The Arab learns to use these terms and in so learning, learns to make the discriminations required to use them correctly. In this sense the word necessitates the discriminations. But on the other hand, an Arab must learn to deal with camels —they are an economic necessity to him. Indeed, his life may often depend upon them. This economic necessity, then, determines that he make relevant discriminations about camels, and the frequency and importance of these discriminations will lead

to the development of single words which reflect the discriminations. So at this level, it is the economic determiner which is the underlying cause of the cultural discrimination. Thus, whether you wish to maintain support for the Whorfian hypothesis on the basis of this sort of evidence becomes a matter of saying what sort of causality you are looking for and what you are willing to call *determinism*.

It is areas such as these in which we encounter another set of problems which center about the problem of translation. In order to determine the effects of a particular language on the behavior of speakers of that language, we must, of course, know what the terms in that language mean. We must translate and say whether or not a given term has an equivalent term in our language. But the notion of whether or not two terms mean the same thing, or essentially the same thing, is quite arbitrary. In general, it is correct to say that it is impossible to translate literally from some languages into others. That is, it is impossible to find a single word in English to correspond to each single word in, say, Iakuti. This lack of word-for-word correspondence between languages can be taken as evidence in favor of the Whorfian hypothesis—that is, as indicating a basic difference in the categorizing of the world by the two language systems. It appears that Whorf himself treats the lack of word-for-word correspondence in this manner—at least in some cases.

On the other hand, it is quite possible to translate anything in one language into any other language if one does not insist upon this totally literal translation. If one is permitted to substitute phrases for words, and the like, then translation is less of a problem. Thus, if we permit free translation we get the picture of a commonness between languages; they all seem to talk about the same sorts of things, and hence it seems that there is no basic difference in the categorization of the world among languages. This would clearly contradict the Whorfian hypothesis. Methodologically, then, we must decide what sort of translation we are going to permit in order to evaluate our comparisons of cognition and behavior between language systems. The issue is confused because Whorf is himself contradictory. He classifies American English among what he calls "standard average European" languages, which include French, German, Italian, Spanish, the Scandinavian, and, apparently, the romance and Germanic tongues in general. Within these standard average European languages Whorf is willing to permit free translation. The most sensible rendition of the sense of an utterance in one language is permitted in the other language.

On the other hand, when it comes to translating between a "standard average European" language and one which is not, he sticks to more literal translation. Clearly this sort of procedure emphasizes the similarities among languages which we knew to be historically related, and emphasizes the differences between those which are not so related. But it is, to say the least, a methodologically suspect procedure. We tend to get a picture of the American Indian tribes—from whom he takes most of his non-European examples—as being radically different in their cognitive structure from Europeans. And, of course, we tend to see all Europeans as being essentially the same, both of which conclusions are probably invalid.

To take an example which purportedly shows the difference in cognition between different language groups, we find that the statement, "I was cleaning the gun with a ramrod," is translated (approximately) into Cherokee by the statement, "I was drying the interior of a hole by the motion of a tool" (Whorf, 1956, p. 208). Now here we have two clearly different ways of categorizing the same state of affairs, both of which are equally accurate descriptions. The question is whether or not these linguistic differences reflect anything other than the differential availability of words in the two languages. An adequate answer to this can be obtained only by asking what sorts of things would follow from there being a cognitive difference associated with the differences in lexicon and categorization? It is not easy to determine exactly what the further implications of this use of words would be. There is, indeed, no evidence from the language alone that the Cherokee sees this state of affairs any differently than an English speaker does. And there is certainly no evidence that his behavior with respect to guns, ramrods, cleaning, and the like, is any different because of the linguistic difference; indeed, there is no difference of any sort which has been established other than the vocabulary difference. If this is all that there is, we need not get particularly concerned about it. The unfortunate point is that *we do not know* whether or not this is all there is. Whorf does not give us the necessary evidence, nor is it intuitively obvious what such evidence would look like. But there may be such evidence. It is certainly interesting to speculate about it, but such speculation does tend to be rather academic at this stage.

Let us instead consider an example of the other sort—that is, a case where Whorf permits free translation. The statements /Je vais aller./ in French and the statement /Ich werde gehen./ in German are both translated as /I will go./ in English. On the other hand, literal translation of the French would be /I go to go./ and of the German /I become to go/. Taking only this as evidence, we can easily see that one can speculate madly—and perhaps even validly—about differences in time perception implicit in the English, French, and German languages. Clearly, to the German, the future is a passive event—it happens to him— while for the English speaker, it is an act of volition on his part, and for the French (and English) speaker it is an action, or has the attributes of an action. I do not necessarily maintain this position seriously—although I must admit that it intrigues me —but I will simply use it to point out that if one insists upon literal translation, one can find large and significant linguistic differences between the "standard average European" languages also. Clearly, if we are to test this aspect of the Whorfian hypothesis, we will require a good deal more in the way of methodological specification than the ambiguous one with which Whorf provides us. The rules for translation must be specified in advance, and they must hold for all languages.

Now in fact, this particular interpretation of the Whorfian hypothesis is not the most important statement of its position. As we have seen in our brief description of color names, the availability of words does not necessarily imply anything further about behavior or cognition. Or, to be more accurate, it may imply things about some levels of cognition but not about others.

So even here we would require a good deal more specification about how exactly to interpret the Whorfian hypothesis. Clearly there appears to be something much more psychologically basic about the seeing of color than about the choice of paints for one's bedroom, to use the example given earlier. Various interpretations of the relationship between vocabulary and cognition differ in their generality and importance. Some interpretations of it are clearly true but trivial. Others are much more important but much more dubious in validity. For the moment, then, let us leave this particular interpretation and proceed to the last two.

(3) The grammatical structure of the language will determine the structure of behavior. We can treat this simultaneously with the fourth interpretation.

(4) The grammatical structure of the language will determine the general cognitive structure of the individual. Here we have essentially an hypothesis which purports to explain our ordering and structuring of events in terms of the ordering and structuring rules of the language which we speak. There is little question about the fact that language consists of a large body of grammatical rules, and there is little doubt but that similar rules could be applied to non-linguistic events, such as other sorts of behaviors, thinking, and so on, in which the ordering and relating of events to one another is required. The empirical question, of course, is whether or not this actually happens.

Now, it is a fact that we do think in words—perhaps not always but sufficiently often to worry about the problem. Here we return to the old issue of whether words are the tool of thought —that is, whether their use is required by extralinguistic variables—or whether they actually regulate the thinking itself. We can, if you will, contrast the Whorfian hypothesis with the recent quote of President de Gaulle that "[t]he wonderful thing about the French language is that it expresses thoughts in their natural order." This latter statement will probably appear somewhat amusing to most of you, but why? Because, first of all, why should French be a better expresser of thoughts than any other language? And secondarily because, clearly, English expresses thoughts better than any other language! To a monolingual, thinking in a language other than his own is a difficult concept to comprehend. Indeed, the very names of a language often seem to have a sanctity; one cannot always avoid the reaction that there is something peculiar about foreigners because they call such "obvious" things by such "peculiar" names. The average speaker, then, has a paradoxical feeling about language; he does not feel that his thought is bound by his language—he never wishes to admit any determinism of any sort—hence, any language is as good as any other. Yet, simultaneously there is something privileged about his own language. He is unable to really conceive of acting without it, or that one can really be as fully competent in any other language. Our average speaker is Whorfian at least in part.

But, clearly, while this feeling of dependence of a language is consonant with the Whorfian hypothesis, it is not by any means sufficient proof of it. The hypothesis at this level states that the structure of man's language becomes the structure of his mind in general. He need not necessarily think in the language, but he thinks the way he does because of the language he speaks. Given this sort of hypothesis, then, we can conceive of speculating about the following sorts of "problems": Logic developed in the European languages rather than in some other because of the subject-verb-predicate (or subject-predicate-verb) structure of these languages. It is only within this sort of structure that one can create propositions of the sort which can be operated on by syllogistic laws, and the like. It is, then, no accident that a thinker such as Aristotle was a speaker of Greek—or that French speakers should tend to stress objects more than properties of objects, while English speakers should do the reverse because the French put their adjectives after nouns, while the English their nouns after adjectives. Or Germans should tend to minimize action over substantive aspects of the world, as evidenced by the fact that they put their verbs at the ends of their sentences. And likewise for Romans.

One could go on in this vein almost indefinitely, and in the course of this speculation one may very well tap some lode of psychological knowledge which is of profound importance. But there is no *guarantee* that this is so, for the above arguments are quite arbitrary and have a subtle but very fallacious aspect to them. Take the adjective example. To an American, in some situations at least, what comes second is of lesser importance than what comes first. Hence, to this American it would follow that the French see their adjectives as less important than their nouns. But this is attributing to the French our cultural values, which is not only a dubious procedure, but, if the Whorfian hypothesis itself is true, completely invalid. Thus, one cannot use this sort of evidence to validate the Whorfian hypothesis, since to do so requires an assumption which itself invalidates the hypothesis.

So where are we? At some level, the Whorfian hypothesis seems almost incapable of empirical proof—and, if this is the case, it seems reasonable to question the desirability of maintaining the hypothesis. The evidence which appears to be most strongly in favor of the hypothesis has an air of triviality about it. Thus, the fact that the language favors a certain emphasis among the many possible ways of structuring a given environment and that the behavior of an individual also shows this structure is, in fact, very weak evidence. Consider the fact that Navaho verbs have endings which are dependent upon the shape of the object which is the subject of the sentence. If, then, we give Navaho children objects to match asking them essentially which is the better match, color or shape, we might expect shape to be dominant. Indeed, this is the case, as shown by a study conducted by Carroll and Casagrande (1958). For American children, this should not be the case, nor should it be for English-dominant Navaho. The latter prediction has been verified, but for the English speakers there seems to be an inexplicable predominance of Navaho-type matching. What exactly this does to the hypothesis is not clear. But even if we neglect it, it can be quite easily assumed that the matching behavior and the language behavior both reflect some third, unspecified cultural cause or pressure. The establishment of a correlation between language and behavior is not equivalent to establishing a causal determinism—which is what the Whorfian hypothesis assumes.

In conclusion, we come to a rather pessimistic evaluation of the Whorfian hypothesis. And yet this does not necessarily mean that the theory is really false. The difficulties with the theory are in its validity—which at worst has simply not been demonstrated. It certainly has never been disproven. The problem is that it would be very difficult to either prove or disprove it. And this is because certain quite critical terms are left undefined. If we are to test an hypothesis about meaning, we must have some notion about what meaning is. If we are to test a hypothesis about the mind—in any of its manifestations—we must have some idea of what it is we are looking for. To test a theory about the effects of language on any non-linguistic events, we should have some concept to explain how language functions so that we can make meaningful predictions about what we should observe. In other words, we need a *psychological* theory in order to evaluate this hypothesis—a theory of the mind and of language. Only then will we be able to say whether or not language can effect the mind, and only then can we specify the conditions under which it does effect the mind. Whorf has not provided us with this—for the simple reason that he does not think it necessary. In this sense he is clearly wrong, for we see that without theories of meaning and the like, we can get nowhere. To fairly evaluate the Whorfian hypothesis, then, we must go beyond Whorf, and consider language in the light of a general psychological theory. Then we can see what effects the language per se may have on the mental life of man. This we shall do in the next chapter.

Bibliography

Allport, G. *The nature of prejudice.* Cambridge, Addison-Wesley, 1954.

Brown, R. and Lenneberg, E. A study in language and cognition. *J. abnorm. soc. Psychol.,* 1954, 49, 454-62.

Carroll, J. B., and Casagrande, J. B. The function of language classifications in behavior. In Maccoby, Newcomb, and Hartley (Eds.) *Readings in social psychology.* New York, Henry Holt & Co., 1958.

Dollard, J., and Miller, N. *Personality and psychotherapy*. New York, McGraw-Hill, 1950.

Fishman, J. A systematization of the Whorfian hypothesis. *Beh. Sci.*, 1960, 5, 323-39.

Freud, S. The Instincts and their vicissitudes. In Rieff, P. (Ed.) *Freud: general psychological theory*. New York, Collier Books, 1963, pp. 83-103.

Kuenne, M. Experimental investigation of the relation of language to transposition behavior in young children. *J. exp. Psychol.*, 1946, 36, 471-90.

Luchins, A. S. *Mechanization in problem solving: the effect of Einstellung*. Evanston, Ill., The American Psychological Association, 1942.

Maier, N. R. F. Reasoning in humans. II. The solution of a problem and its appearance in consciousness. *J. comp. physiol. Psychol.*, 1931, 12, 181-94.

Osgood, C. E. Studies on the generality of the affective meaning system. *Amer. Psychologist*, 1962, 17, 10-28.

Sapir, E. *Culture, language and personality*; selected essays edited by D. Mandelbaum. Berkeley, University of California Press, 1956.

Spence, K. The differential response in animals to stimuli varying within a single dimension. *Psychol. Rev.*, 1937, 44, 430-44.

Whorf, B. L. *Language, thought and reality*. New York, John Wiley & Sons, 1956.

Zipf, G. K. *Human behavior and the principle of least effort: an introduction to human ecology*. Cambridge, Addison-Wesley, 1949.

X

Language as a Weapon

With this chapter we arrive full circle, back to language as a social behavior. Language and meaning evolve, culturally and individually, in a social context. The function of language is in this sense always—and in countless ways—social. Language, for example, is a weapon by means of which man attempts to compel his fellow man to do his bidding. We must now discuss some examples of this aspect of language—in both its obvious and its more subtle guises—to see why these sorts of things can be. We will then see something close to the true relationship between language and the mind. Indeed, we will have arrived at a picture of man as a whole—which is, of course, the task of any psychological endeavor.

The most obvious and direct example of linguistic influence is the command. Perhaps we should use Skinner's terms and refer to it as manding in general. Here we tell a person what he is to do. His behavior is to correspond to the behavioral description we have given in our utterance. At one level the problem may appear to be quite simple. If the listener is a member of the speaker's language community, he of course knows what the speaker means when he utters the mand. The listener may then obey it or not as the case may be. But the issue is not quite this simple, for there are some people who are more likely to obey than are others. And there is certain training which can produce what we might call habits of obedience. To understand the effectiveness of a command, we must understand such habits of obedience—whatever they may be.

First let us consider what we mean by meaning—in a theoretical sense. We have defined meaning as the set of readinesses to respond which have been associated with a word or utterance in the language. In addition, a perception is also defined as a set of readinesses to respond which have also been associated to stimuli. Now, to the extent that a word has meaning, there is a behavioral readiness present. For a command to be translated into action, one need only translate the relevant behavioral readiness, which is the meaning of the utterance from a readiness per se into an overt action. A translation from potential into action can be accomplished by manipulating the external situation, the individual's motives, the rewards present, etc. until the proper combination has been found so that the meaning of the command produces the overt behavior which corresponds to the meaning of the utterance. Thus, /close the window/ may not produce overt behavior by itself alone. But if there is a draft on the listener, if he is threatened with a spanking for not acting, if he is not too fatigued, and so on, then he will in fact close the window when he is told. But clearly, in this relatively normal situation, the verbal utterance is not sufficient to account for the obedience. The situation of normal command, then, requires extraverbal factors for its effectiveness. This situation is of very little concern to us now.

Of more importance is the situation in which someone's "word is law"—the situation in which the command is *immediately* translated into action. How is this achieved? There seem to be two ways in which this state can be achieved: one essentially motivational and the other involving a change in the language itself. Certain attempts to influence the behavior of an individual by verbal means alone do not appear to be successful, however. I refer specifically to attempts by certain advertisers to affect the buying behavior of people through subliminal stimulation. Thus, it was assumed that the flashing on a movie screen of /buy Cocacola/ —too rapidly for the individual to see on a conscious level

—would in fact make him buy the product. There is absolutely no empirical evidence that such an effect can be obtained. Indeed, there are no theoretical grounds for assuming that it should be obtained. Why this simple sort of stimulation should be translated directly into action is not easy to see. The assumption that such will be the case seems quite naïve. At best it is a serious misreading of Freudian theory.

But there *are* cases in which verbal stimuli are translated directly into action. In some ways the most striking of these may be the state of hypnosis. The word of the hypnotist is quite literally law. Each of his utterances is a command; even the nuances of his speech, of which he himself may be unaware, are commands. Thus, we find the hypnotic subject obligingly producing "memories" of, for example, how he will behave in the *future*—not because he has any such memories, of course, but because he correctly interprets the hypnotist as desiring such memories (Weitzenhoffer, 1953, p. 193). We should have no doubts about this: the practiced hypnotic subject will apparently do anything his hypnotist desires. There are reported cases in which the subject attempted acts of violence on another person at the hypnotist's request, despite the general assumption that one can do nothing under hypnosis that one would not do in the waking state. Such studies have been criticized on the grounds that the subject "knew" that the hypnotist would not "really" require him to do anything immoral. But there is in fact no evidence that this is the case. And, if the meaning of the word /kill/ is really a readiness to respond, then to the extent that we know this word, we have a readiness to do the relevant act. /Kill/ is no different than any other word in this respect, and there seems to be no good reason to assume that it will behave differently under hypnosis.

But we need not consider such an extreme case. The simplest commands of the hypnotist are carried out immediately and with a sureness which is in many cases quite uncharacteristic of the waking state. Beyond the direct behavioral effects, we see that the hypnotist can command purely "sensory" occurrences as well. He can produce hallucinations in his subject; he can have the subject see things incorrectly, hear things which are not there, and so on. Insofar as hypnotism depends upon the manipulation of meaning, this is not surprising, for the meaning system and the perception system appear to be identical as far as the underlying psychological determinants are concerned. The hypnotist is merely activating readinesses to respond. The fact that some of these are "perceptual" is not too important theoretically. However, it does indicate that at least in this case, the perception has been associated to the word. The word as a stimulus can call out readinesses to respond which are characteristic of non-verbal stimuli. In this sense, we can see that there is a dependence of perception on the vocabulary of the language. In case there is any doubt about this, we should point out that these imaginary things which the hypnotic subject experiences are quite real to him.*

The hypnotist, then, can translate the meaning of a word directly into behavior and experience in his subject—providing, of course, that the subject is a good one. Here, of course, seems to be the crux of the problem of how hypnotism works. Some people are almost impossible to hypnotize; others can be put in a trance at the simple command of /Go to sleep/. If we can account for these individual differences, we will probably have some understanding about the nature of this sort of command. We cannot give a full answer since the data is not yet available. What we do know suggests strongly, however, that there is a motivational effect here, or an effect which may be described as the prior learning of the ability to be dependent.

A major individual difference related to the susceptibility to hypnosis is birth order, i.e. whether one is an only child, the first child in a multi-child family, the second child, etc. Susceptibility to hypnosis increases with the birth order as listed above. An only child is a very difficult subject. A second child is a "push over." The crucial variable seems to be related to dependency, or

---

* Once when I was hypnotized, I saw a rather vivid color—which was not there—and then actually experienced a negative after-image from it. The latter did not take place at the suggestion of the hypnotist and, hence, suggests that he had elicited in me a "real" perception.

to a tendency to put oneself at the disposal of others. This, of course, is really just another way of saying that one "pays attention" to what others tell him—i.e. that he obeys. We would probably be better off if we considered it this way: As you recall, we found that we could not account for the understanding of a linguistic stimulus by a listener in terms of the stimulus alone. We had to look to certain internal states which could generally be described as the intention to perceive meaning, the desire to listen, etc. We do not know what these states are, but we can assume that they involve readinesses to respond and that they are acquired. Only by making such an assumption can we account for the selective understanding shown by speakers and listeners—the fact, for example, that they hear only what is relevant to their on-going conversations. Can we not say, then, that the dependent person has these internal states associated with the presence of other people, or perhaps to other people who have certain more definite characteristics—e.g. older people, men, etc. Thus, for him, to a greater extent than for the only child—who is generally exposed to fewer people in his immediate home environment—the presence of another becomes a necessary stimulus to the perception of meaning. With only a slight additional assumption we can see that another person can be the necessary stimulus for translating meaning into action as well. How the hypnotist produces the effects that he does is still somewhat of a mystery; nevertheless it can be considered as an extreme case of what happens in the normal life of the individual. Obedience in this case becomes a matter of another person's providing the necessary stimuli for meaning to be apprehended, and for meaning to be translated into action.

One may characterize this easily influenced individual derogatorily as dependent or conforming or even subservient—and with a certain degree of justification. Nevertheless, his case is far from hopeless, for not only can he acquire new habits, but he undoubtedly already has many of them. Other people may be sufficient to produce the meaning-perception conditions, but other non-human stimuli may be also. There is nothing mutually contradictory about such an assumption. Moreover, so long as the individual is actually responding to the meaning of a word, there will always be a degree of independence of his behavior from the intentions of any other person. Meaning, as we have seen, involves uncertainty; it exists only when there are alternative modes of responding; meaning is derived from the individual's having choice. Thus, we can see that the intent behind the command of the hypnotist may not necessarily be correctly translated by the subject; he may well produce one of the other aspects of the meaning of the words. And this will be even liklier when one leaves the hypnotic situation for real life. Meaning can never result in unambiguous behavior, and as a result we can infer that meaning and total command are in some sense incompatible. The other sorts of total command seem to realize this and to capitalize on it.

Let us consider this other sort of command, which is exemplified in the military situation where the word of the commanding officer is law to the subordinate. It is characteristic of the well-trained soldier that he executes commands immediately and without question. He quite literally acts before he thinks and, indeed, probably does not think at all in many situations. The response to the command is, in fact, often quite unconscious, and it is this fact that gives us a clue to its nature. This situation is, in other words, often unlike the hypnotic situation in which the subject willingly and willfully *gives* obedience to the hypnotist and in which a strong desire not to obey can, in fact, result in the subject's breaking out of the trance in some cases.

Before trying to elucidate the true nature of military command, let us eliminate one possible reason for it—the threat of physical harm. There are, of course, situations in which the failure to execute a command correctly and immediately can result in the death of the soldier. Such insubordination may result in his putting himself in a position of physical danger. Or he may have to suffer actual punishment for failure to execute the command; that is, he may be executed for insubordination. These things *can* happen, but they are by no means universal threats. There are cases in which commands can be disobeyed without such bodily harm resulting, although negative sanctions are al-

ways possible. But clearly the soldier does not really think about
the possibility of punishment when he executes the command.
In some cases, his action is too prompt for there to have been
time for such thought. The threat of punishment does, indeed,
play a role in the *training* of obedience, but it cannot itself account for any specific act of obedience. It cannot, for example,
account for the numerous examples of blind obedience which
resulted in acts as morally depraved as those seen in the German
concentration camps, or in the bombing of innocent civilians by
our own countrymen in Vietnam. The term "blind obedience"
is the key. It is obedience without thought or reflection that we
must explain.

Let us return to a definition of consciousness or awareness. We
have defined consciousness as a set of readinesses to respond—
that is, a collection of tendencies to make certain movements
(behaviors or acts in the adult) to certain stimulus arrays. The
stimuli, of course, consist of the entire external and internal
arrays present at a given moment of time. The point of importance here is that consciousness requires *a set of several* such
readinesses. Consciousness is, in fact, the result of ambiguity,
of uncertainty, or of the possibility of choice. The opposite of
this situation, complete certainty or rote behavior, in which one
stimulus always produces one and only one response readiness,
we have called unconsciousness. There is a tendency to respond
to a stimulus, but there is only one such tendency at a given
moment. Following the assumptions of our theory, the subject
will not have any awareness of the stimulus array which calls
out one and only one such tendency to respond.

Let us consider specifically the case of language and meaning.
We have defined meaning as a set of tendencies to respond to
a given word—that is, to the stimulus array produced by having
the eyes or ears stimulated by the hearing of or the seeing of the
written characters of a word. Since meaning too involves ambiguity and uncertainty, it is, by definition, conscious. Now this
does not mean that every time one hears a word one will immediately *think* of a definition of it, or of a paraphrase of each
utterance, or any such thing. Rather, it means that the under-

standing and use of language, of the system of meaning which
is language, is a conscious process. That is, we know what is
meant; we understand language; we are aware of its significance.
If we equate meaning with conscious processes in general, we
can see that according to our theory if some word were to acquire
only *one* tendency to respond, it would *not* be conscious and
would *not have meaning* in the way that other words do. The
word with only one tendency to respond is not a part of our
conscious knowledge, is not reacted to consciously and, in fact,
does not have meaning. It is my contention that the teaching
of obedience involves the systematic elimination of meaning from
the words of the language to the point where each word has one
and only one response tendency connected to it for the context
in which the commands will occur. One cannot, of course, take
a real functioning word in the language and eliminate all but
one of the response tendencies which it has, at least not in all
contexts and situations. But one can make a pretty good stab at
this for at least some words in some situations. And one must
face the uncomfortable possibility that the rigidities of one era
may be passed on to the next. But more of this in a moment.

Let us first discount one possible objection. We have claimed
that all meaning involves ambiguity and uncertainty. To this it
might be retorted that this eliminates any possibility of precision
in language. It is clear that the physical sciences tend to be quite
precise in their terminology and that, indeed, their excellence is
in some way dependent on this precision; does this not tend to
invalidate the ambiguity theory of meaning? The answer is, of
course, no; for the precision of technical terms lies only in the
fact that scientists agree about the *range of ambiguity* which constitutes the meaning of that term. Thus, most scientific terms
are class names of some sort. They could not be true proper
names in any sense, for the true proper name denotes one and
only one specific state of affairs. A science, which by definition
deals with general laws, would have little or no use for such
specific terminology. But the fact that scientific words are class
names signifies that they denote collections of things and, since
no two things are absolutely identical, the identifying marks of

belonging to a certain class must be some sort of *similarity* or *resemblance* rather than identity. In other words, scientific classes consist of collections of different things, but where the *differences among them are systematic or orderly in some manner*. To take a specific example, all scientists would agree upon the use of the term "visible light." It denotes a specific *range* of electromagnetic radiation frequencies or wave lengths. But since a range is involved, it is clear that to that extent the "meaning" of the term "visible light" is ambiguous. It could refer to this wave length or to that wave length or to some other, etc. The precision of this term lies, as we have said, in the fact that scientists would agree about the nature and the scope of the ambiguity which constitutes the meaning of the term. A little consideration will convince you that this is the case for all scientific terms. The precision of science in fact gives us support for a theory of meaning based upon uncertainty.

Now then, the military command situation is really quite simple. So-called basic training involves essentially the compelling of soldiers to execute a series of quite arbitrary actions in response to the verbal command of the officer in charge. The compulsion is, of course, of the essence here. In training, the word *must* be followed by the action, and it must be followed *always*. The training procedure is one in which failure of obedience is severely punished and in which physical force is used if necessary to elicit the necessary action from the soldier in training. In other words, each time a word is uttered, one and only one action is permitted, and one and only one action actually occurs. No deviations are allowed, and the action is forced if necessary. We have, then, the military context set up for the acquisition of a one-stimulus, one-response situation, with no ambiguity present at all. That punishment is evoked, or at least the threat of it offered, has two implications. It of course provides a kind of reinforcement for the new learning. The avoidance of pain or anxiety is a well-known and highly efficient motivator and reward. There is no doubt that the learning of the correct response to the stimulus (in this case the verbal command) will take place in such a circumstance. But, in addition, the punishment insures the *extinction* of all of the old responses which may have been previously acquired to the verbal command. We have, then, the building up of one response tendency simultaneous with the eliminating of all others to the words of command.

One other device insures the final desired outcome—the demand for immediate and rapid action or the acquisition of generalized habits of obedience associated with the military context. It is crucial to the system of command that the soldier never develop the habit of stopping and thinking about what he is doing, for that would automatically throw ambiguity into the situation. Thinking itself would be another response to the command, and, given this other response, there would always be the possibility that the command would not be obeyed. In the military context, the man who thinks too much is quite dangerous, for he undermines the entire command situation. Thus, the training emphasizes rapidity, with the result that no possibility or opportunity of thinking about anything arises. The action follows the word with no mediators at all.

So we end with the well-trained soldier who can be characterized as something less than human, for his training in the military ways has eliminated from him that which makes him human—his awareness and his use of symbolic meaning systems. Now, given the word of command in the military context, he quite literally has no alternative but to obey. And this obedience is exacted at the price of a part of his mind. The words no longer have meaning for him; his awareness has been lessened by that amount. And it is only through this elimination of meaning that command can be exercised to its fullest and most efficient extent. It is only through the lack of meaning that the necessary rigidity and the necessary lack of reflection can exist. Obedience, of course, cannot be depended upon as long as either ambiguity or its corollaries, reflection and awareness, exist. We must conclude then, that command is effective not because words have come to mean certain things, but *precisely because they have come to mean nothing. They are no longer words* but are mere stimuli which reliably elicit one and only one response tendency. Nothing can break this cycle once it has been established save some radical change in the stimulus situation or context. Put an individual in a truly new world and he may reacquire meaning. But to the extent that command is exercised in wider and wider spheres to life, to that extent escape from its influences becomes increasingly remote. Moreover, we must face the fact that language and meaning are social phenomena; they are taught by people to people. And a person who has a vocabulary with no meanings, but only with single rote responses connected each to its own verbal stimulus, cannot teach anything but these to another person. Having been trained to obey, then, one can teach others nothing but obedience as well. We have, then, the verbal counterpart to what Adorno and his associates (1950) called the *authoritarian personality*—the individual who desires and "lives for" obeying and commanding simultaneously. The military situation and any other command situations which resemble it, can be the training grounds for a verbal totalitarianism.

This, of course, is an extreme example of the power words have to influence people; yet, it has within it the germs of most other contemporary examples of verbal influence. Consider another sort of extreme example, the phenomenon known as *brainwashing*, which came to prominence during the Korean war. Essentially, brainwashing refers to an attempt to induce a person to abandon one ideology and accept an alternative, and to do this completely and utterly, so that he believes in and reacts to the new ideology as he did to the old one. This represents a large-scale attempt to eliminate one set of meanings for certain terms and substitute another set for them and is based on the assumption that any ideology consists of a set of meanings for some particular cluster of terms. In this case, the ideologies are political, and the crucial terms are those such as "democracy," "freedom," "imperialism," "Communism," and so on. To any American each of these terms has a meaning*—that is, a set of potential responses associated to it. We know the meaning of these terms insofar as we can use them properly and insofar as there

---

* That these meanings have become clearly limited, almost to the point of non-meaning, need not concern us at the moment.

is some ambiguity and awareness involved in their use. For most people this is the case for the sorts of words in question.

To understand the verbal manipulations involved in brainwashing, we must take a specific example. Let us consider /democracy/. To an American this term has a definition which involves something about the government's being responsible to the wishes of the people. Typically this would imply something about the government officials being, at least in part, elected by some form of wide suffrage. We use the term "democratic" in situations which involve majority rule, popular voting, and so on. Implicit in it is the tolerance of a certain amount of dissent (although, of course, not too much) and certainly no opposition to the majority-rule notion. It should be clear that this definition has little or nothing to do with the actual governing of the United States. Our elected officials are generally selected by political parties over whom we (the electorate) have no control. They are elected by virtue of the size of their campaign budgets: their primary loyalty, therefore, is to the men who have financed them, not to the voters. Their government is for the few, not for the many. While there is indeed majority rule, the choices given to the voters are so narrow as to be almost without significance, and these choices in no way effect the behaviors of the elected. But when we wish to refer to this form of government, we use the term /democracy/; hence, we must say that this is what "democracy" means. Meaning is not logical; "democracy" can mean simultaneously the rule of the many and the rule of the few.

When a member of a Soviet Communist country uses the term /democracy/ he means something quite different. To him a democratic form of government may be one in which the will of the proletariat or working class is exercised. It is a "dictatorship of the proletariat" which is democratic by virtue of the fact that it represents the will of the vast bulk of the people—the proletariat. Since Marxism is an historical theory which, among other things, attempts to predict the course of political evolution, the will of the proletariat can be defined in historical terms. That is, it is the will of the masses of people that certain events

will occur in history—that is, in the future. Anyone well trained
in the theory can know what is supposed to happen and, hence,
can represent the will of the people—as defined by the theory.
Thus, "democracy" can mean the rule of a small number of
people—the Communist party central commissions—since by
definition the party represents the people, and the leaders represent the party and are cognizant of the historical necessities of
the proletariat. Democracy exists because the will of the majority
is presumably being exercised even though the majority have in
fact no say about what happens. We may find this sort of reasoning foreign and bizarre. It is certainly "un-American." But it is
probably no more senseless than our own reasoning.*

In the case of /democracy/ we are dealing with a term that is
quite arbitrarily defined and which simply has a use in a language, as all real words do. That this use may imply behaviors
which are quite contrary to reality must also be born in mind.
The question now is: how do we substitute one set of uses for
another? The brainwashing procedure accomplishes this substitution in quite an interesting manner. First of all, the prisoner
to be "brainwashed" is completely isolated from any social contacts. It is clear that for a meaning system to be manipulated, no
distracting or contradictory influences can be present. One cannot have the prisoner reinforcing his old meanings by association
with his old social reinforcers. This isolation may be physical,
but it may also be accomplished by sowing suspicion among the
prisoners through the planting of spies and informers among
them. Thus, no one trusts anyone else—and from a lack of trust
grows lack of reinforcement.

Only the captors can control the reinforcements, both because
they have the power of life and death over their prisoners and

---

* It is of some interest that the rule of the few has always been considered
democratic by the Russian elite. Even the Tsar considered himself to be a
democratic leader because he conceived of himself as personally exercising
the "real" will of the people. But the Russian heritage of such thinking, and
the fact that Communist thinking has often become tinged with a form of
Pan-Slavist chauvinism, should not mislead us as to the fact that this definition is as valid ("useful") as our own.

because the prisoner has no one else from whom to get reinforcement. The next step involves extracting a "confession" from the prisoner. This confession is a repudiation and condemnation of everything that the prisoner has believed in; it is a castigation of his political ideology, among other things. Now it is easy enough to get the prisoner to write such a confession, for he is, after all, at gun point, and it is, after all, "merely" some silly piece of paper he is submitting. But this is just the beginning, for he must now rewrite the confession time and again, and he must discuss, rehearse, and defend it to his interrogators. But language is a social thing. It is based on consensual validation—the agreement among people as to meanings, uses, and the like. Our prisoner can use language only in a social manner, but his society is now restricted to his captors and interrogators. It is only a matter of time before his uses of language conform with his captors'. By the rote practicing of ideological statements where certain uses of terms are punished and other uses are rewarded, old meanings can be obliterated and a new set substituted. This is not a case of just making something meaningless, but rather of substituting a new range of permissible ambiguity for a given term. The word acquires a new meaning and a meaning which is quite genuine.

Now there are still several mysteries about this situation to be clarified. One would think that the knowledge that this was done under the threat of physical violence would somehow negate the entire procedure. And indeed it would, except that this knowledge becomes unconscious. The entire proceeding has a rote aspect in that the manner of extracting and treating the confessions themselves is routinized. Each day, in the same general situation, the prisoner undergoes the same sort of procedure. The words which he says are very much alive to him, since he is required to analyze them, criticize them, revise them, and so on. Then the surroundings become vague, for it is the same thing over and over again. What we have here is a variety of the command situation in which the interrogation situation itself always comes to evoke the same response. It then becomes meaningless and its significance unconscious. The threat no longer exists, and the prisoner finds himself uttering words, expressing opinions which are contrary to everything he ever believed in, and doing this for reasons which he *cannot* know. One can use some version of Festinger's theory of dissonance (1957) to explain this—that the conflict between what the prisoner says and what he believes gets resolved in favor of the utterances. Or one may simply say that saying something without questioning why we say it is what we mean by belief. At any rate, a term like /democracy/ eventually no longer means the same thing to the prisoner—he has lost all its old uses and acquired a new set. As a result he can be set free; he has been re-educated. He is a different man with different meanings and, as a result, a different awareness.

Here, then, we return to the Whorfian hypothesis, for there can be no doubt that the world looks significantly different to this individual. He has gone through an episode of strictly verbal training which has resulted in the abandoning of one meaning set and the assumption of a new one. /Democracy/, for example, now means something quite different to him. And as a result of this new meaning, he now *acts* differently with respect to objects which might be labeled "democratic." Whereas he once would have referred to the government of the United States by this label, he would now use it to refer, for example, to the Peoples Republic of China. But as we all "know," the latter government is far from democratic.* The point of interest is that his actions and behaviors are changed. From our definition of meaning as a set of tendencies to respond, this change in behavior which follows a change in meaning is hardly surprising. But it would also seem to imply that the object referred to is perceived differently. How, otherwise, would we account for the change in behavior?

Thus, if a particular form of government "looked" or appeared the same to the individual after brainwashing as it did before, why would he change his behavior? Why would he not simply

---

* Needless to say, there is no question about there being "real" or "true" names for objects or of there being "real" or "true" meanings for words. The meaning of a word lies in its use—and that is the only truth involved. Our brainwashed individual is not misusing the word "democracy"; he is simply using it differently.

bring this behavior into line with his perceptions of the institutions? Certainly there is no reason to assume that meaning is somehow prepotent over perception or other forms of cognition —at least there is no reason to assume this if we suppose that they are relatively independent mental systems. But, on the other hand, what if they are basically different forms of the same system (which is essentially what we are assuming)? If perception is also a set of tendencies to respond, how are we to separate these from the tendencies to respond which constitute meaning? More specifically, how is the particular individual in question to separate them? The answer is, of course, that he cannot do so. A given tendency to respond may be equally effective in determining what we call perception and what we call meaning. A change in meaning, then, is equally a change in perception, cognition, thinking, and the like. This hypothesis is supported by the fact that the changes in meaning produced by brainwashing do in fact often produce relatively long-lasting changes in behavior—a fact which could not be explained unless there were changes in perception as well.*

We have outlined here an extraordinarily difficult but effective exercise in influence and command. It is accomplished through an actual change in the meanings of an individual's words—that is, in his tendencies to respond to the word and use it—and these effects influence the mind and its functions in their entirety. We can learn two important lessons from this consideration. First we see that our behavior can be profoundly affected by the linguistic categories which we have; they put blinders on our behavior so to speak. Once we have learned the meaning of a word, we will tend to *see* evidence which will confirm that meaning, since the meaning mechanism and the perceptual mechanisms are identical. What we find, then, is that *all* language learning

---

* Perception cannot, of course, be altered so that it is directly contradictory to the world without that alteration's breaking down. It is this fact that doubtless accounts for the eventual failure of many of the brainwashing attempts made by China in the Korean war. This does not mean that brainwashing could not be complete and permanent. It merely means that China's attempts were crude.

is a form of brainwashing, for it involves learning a completely arbitrary set of uses for words, wherein the only definition of correctness is one provided by social means. It is a definition established either by a person with power, or by some indefinable and intangible consensus of opinion and habit. By these means you are controlled as much in your meaning of the term /democracy/, say, as is the unfortunate subject of brainwashing. Things are not all this gloomy, but we shall have to wait a bit to see the positive side. We learn, then, that language controls us and that this control may be completely arbitrary or basically irrelevant to any criteria of "essential" truth or falsity, correctness or incorrectness.

You may have already seen a way out of the brainwashing procedure itself, for the technique as practiced does not have to be effective—either in the prison camp or in your home. The system works; indeed, meaning becomes compulsion to the extent that there are *few* response tendencies connected to the word. Since brainwashing must destroy an original set of meanings to given words, it must operate just as the military-command situation does, by eliminating various response possibilities until the individual is no longer conscious of the meaning of the word. Once meaning is unconscious, a new set of tendencies can be built up at the discretion of the interrogator. There is nothing to hinder him now since there is no meaning to contradict anything he might say. Since meaning and perception are so intimately connected, no contradictory information can possibly be achieved by sensory means, at least not for an "object" as intangible as democracy. But we have also suggested that speed is essential in eliminating meaning: one cannot permit the prisoner—or soldier —time to think about what he is doing.

Thinking must involve the excitation of tendencies to respond, as does any mental process. Thus, if one consciously thinks of or about a word, one must be arousing various tendencies to respond to it. Any thinking to verbal stimuli at least maintains, and probably even raises, the number of response tendencies associated to the word. Thinking, therefore, raises the response ambiguity which the word has and increases its meaning, by definition. Thinking, of nearly any sort whatsoever, maintains meaning. Even though meaning may quickly become something other than the consensually valid meaning of the rest of the language community, it is meaning nevertheless. Clearly, if the prisoner could be trained to stop and think about everything which he said and wrote in the interrogation, he could resist the brainwashing procedure and could probably do so almost indefinitely. Since the military authorities have expressed some concern about our soldier's tendencies to succumb to brainwashing, we can suggest to them that all they need do is train the soldiers to think about everything which they hear and say.

Needless to say, this will never be done for the simple reason that it contradicts the necessities of the military-command situation. Once soldiers start thinking about what they hear or say, chaos reigns—from a disciplinary point of view. Thinking soldiers are not good soldiers any more. It follows, then, that the very training which goes into making a good soldier is training that makes him the most suitable and easy material for brainwashing. I doubt that the authorities will wish to attempt to resolve this paradox.

This analysis, then, suggests that thinking is always detrimental to the maintainence of stable and relatively restricted meaning systems. It is for this reason that governments of all forms tend to resist so strongly discussion and questioning about at least some of their policies or the underlying assumptions behind those policies. Thus, in the Soviet Union, we are told, one cannot question the party, and in the United States any serious questioning of capitalism and free enterprise is often treated as un-American and sanctions are placed against it. This must be done if these basic premises are to be maintained. If truly free thought were permitted, we might be subject to all sorts and varieties of revolutions; governments would fall, economics would totter, and the like. Of course, we would all be considerably richer human beings because of it, but evidently that is not as important as the status quo.

We have been working under the assumption that there is an intimate connection between meaning systems and other mental functions. Things which affect one function automatically affect others as well. In other words, we have argued that the Whorfian hypothesis is true. And the data we have considered so far is certainly consonant with this assumption. We have also assumed that there is an intimate connection between meaning and behavior or action. Meaning is a tendency to respond in a particular manner in a particular situation; and the more different tendencies to respond there are connected to a particular word, the more meaning it can be said to have. Meaning, then, resembles an attitude, as it is often defined—i.e. a tendency to behave in a particular manner, or to feel in a particular manner. In fact, we may call meaning a type of attitude if we wish. Such an approach to the problem of meaning allows us to understand another effect of language, that which is sometimes known as *word magic*.

We can describe word magic as either the equating of the name with the thing itself, or as the asking of something with the actual doing of it. Various forms of word magic can be observed, the most visible of which is found in relatively "primitive" societies, and particularly in preliterate societies. In these societies we find the phenomena of cursing and incantation, and the various rituals associated with the naming of people and the knowing of their names, all of which involve some form of word magic.

Consider, for example, the curse. Here the saying of a certain set of words, sometimes ritualized and sometimes extemporaneous, is presumed to bring about some event, generally bad, upon some person in the future. Similarly, an incantation is a verbal summoning of some person or thing to the speaker. In both cases, the speaker works under the tacit assumption that the saying of something is a cause of or equivalent to actually doing something to the individual. Saying harmful things is equivalent to actually harming; a verbal summons is equivalent to actually going out and getting or compelling the thing to come, and so on. We have two things to explain here. First of all, why people believe in cursing and incantation and, second of all, why they do in fact appear to be actually effective in some cases.

A clarification of these questions may be gained if we consider the peculiar word magic related to names. In some cultures, each individual actually takes on a secret name which no one at all ever knows but himself. In other cultures, we find individuals changing their names with relative frequency as a result of something which has happened to them, as the result of something they desire, or as the result of some intervention by the "spirits" in their life. This type of behavior is often connected with religious matters. The "real" name of God is concealed from people—as was the case with Moses, for example. Finally, we should point out that the so-called civilized societies are by no means free of this sort of ritual. Most students faced with their first Russian novel are staggered by the bewildering array of names—Christian names, surnames, patronymics, nicknames, etc—which are attached to the characters. In Russian society, of course, one is called by one's family name by a certain group of people—those not close to one—by one's surname and patronymic by those closer, by one's surname by those even closer, and by one or several nicknames by one's intimates. We in America practice essentially the same thing, but in a relatively less complex form.

In the case of cursing and incantation, we clearly have the equation of saying something with doing something; the word and the deed are seen as equivalent. The word magic involved with people's names seems essentially a subclass of this, for in it we see that people *feel* that being able to manipulate someone's name is equivalent to actually having control over the individual. I am somehow under the control of the person who knows my name; but I can control him through the use of names too, through curses and the like. Some evidence of this sort of thinking is given by Lévi-Strauss (1961) when he asserts that literacy was essentially used as a source of power by the literate over the illiterate in many ancient and primitive cultures. Citing observations made on Brazilian Indians, he shows how an individual in one non-literate tribe was able to assume power because he got possession of a written list of names of his fellow tribesmen; in this case the names were actually written by Lévi-Strauss. While this individual was illiterate, his possession of the written names and his "acted" reading of the names were sufficient for him to achieve the leadership of the tribe, at least for some time. We would have to assume that this could happen only in a situation in which the people in the society felt that words and deeds were somehow equivalent, where words themselves conveyed power.

To fully understand this effect, we must come to grips with the fact that the ascribing of power to words and names is *totally and universally natural and normal*. All people do this, at least in their childhood. The real problem of psychological interest is why some people stop doing it. Let us start with a child in our culture and observe his word magic. Following Piaget (1959), we can assume that at the beginning of language acquisition, the name for a thing and the thing itself are not perceptually differentiated. This is hardly surprising since meaning and perception are but two sides of the same process in all situations. For example, when the child manipulates an object he is also—in his awareness— manipulating the name for it as well. The stimuli arising from the object and the stimuli arising from the hearing of the name both have essentially the same set of tendencies to respond attached to them for the child. Of course one is seen, we presume, while the other is heard; but in terms of the *functional significance* of the stimulus, in terms of what the child can *do* with it, how he can have intercourse with it, and so on, the learning situation is such that the object and the word will have similar sets of tendencies to respond. This means, then, that the perception of the object and the perception of the name will be similar and, moreover, that the perception of the object will tend to produce the perception of the name and vice versa. Thus we can say that when the child interacts with or manipulates the object, he is manipulating the word as well. As with equal justification we can say the opposite; when he manipulates the name this is equivalent to manipulating the object. In other words, from the beginning he operates under word magic. The essence of meaning is action; meaning is what can be done to the word and to the object to which it refers. The connection, then, between the word and overt action and behavior is not only intimate, it occurs by necessity. Manipulating the word is in some sense phenomenally equivalent to manipulating the object, for the child.

It is only gradually that the child learns otherwise, which he does first of all through contact with the world. He discovers that his environment does not always co-operate with him. If he attempts to verbally summon his rattle to him, the rattle is not likely to come. And, moreover, neither will his parents in many cases. Through this very simple and natural independence of the environment from the child, he learns that the word and the object are separate. But there are cases in which this sort of learning will be retarded. The first such case is with proper names. People, when they are called, have a habit of appearing since, after all, a legitimate use of a name is to summon someone. But by this very fact, proper names retain a vestige of word magic when other more common words have lost it. Proper names are, in fact, controllers of others; hence they retain their magic. I do not doubt that it is because of this latent magic possessed by proper names that children are so curious about them. It is the rare child who is at home with a stranger until he knows the person's name. And it is the rare child who would not like to know the names of nearly everyone he sees. Children, in fact, often display their intimacy with others by "playing" with their names, rhyming them, and just "using" them. All this is quite consonant with the notion that in some fashion the child feels that the name gives him some control over—or at least security from—the person whose name it is. And he has, of course, that most magical name of all at his disposal—his own.

Whatever faults there may be in the magic of other person's names, there is always one name which is completely magical—one's own. For the child at least can control his own behavior completely by using his own name. If you observe the child talking to himself, you will hear that he does tend to call himself by name. Through this sort of self-conversation, the magical power of his own name is retained. A great deal of what he says about himself does happen, because, after all, he is just describing what he is doing. Nevertheless, despite its arbitrariness and irreality, it is sufficient for the retention of this sort of word magic, and for its generalization to other proper names as well. Bear in mind that this does not suddenly disappear with adulthood. One's own name is always in some sense sacred and an intimate part of one's self. It is the rare adult, no matter how educated and sophisticated, who can imagine his being called by another first name. Children definitely, and adults often enough, get upset at the notion that they might have been differently named. And, as Freud points out (1948), the meeting of someone with one's own name is always an occasion of some strain; after all, in our terms, he might have as much magical control over you as you yourself do. Notice, in case there is any lingering doubt in your minds about the power of names in the adult mind, that people who change their names are almost entirely treated as, or found among, the marginal members of our society. We find two large classes of people with whom the practice of name changing is commonly associated—actors and criminals. The latter are pariahs, outcasts of society; the former are almost so to the average man. There is little doubt but that many people feel that the mere changing of their names is evidence of their unacceptability; they have done something which every normal person feels is somehow wrong or at least of questionable taste—although it has a certain "magical" function as well.

As we have shown, within limits the child can learn to give up his initial and natural word magic because the world about him does not reinforce this sort of attitude—at least not completely. Of course, the more divorced any particular part of the language is from any *direct* participation in environment, the more resistant it will be to this sort of "reality principle." Some words retain a magic because that is their nature; hence, the above discussion of proper names. Other words remain magical because they have no immediate consequences in the world; these words are what might be called abstract, a word such as /democracy/ for example. There is nothing to which one can point which is the proper referent of this term. There is very little which one can do which is directly relevant to the meaning of the term. One's individual day-to-day behavior is very little influenced by such concepts. The meaning of /democracy/ lies, of course, in the other words which one uses in connection with it. Hence, its meaning resides in "free speech," "free enterprise," "popular election," "the will of the majority," and so on. And once again, these concepts have little bearing on direct action, except in relatively rare and restricted circumstances. Such abstract terms —and there are many of them—can be used in all their magical sense with very little opportunity for them to run afoul of reality. They are the conjurings and curses of the present day.

A child can call one of his playmates a /rat/ and have this verbalism "hurt" as much as if the playmate had actually become a rat. To call someone a name means that the person thus called has acquired some of the characteristics of the name. This is an essential consequence of the nature of childlike meaning, i.e. the name and the object are somehow inseparable. There is no question but that both youthful parties to the name-calling episode are agreed about this. The caller intends to hurt and the called is hurt by this action. Such concrete name calling diminishes as concrete words loose their magic, which they do when it is seen that they are ineffective. But the abstract words, on the other hand, are the names to be called in adulthood. Thus /communist/ serves an adult equally as well as /rat/ does the child. And even the most naïve student of current affairs can testify that once a given individual has been called a /communist/ he may be treated by some people as though he actually were one. He is, as they say, branded; this label has become a part of him, inseparable from his other characteristics. And since there are few, if any, ways in which a term like /communist/ is directly relevant to the activities of the average man in our society, there is no possibility for anyone to prove that he is not a Communist, if he so desires. This word has retained its full magical value.

We have maintained that it is possible to escape word magic through contact with reality; that is, by observing that one's behaviors in the world do not correspond to those behaviors suggested by the meaning of the term. In this case the new, functionally relevant behaviors may become the new meaning of the term. Some philosophers have attempted to apply a criterion of functional relevance to philosophical terms and have discovered that many of those terms have, in fact, no relevance at all to non-philosophical behavior. Hence, they have dismissed them as meaningless and irrelevant for further study. This sort of dismissal is suspect, for the use of a term in connection with other terms within a scholarly discipline is as legitimate a use as one in connection with the real physical world. How is it, then, that some people are able to avoid word magic even for abstract, non-concrete terms?

There appear to be two other ways of accomplishing this divorce between language and the world. The first is through literacy. While literacy is by no means a sure-fire technique, it does seem that literate cultures are often less likely to use word magic than non-literate ones.* Literacy per se appears to be the reason for this. As we tried to indicate earlier, writing can present the word to a person as an object in itself. More importantly, he can say /This is the word and this is the object./, a statement which may not be the best logic in the world but one which is of some functional significance. In other words, he can now *see* the independence of the word and the object; he can *see* that there is no necessary connection between them. To the extent that he does see this, I would assume that he would tend to give up word magic. One tends to be less impressed by the *label* /communist/ per se, if one treats it as "just another word." And writing helps one to see that all words are just exactly that— words.

Thus, we find another escape from word magic. But this escape may have its price also. For it can tend to produce an ignoring of the fact that while terms like /democracy/ and /communism/ are just words, they also do in fact have meaning and, moreover, that this meaning is just like any other meaning—it is a set of tendencies to respond in particular ways. These words do have implications for behavior despite the fact that they are

---

* Of course there is a price to be paid for this. When one does find an example of word magic in a literate society, it will tend to be a very subtle one. Non-literate societies often *admit* to themselves the power of words, while we do not. Unaware of what word magic we have, we do not have control over its power over us, and its effects are perhaps more pernicious than in primitive societies.

independent of the world in any direct mechanical sense. Knowing what /communism/ means implies knowing how to behave communistically—whether one chooses to do so or not. Writing may lead one from the pitfalls of word magic, but abandoning of word magic should not lead to the assumption that "it's all the same," that nothing really means anything, a conclusion which is decidedly false. And, of course, if one carries this far enough, the loss of meaning acquired in this fashion leads the individual into susceptibility to the types of influence which we have discussed in connection with brainwashing, for these commands tend to depend on a loss of meaning for their efficiency. Thus, literacy itself may contain the seeds for the loss of individual freedom—if it is treated without proper caution.

We now have two methods of avoiding word magic. The first stems from the knowledge that the world is in fact independent of oneself, and the second from the fact that one can see, in writing, the separation of the word and the object. But these clearly are not sufficient. We are faced with the uncomfortable fact that neither of these two methods has any *guaranteed* effectiveness, particularly concerning the words which enter into the ideologies which shape our lives. We can find hope—and puzzlement—in the fact that some people seem to avoid even this sort of word magic. The question we must still answer is how this is possible.

I suspect that the final method for avoiding word magic lies in the antithesis of the first method. That is, the individual finds out that the world about him is independent of his control. And at the same time he can discover that he is, in turn, independent of the environment's control. His behavior is *not* compelled by any feature of the environment. More specifically, he does not have to do what other people want him to do.* Given a par-

* As a psychologist I, of course, subscribe to a variety of mechanical causal theory of psychology. However, it is clear that not all the causes of behavior are *external* to the individual; his behavior or mind will never be fully explained by externals only. Moreover, we are now talking about what the individual himself experiences. And it is clear that he does not experience himself as a deterministic machine. The reason for this would appear to be quite

ticular stimulus, of whatever sort one chooses, one of the logically possible responses to that stimulus is to not respond, to not move. Many theorists have found it necessary to make the almost paradoxical assumption that not responding is a response. There are many sound theoretical reasons for doing just this, beyond the one we are about to discuss. Let me point out, that if one is going to *maintain* a given bodily position and orientation for a certain period of time—i.e. not move or respond—this requires as much control and enervation of the muscles as moving does. The opposing muscle groups have to maintain themselves in a state of equal and opposite tension. Not moving is not achieved by relaxing the muscles—this would simply lead to collapse. Not moving is achieved by maintaining the present status of tension, rather than changing it, which results in moving. From the point of view of the central nervous system, then, not moving is quite as much of a response as moving is.

We need not concern ourselves with how the response of not responding is acquired. There are countless occasions when this can take place. Let us merely assume that we are dealing with an individual who has this response in his repertoire. There may, of course, be those who do not have it—they can never say /no/ as it were. For them we can only have pity. Our concern is for those who can say /no/. And this statement is more than a figure of speech. For how are we to account for the fact that the word /no/ has meaning if not through this sort of mechanism? That is, /no/ means that one does not respond appropriately, or just does not respond in general, to an otherwise "adequate" stimulus or context. To the extent, then, that the word /no/ has meaning for an individual, we are in a position to assume that the tendency not to respond is part of his behavioral repertoire.

Now then, what can we do with this tendency now that we have it? One thing appears to be clear; once one has *refused* to

simple—without long and sophisticated reflection, the factors which may, in fact, control his behavior are not part of his awareness. Hence, he does not see himself as "caused" in any significant sense of the term. At any rate, he does not see his behavior as being necessarily determined by the behavior of others or at least he can come to see this given an appropriate environment.

respond to a stimulus, one has effectively removed oneself from its domination. If that stimulus is a word, then not responding to it removes one from the control of that word and, of course, removes its control over oneself. In other words, it destroys the magical power of the word. By not responding to the word, the word must be seen as independent of oneself and as independent of the object or state to which it refers. Once this is accomplished, of course, one can see that the word does not have power over anything. The denial of the word has given one freedom from it.

But interestingly enough, the fact that not responding to a word has added the tendency of "not responding" to that word's collection of acquired response tendencies and has thus accomplished something else. It has given the word meaning or increased its meaning. For each additional response tendency is an additional bit of meaning. One has achieved two virtues, as it were. One has achieved an independence from the domination by words and from the assumption that words control things, and one has done this not at the expense of meaning, but by increasing it. Clearly this sort of activity will work as a counteractive to any form of influence which attempts to achieve control by eliminating meaning. The refusal to accept, the refusal to respond to a stimulus, even for the briefest period of time, is sufficient to add meaning to the word. Thus it is that reflection is the proper medicine for brainwashing. For all that reflection is, is a hesitation, a temporary not-responding, a brief period in which the tendency to respond is not converted directly into action. And this tendency not to respond becomes part of the meaning of the word and preserves the existence of meaning.

The reader may detect a not entirely coincidental resemblance between this reasoning and the sort of systematic denial of knowledge practiced by Descartes (1950). To Descartes, truth was arrived at only by first refusing to accept anything as truth and seeing what remained when this had been carried to its extreme. But of course, once this point was reached, he then proceeded to try to put the world together again; from the basic truths he would reconstruct the apparent truths of the world.

The individual must do this too, for denial, while therapeutic, does involve not responding. If carried to its extreme, the result is a vegetable and not a man. The point of the not responding is not the destruction of meaning, but the attempt to realize exactly what meaning is. Given this realization, one can then react to meaning in a more realistic sense. One can use words instead of being used by them. By always having the possibility of negating a perception or a meaning, one can then arrive closer to the position in which words are the tools of the mind rather than the mind's being the construct of the words.

But we cannot and should not avoid the obvious. The history of words is a history of word magic. Meaning arises from word magic and it can never deny its historical roots. We can overcome the roots, and we can grow in our ability to use meaning. We can even state a generality that the more meaning, the better; for each additional meaning allows that much more escape from the simple one-to-one control of the mind by words. Meaning is freedom, if you will. And it is the implicit realization of this which makes the totalitarian members of our society condemn the free exchange of ideas as being opposed to the very basis of society. Indeed, it may be just exactly that. And we cannot deny the intimacy between language and other mental activities which this entire argument presupposes. They cannot be separated. A change in one is a change in them all. And it is probably for this reason that it is difficult to prove the Whorfian hypothesis even though the Whorfian hypothesis is so clearly correct. For it would appear that the differences among languages are so small in contrast to the effects of just *having* a language, whatever that language may be, that they become almost undetectable. The major factor is just having a language. Since the nature of language is the same for all languages, and since it is this nature which has the most predominant effect on the rest of the mental apparatus, the minor structural differences produce effects which are vanishingly small.

In conclusion, then, we see that language starts as a weapon. But we see that the nature of meaning itself is a method for counteracting that weapon. Our success at this endeavor will depend upon how much meaning we are permitted to acquire. For there is little doubt but that—with sufficient control of the physical environment—one can restrict the possibilities of acquiring meaning almost *ad libitum*.

Bibliography

Adorno, T. W., *et al*. *The authoritarian personality*. New York, Harper, 1950.

Descartes, R. *A discourse on method*. New York, Liberal Arts Press, 1950.

Festinger, L. *A theory of cognitive dissonance*. Evanston, Ill., Row Peterson, 1957.

Freud, S. *The psychopathology of everyday life*. London, Ernest Bewn, 1948.

Lévi-Strauss, C. *Tristes tropiques*. New York, Criterion Books, 1961.

Piaget, J. *Language and thought in the child*. New York, Humanities Press, 1959.

Weitzenhoffer, A. *Hypnotism: an objective study in suggestibility*. New York, John Wiley & Sons, 1953.

Index

(Bibliographic references are indicated by figures in italic type.)

327

11